CAREER EDUCATION: PERSPECTIVE AND PROMISE

KEITH GOLDHAMMER
Michigan State University

ROBERT E. TAYLOR
The Ohio State University

CHARLES E. MERRILL PUBLISHING COMPANY
A Bell & Howell Company
Columbus, Ohio

THE MERRILL SERIES
IN CAREER PROGRAMS

Published by
Charles E. Merrill Publishing Co.
A Bell & Howell Company
Columbus, Ohio 43216

International Standard Book Number: 0-675-09078-4

Library of Congress Catalog Card Number: 72-83231

2 3 4 5 6 7 — 77 76 75 74 73

Printed in the United States of America

THE MERRILL SERIES IN CAREER PROGRAMS

In recent years our nation has literally rediscovered education. Concurrently, many nations are considering educational programs in revolutionary terms. They now realize that education is the responsible link between social needs and social improvement. While traditionally Americans have been committed to the ideal of the optimal development of each individual, there is increased public appreciation and support of the values and benefits of education in general, and vocational and technical education in particular. With occupational education's demonstrated capacity to contribute to economic growth and national well being, it is only natural that it has been given increased prominence and importance in this educational climate.

With the increased recognition that the true resources of a nation are its human resources, occupational education programs are considered a form of investment in human capital—an investment which provides comparatively high returns to both the individual and society.

The Merrill Series in Career Programs is designed to provide a broad range of educational materials to assist members of the profession in providing effective and efficient programs of occupational education which contribute to an individual's becoming both a contributing economic producer and a responsible member of society.

iii

69257

The series and its sub-series do not have a singular position of philosophy concerning the problems and alternatives in providing the broad range of offerings needed to prepare the nation's work force. Rather, authors are encouraged to develop and support independent positions and alternative strategies. A wide range of educational and occupational experiences and perspectives have been brought to bear through the Merrill Series in Career Programs National Editorial Board. These experiences, coupled with those of the authors, assure useful publications. I believe that this title, along with others in the series, will provide major assistance in further developing and extending viable educational programs to assist youth and adults in preparing for and furthering their careers.

Robert E. Taylor
Editorial Director
Series in Career Programs

PREFACE

Career education is an idea whose time has come. It has been nurtured by research in career development and related areas, by the rising expectations of people for living a fulfilling life, and by legislative support. Career education is a response to the pressing human issues of the day and provides a new paradigm for education. It is designed to capacitate all individuals for their multiple life roles. The conceptual structure for career education grows out of career development theory. In practice, it is designed to enhance self-awareness and to enable individuals to make increasingly rational decisions as they pursue their careers and become participating, contributing and fulfilled members of society.

We hope this publication will provide fresh insights and perspectives to the various dimensions of career education and its potential for delivering on the educational promises of many decades. We wish to thank the several authors who have permitted us to include their papers in this book and several others who have contributed material, among these Dale Parnell, Edwin L. Herr, Gordon I. Swanson, Frank C. Pratzner, and Louise J. Keller.

Keith Goldhammer
Dean-elect, School of Education
Michigan State University

Robert E. Taylor
Director
The Center for Vocational
   and Technical Education
The Ohio State University

PUBLISHER'S NOTE

The authors have waived all royalties in order to expedite the publication of this book at minimal cost, as a means of facilitating the dissemination of career education concepts.

v

CONTENTS

INTRODUCTION: CAREER EDUCATION PERSPECTIVES

To the casual observer, career education may appear to be a totally new conceptual focus for American education which burst on the scene full-grown and received initial visibility and emphasis when U. S. Commissioner of Education Sidney P. Marland, Jr. issued his call for "Career Education Now" to the National Association of Secondary School Principals in Houston in January, 1971. Additional review, however reveals that significant dimensions of the concept have historical roots deep in American thought and action. At least three major sources have contributed substantially to the evolution of career education as a major conceptual framework for American education. These three sources are (1) statements of the major goals of education enunciated by various groups, (2) educational legislation reflecting society's collective intentions in this area, and (3) the accumulation of research findings concerning individual development.

Significant elements of the career education concept have been included and reemphasized in practically all of the major statements of goals for American education.

"Vocation" was among the seven objectives listed in the 1918 publication by The Commission on Reorganization of Secondary Education entitled *Cardinal Principles of Secondary Education.* According to the Commission, "a good citizen earns his living, contributes to the gen-

1

eral welfare by working, and maintains desirable relationships with fellow workers."[1]

The Educational Policies Commission of the National Education Association[2] in 1938 listed four current school objectives—third among them, "Economic Efficiency." The school should produce an individual who selects his own vocation, understands and lives according to the requirements of his job, improves his working efficiency and plans his own economic life.

The first of ten imperative needs of youth, according to the Educational Policies Commission[3] of 1944, was: "All youth need to develop salable skills and those understandings and attitudes that make the worker an intelligent and productive participant in economic life. To this end, most youth need supervised work experience as well as education in the skills and knowledge of their occupation."

A further statement by the Educational Policies Commission in 1961 stated that the central purpose of education is the development of rational thinking, but also reiterated the school's traditionally accepted obligation to teach the fundamental processes:

> More than ever before, and for an ever-increasing proportion of the population, vocational competence requires developed rational capacities. The march of technology and science in the modern society progressively eliminates the positions open to low-level talents. The man able to use only his hands is at a growing disadvantage as compared with the man who can also use his head. Today even the simplest use of hands is coming to require the simultaneous employment of the mind.[4]

While occupational and career development have been included in earlier statements of educational purpose, it should be emphasized that career education is not more of the same. It is not a synonym for vocational education. It is not a reiteration of traditional and good educational goals. It retains the essentials of education but introduces a new sense of purposefulness—career development. It places career development as the central unifying element for education.

In addition to statements of educational purpose articulated by various elements of the educational profession and other responsible groups, American education has also been influenced in a major way through federal legislation. The Morrill Act, which established the land-grant college system, the Smith-Hughes Act, which is the National Organic Act for Vocational Education (later supplemented and refined by the George-Deen, George-Reed, George-Ellzey and George-Barden acts), and the National Vocational Education Act of 1963 and its 1968 amendments have all contributed materially to extending and strengthening the concept of career development. The National Defense Education Act of 1958 and its subsequent amendments placed increased emphasis on counseling and guidance at all levels and hence provided additional momentum toward the conceptual integration of various elements of career education.

Over the past century, Congress has reflected our country's goals through legislation by incrementally, but nevertheless steadily, moving toward recognition and support of career education. The legislators have recognized the importance of providing increased opportunity for all citizens to prepare themselves for vocations consistent with their individual interests, needs, and employment opportunities.

A third source of influence in the evolution of career education has been the growing body of knowledge accumulating from research and development efforts. As indicated in Herr's paper later in this book, the work of Super and others has contributed to a "developmental" view of individual progress. It is further evident that the "state of the art" concerning careers, career planning, and individual development, fused with concepts emerging in manpower planning, will make possible a more direct and effective structure to facilitate individual career preparation.

The convergence of the three sources of thought and action into the current concepts of career education should have been predictable. There are linear indications from each of them.

A fourth dimension which has contributed materially to the rapid acceptance and widespread support of career education can be found in the disillusionment with education that is evident in the current context.

Context for Career Education

It is not necessary to enumerate in detail the range, magnitude, or intensity of the problems currently faced by society and education in preparing individuals to become effective, contributing members of society. Among youth we find truancy, alienation, drug addiction, unemployability, misunderstanding, and total ignorance of the world of work. Dropout rates are reaching alarming proportions. Hence, we find individuals graduating or leaving schools ill-equipped to cope with the complexities of a modern technological society.

Today, less than 20 percent of the secondary population receive some kind of specific occupational training, while 80 percent of our youth do not graduate from college.[5]

During 1970–71, 3.7 million young people left formal education. Of these, nearly 2.5 million lacked skills adequate to enter the labor force at a level commensurate with their promise. Many left with no marketable skill whatever. Some 850,000 dropped out of elementary or secondary school; 750,000 graduated from high school general curricula; 850,000 left college without a degree or completion of an organized occupational program. These people represent an educational outlay of $28 billion—about one-third of the amount spent on education in the country last year.[6]

Men and women are faced with difficult problems in adjusting to, and preparing for, the dual roles of family member and worker. We witness adults faced with mid-career decisions and redirections who have experienced an erosion of their employment skills and who need help in their further career planning and development. Overlaying all these groups are the severe problems of the disadvantaged—those who represent the failures of our present social systems.

At the same time, our position of leadership in the free world demands a strong economic base which, in turn, requires new skills and increased levels of efficiency and productivity if we are to survive in world competition. In these rigorous times of accountability, performance contracting, the efficiency cult and management by objectives, it is easy to forget that the individual is paramount in our free society. The problem, then, becomes one of balancing the requirements of society against the essential freedom of its individuals.

Traditionally, our society has looked to the school to transmit our cultural heritage, to preserve and extend our democratic system of government, and to energize our economic system. However, recently the high esteem for schools and the almost blind faith that society has traditionally placed in the educational system appear to be in jeopardy.

Large numbers of high-school and college graduates, as well as the recipients of doctoral and master's degrees, are unemployed, and everyone —students, parents, employers and policymakers, each with his own personal and institutional interests—is asking why. When we consider the enormity of personal and social investments, the loss of self-esteem and self-confidence, the billions of educational dollars spent for inappropriate, non-relevant education, and the cost of remedial, correctional, and welfare programs, the implications for efficient human resource development and utilization are staggering.

There are no ready-made panaceas or shortcuts to resolving the educational implications of these problems. It appears, however, that career education, which has grown out of a new social consciousness and the research tradition of career development fused with concepts of manpower planning, shows considerable promise as a construct for orienting and deploying our educational resources. It provides a new, vigorous sense of purpose and mission for the school enterprise. Regardless of whether we educators are ready to accept this new direction, legislative groups at the state and federal levels already have taken specific actions. In addition to the legislative ferment on the national scene, several state legislative groups have recently passed acts which are significant for career education. For example, Senate Bill 5 (1971) in Arizona made available approximately two million dollars for initiating statewide activities in the career education field. The New Jersey state legislature also has appropriated funds to finance pilot projects of career education. Three such projects were conducted with success during the 1970–71 school year. The California state legislature passed Assembly Bill 102 (1971), which states:

> The Legislature hereby recognizes that it is the policy of the people of the State of California to provide an educational opportunity to every individual to the end that every student leaving school should be prepared to enter the world of work; that every student who graduates from any state-supported educational institution should have sufficient marketable skills for legitimate remunerative employment; and that every qualified and eligible adult citizen should be afforded an educational opportunity to become suitably employed in some remunerative field of employment.[7]

State and local boards of education are evolving new position statements relative to the school's responsibilities for career education. The Los Angeles City Board of Education on October 28, 1971, adopted a position of providing career education for all youths and adults of the city schools, committing the school districts to:

> . . . preventing as far as is possible any student who is not prepared to enter the world of work from dropping out of high school, preparing each student who graduates with a salable skill for productive work, or with an academic background sufficient to successfully complete a college course, and offering every adult an educational opportunity which will ensure his appropriate employment.[8]

Nationally, one of the most heartening and promising factors on the horizon is the wholehearted endorsement and support of career education by the U. S. Office of Education. If public education is to meet the challenges of the seventies, leadership from the highest level of the profession and government is essential. The two speeches by Marland included in this book reflect this leadership and commitment.

What is Career Education?

Probably the most accurate and honest statement to be made at this time is that career education remains to be precisely defined. Although Commissioner of Education Marland and other educational leaders have given considerable attention to this "movement," it is not yet guided by a universally accepted definition. In fact, the strategy is to leave the matter of definition open to as much dialogue and interaction as possible.

Career education introduces a new polarity and sense of purpose into education. Some view it as the new paradigm for education, focusing on career development. Career education considers curriculum to be systemic —an integrated and cumulative series of experiences designed to help each student achieve (1) increased power to make relevant decisions about his life, and (2) increased skill in the performance of his life roles.

Specifically, career education is designed to capacitate individuals for their several life roles: economic, community, home, avocational, religious and aesthetic. It recognizes the centrality of careers in shaping our lives by determining or limiting where we work, where we live, our associates, and other dimensions that are significant in defining our life style. Designed for all students, career education should be viewed as lifelong and pervasive, permeating the entire school program and even extending beyond it.

Career education is a systematic attempt to *increase* the career options available to individuals and to facilitate more rational and valid career planning and preparation. Through a wide range of school- and community-based resources, young people's career horizons should be broadened. Their self-awareness should be enhanced. The framework for accomplishing these goals are the phases in the career education program: career awareness, career exploration, career preparation.

The educational program should be sequenced and postured to optimize career development and should provide as broad a base of understanding of self and the world of work as possible. It should be designed so youngsters will, in fact, have two options at several levels: continuing education or employment. Career education provides those options and is designed to strengthen and achieve student self-actualization. It builds upon the strong motivating force of career interest, career development and preparation. It provides a means of making other elements of the school relevant to life purposes and stimulates student interest and participation in these "supporting" areas. Subject matter is not an end, but rather a means of helping individuals optimize their career development. Knowledge is viewed as applicative; not merely descriptive. In the vernacular of the day, career education "puts it all together."

The Career Education Models

What is being done to further refine and develop these concepts? Many school districts are already well under way in implementing them.[9] The U.S. Office of Education's research and development initiatives to facilitate career education are substantial and yet varied. They should ultimately make an empirical contribution to shaping and further defining career education. The Federal Government has already made available more than 86 million dollars through a variety of programs for research, development, and implementation of career education concepts.

There now exist four alternative conceptualizations of career education or, more accurately, four alternative ways of delivering or facilitating career education goals. In a research and development sense, the four models may be viewed as alternative means of delivering on our career education commitments. The four models are:

1. Comprehensive career education model—the school-based model
2. The employer-based model
3. The home-based model
4. The residential-based model

THE SCHOOL-BASED MODEL

The U.S. Office of Education has designated The Center for Vocational and Technical Education, located at The Ohio State University, as the prime contractor to develop, test, and install the school-based Comprehensive Career Education Model. The model is being developed in six local school districts selected by the Office of Education. They are: Mesa, Arizona; Los Angeles, California; Jefferson County, Colorado; Atlanta, Georgia; Pontiac, Michigan; and Hackensack, New Jersey. The development network encompasses many diversities. There are variations in school district size, geographic setting, and the cultural and ethnic mix. Specifically, the network involves the staff and students from 112 school buildings. Over 3,900 teachers and administrators are working with 83,300 students in this development effort.

The object of the model is to develop and test a career education system (K–12) in these districts which will help students develop (1) a comprehensive awareness of career options; (2) a concept of self which is in keeping with a work-oriented society and includes positive attitudes about work, school, and society, and a sense of satisfaction resulting from successful experience in these areas; (3) personal characteristics, such as self-respect, initiative, and resourcefulness; (4) a realistic understanding of the relationships between the world of work and education which assist individuals in becoming contributing members of society; and (5) the ability to enter employment in a selected occupational area and/or to go on for further education.

As the prime contractor for the model, The Center is obligated to have programs "up and running" in the six sites, starting September 1972. The general project strategy is further refining and operationally defining, in terms of student outcomes, the conceptualization of the school-based model. A national inventory of materials and programs (treatments) will be undertaken which produces the prescribed outcomes and is congruent with the model. Simultaneously a diagnosis will be made of programs in the six site schools to determine what portions of the model are already in place and operating. Prescriptive treatments will be formulated, carefully evaluated against desired outcomes, and recycled if necessary. The iterative cycle of diagnosis, prescription, treatment, assessment, accepting, rejecting, and recycling is the central project strategy. Concurrently, the benchmark data to establish the present state of affairs—student, school and community— will be assembled and analyzed. A contract has been let for an outside (summative) evaluator to complement and reinforce the formative evaluative capacity of the project staff. Extensive staff development programs will be initiated in the local education agencies (six site schools).

  Full-time interdisciplinary development teams employed in the participating schools under the project and from The Center are at work in the six cooperating school districts. A central planning, management, and consulting staff is headquartered at The Center. Extensive involvement of school and community personnel will characterize the development process. A longer-term research and development program will be evolved to work toward a totally integrated and valid model.

  This joint effort of a national research and development center and six LEA's operating in a consortium should not be viewed as just another curriculum development program, but rather as a systematic research and engineering effort. The approach requires that instructional components (treatments) be stated as hypotheses to be tested and not as established guides for achieving predetermined goals. The engineering aspect includes the requirement that times and places, as well as means, be found and alternatively tested for the delivery of the experiences necessary for a comprehensive career education system.

THE EMPLOYER-BASED MODEL

  The goals of the employer-based model are (1) to provide an *alternative* educational program for students, aged 13–18, in an employer-based setting; (2) to unify the positive elements of academic, general, and vocational curricula into a comprehensive career education program; (3) to increase the relevance of education to the world of work; and (4) to broaden the base of community participation, particularly by involving public and private employers more directly and significantly in education.

  It is anticipated that the program will be operated by consortia of employers. Each consortium will encourage the assistance and active support of such diverse community elements as unions, schools, parents, PTA's and Chambers of Commerce. The program contemplates year-round operation and open entrance and exit of students. It will emphasize educational experiences that take place in a variety of settings such as laboratories, production lines, parks, museums, hospitals, and construction sites. The aim is to make the community the classroom. Planning studies are under way at the Far West Laboratory for Educational Research and Development, Berkeley, Calfornia; at the Northwest Regional Educational Laboratory, Portland, Oregon; and at Research for Better Schools, Philadelphia, Pennsylvania. Experimental classes will begin in the fall of 1972 for 50 to 100 students in Oakland, California; Tigard, Oregon; and Philadelphia, Pennsylvania.

THE HOME-BASED MODEL

The purposes of the home-based model for career education are (1) to develop educational delivery systems into the home and the community; (2) to provide new career education programs for adults; (3) to establish a guidance and career placement system to assist individuals in occupational and related life roles; (4) to develop more competent workers; and (5) to enhance the quality of the home as a learning center.

The Education Development Corporation in Newton, Massachusetts, is conducting studies in three major areas: in-depth definition of population characteristics appropriate for a career education TV series, development of an evaluation plan for the series, and conceptualization and feasibility studies of supporting components for career guidance and in-home study. The Rand Corporation is completing an analysis of successful media-based educational programs so that the Office of Education can develop a prototype for the implementation of the model.

THE RESIDENTIAL-BASED MODEL

The Mountain Plains Regional Education Center, recently established at the Glasgow, Montana Air Force Base, will develop and begin to implement a resident career education program with services to disadvantaged individuals and families drawn from rural areas of six participating states trying to develop their economies. Program components in the residential-based model will include education, family life and community services, health and health services, economic development services, and research and evaluation activities.

Family units and individuals are now reporting to the training site so that each can develop an appropriate career role through employment, study, home management, or through a combination of these. Employment upon completion of the residency is guaranteed by the home state of each family. Experiences in developing and operating the Glasgow center will be utilized in assessing the potential for other kinds of institution-based career education programs.

IMPLICATIONS OF THE ALTERNATIVE
CAREER EDUCATION MODELS

It is difficult, if not impossible, to assess the full range of implications for each of these models, let alone the synergism among the alternative models. However, the future implications of a successful school-based comprehensive career education model is significantly magnified when considered in relation to the other three. As previously indicated, career education incorporates a concept of an individual's lifelong entitlement to the educational opportunities required for career selection, preparation and advancement. The school-based model may be viewed as the formative developmental program provided for all children and youth in their maturing years. The other models extend the concept beyond the formal school and provide educational opportunities for individuals through all of the successive stages of their lives. When fully developed, the various models will provide a variety of options for individuals who, for one reason or another, need to recycle their career activities, or who desire to advance in their career goals.

As now conceived, the models should provide opportunities for career development and preparation for any person, regardless of his age, regardless of the circumstances under which he must work and live, and regardless of the social or physical barriers he might face.

Summary

If career education is to fulfill its potential and capitalize on its dynamic qualities, several current concepts and assumptions inherent in the present "system" of education must be examined and restructured. We need to develop educational systems that parallel the lifelong educational needs of people. We need to evolve a new view and sense of purpose for the schools. Further, we need to distinguish between education and schooling. If career education is to deliver on its promise and potential, schools must become different kinds of institutions.

We need to question some of our current beliefs and practices—to examine the implications of our heretofore unexamined assumptions, such as the belief in continuous, uninterrupted schooling K–12; the nine-month school year with its lock-step structure; compulsory attendance laws; child labor laws; and the assumption that learning takes place only in the school building.

What would happen *if* we were to think in terms of an educational entitlement which would permit and, in fact, encourage youngsters to move from school to employment and re-enter the school system as new needs and maturity dictate? What would be the effect if we were to enroll youngsters in school on their sixth birthday with the school year being continuous, thereby enabling students to leave or graduate any month of the year rather than dumping all students on the labor market in a single month? Are there not advantages to both individuals and society in encouraging people to transfer from school to other learning and growth environments, such as employment and public service activities, which contribute to their individual development and capacity?

Perhaps school needs to be viewed as the planner and manager of the educational growth of individuals, drawing on and utilizing the full range of societal resources that are available, making extensive use of educative capacities in the community such as resource people, lay career advisers, and advisory committees, availing ourselves of opportunities for cooperative work studies. Surely we can think of numerous other ways which provide a more optimal interface and reestablish the sense of "community" in the educational context.

In summary then, career education should be viewed as a pervasive and evolving concept. It is difficult, if not impossible, to explicate the whole range of interactions and implications inherent in the full implementation of the concept. However, it is accurate to state that it is too big and powerful an idea to go away. As educators, as citizens, we must confront it, think it through, consider it, and shape it, so that career education can more effectively keep its promise of fully capacitating individuals for their multiple life roles.

The following articles, written by national leaders in education, present various perspectives and dimensions of career education in the hope they will contribute to its further development.

FOOTNOTES

[1]National Education Association. *Cardinal Principles of Secondary Education.* Washington, D.C.; U.S. Department of Interior, Bureau of Education, Bulletin No. 35, 1918, p. 7.

[2]The Educational Policies Commission. *The Purpose of Education in American Democracy.* National Education Association of the United States and the American Association of School Administrators, Washington, D.C.: 1938, p. 91.

[3]The Educational Policies Commission. *Education for All American Youth.* Washington, D.C.: National Education Association, 1944, p. 225.

[4]The Educational Policies Commission. *The Central Purpose of American Education.* Washington, D.C.: National Education Association, 1961, p. 8.

[5]Bureau of Adult, Vocational and Technical Education, "Vocational Education for the 70's." Conference discussion paper, Washington, D.C.: U.S. Office of Education, Division of Vocational and Technical Education, March 1971, p. 3.

[6]Sidney P. Marland, "Career Education—A New Frontier." Speech delivered at the Conference of Pennsylvania Personnel and Guidance Association, November 14–15, 1971, Pittsburgh, Pennsylvania.

[7]State of California Assembly, Assembly Bill 102, addition to Section 7504 Education Code, August 24, 1971.

[8]Adopted by the Board of Education, City of Los Angeles, California, October 28, 1971.

[9]See Part III for examples of programs.

BIBLIOGRAPHY

Educational Policies Commission, The. *Current School Objectives.* Washington, D.C.: National Education Association, 1938.

———. *Education for All American Youth.* Washington, D.C.: National Education Association, 1944.

———. *The Central Purpose of American Education.* Washington, D.C.: National Education Association, 1961.

National Educational Association. *Cardinal Principles of Secondary Education.* Washington, D.C.: United States Department of the Interior, Bureau of Education, Bulletin 1918, No. 35, 1918.

Part I   UNFULFILLED EXPECTATIONS IN AMERICAN EDUCATION

The Dilemma of
American Education

If one were to consider the ways in which public education has contributed to American well-being following World War II, he would have to concede that, in spite of deficiencies in the educational system, this nation has been fairly well served by its schools. The nation's gigantic industrial-technical-military-cultural apparatuses have remained functional although beset with problems. A high level of prosperity has been maintained in spite of the persistence of unresolved poverty. Professional programs for the provision of essential human services have been provided and largely improved. In spite of all of the problems which have confronted our times, American society has survived and, to a considerable degree, with a progressive adaptability. This age has witnessed the most specific examination of its social goals and practices and a most profound attack upon the gaps which exist between its ideals and realities. Yet, in spite of the growing heterogeneity of values and interests, American society has made almost impossible gains toward the rectification of its inadequacies and the remediation of its injustices, even though its progress toward these ends has been all too slow.

This responsiveness of American society is an evidence that the schools are doing their work well, at least in part. One of the most inspiring if controversial characteristics of the 1960's and 1970's is the extent to which we have tolerated, if not appreciated, the counter-culture of youth. Its major thrust has been to point out to the older generations the ways in which discrepancies between ideals and practices have been mindlessly tolerated. Evidently, the schools have been successful in teaching a large number of our youth to be concerned about the principles and ideals upon which a democratic society can be established and to help deprived groups achieve the knowledge, skill, and assurance they needed vigorously and constructively to protest and to consolidate gains they achieved through their activism. The schools cannot be denied their impact on hastening the retreat of established discrimination, the reduction of American apathy toward poverty and disadvantage, the recognition of the effects of socially indifferent power upon American society, the environment, and the American image abroad, and the change in the American ethos from a country which universally admired its war policy to one which scrutinized even military operations in the field in accordance with stated values and ideals. Perhaps it could be said that the social traumas of the 1960's and 1970's resulted in part from the quality, not the indifference or ineffectiveness, of the educational institutions.

Its successes led to the startling revelation of its weaknesses. They also led to the recognition of the differentiation of goals which Americans hold for their schools. Criticisms of education have come from those who wanted the schools to be more effective but in even larger measure from those who disagreed with what the schools were accomplishing. Three basic trends of criticism can be discerned. One group felt that there was nothing wrong in the basic design of the educational program, but educators were not effectively carrying out that design. Education, they maintained, exists for the dissemination of knowledge, the preparation of individuals for academic careers, but teachers lack academic depth and sophistication. These criticisms led to the examination of specific aspects of the curriculum by scholars of the various disciplines, the development of new organizations of content by these scholars, and the attempt to make schools more academically rigorous. Unfortunately, many of these improved academic curricula resulted in frightening away increasing numbers of students. An updated content with greater academic rigor resulted in the intensification of the screening process through which students were admitted to these courses and an increasing dropout rate from them. Increasing the academic rigor of instruction has not solved the basic problems of the schools.

A second group of critics saw the schools as failing to instill the social disciplines which were thought to be necessary for the maintenance of the control systems of society. Less concerned with academic accomplishment, they were critical of the schools' attempts to relate to the immediate life needs of students, helping them to become self-directive human beings in a free society. Ever the hallmark of public education, control and discipline were considered weak and in need of strengthening. The older generation can always find reasons for criticizing the lack of discipline among the younger generations, and they frequently blame this deficiency upon the laxity of the schools. Not what is taught, but the disciplined inculcation of enduring values is the important thing about schools. Schools were particularly criticized for their failures to emphasize moral and spiritual values, their emphasis upon "life-adjustment education," and their teaching such things as "sex education." A few schools tried to comply with the requests of these critics, but capping the safety valves doesn't relieve the pressure inside the vessel. In spite of (or possibly even because of) more rigor in control, schools with severe problems became particularly volatile.

A third group, entirely incongruous with the second, criticized the schools for their irrelevance and their exaggerated emphasis upon control and discipline. Studying the educational problems in the inner city led some educators and citizens to see the human wastage which results from the failure to adapt programs and instruction to the needs of all children regardless of their racial, economic, or social class antecedents. Daily, children were subjected to studies which were beyond their powers of conceptualization, irrelevant to their needs for learning how to deal with the world about them, and inconsistent with the patterns of development open to them. The control mechanisms of the schools attempted to maintain discipline, but resulted in discouraging ingenuity and creativity, developing an humbling conformity, and reducing school to a meaningless ritual. Mindlessness, rigidity of control, irrelevance, drive toward conformity and apathetic acceptance, these were the characteristics of the school system particularly identified by these critics.

In spite of the criticisms, not much fundamental change took place within the schools. Little challenge was made to the basic assumptions on which the schools operated. For most critics, the schools were still looked upon as knowledge-disseminating instruments, and the measure of success in school was in terms of grades earned or credits accumulated. Some schools swung in line with the demands of powerful critics. New math and science curricula were adopted. Curricular innovations in the social studies were proposed. Programs in the humanities (to take care of moral and spiritual values, presumably) were instituted. The rigidities emanating out of the system of grading and credits were modified. Open requirements, greater student freedom of choice and action, modified class schedules and organizational structures became experimental variables. In spite of all efforts at reform or accommodation to critics, the basic problems of the schools remained and little fundamental change took place. What was taking place in the American school system could be entitled "Variations upon a Theme." The theme was still the basic paradigm which looked upon the school as a place to teach subjects, and upon learning as the process of memorizing and repeating back for examinations the subjects learned.

Good or bad, the American school system has persisted with all of its credits and debits, but it can no longer avoid confrontation with its basic issues. The most basic issue of all is the examination of the fundamental assumptions, or paradigm, on which it is structured, to determine whether or not the schools are doing that which it is most important in this age for them to do.

The Paradigm Governing American Education

The paradigm which governs practice in American education is relatively simple, as it has been within Europe for several centuries. Fundamentally, education is presumed to be the transmission of knowledge. Skills may be taught if they are the fundamental skills needed for the transmission of knowledge. Beyond this, the teaching of skills is considered to be "training" and unworthy of an educational program. Within the framework of this paradigm, the educational program is structured on the basis of "subjects," and the educational output of the instructional program is conceived to be the mastery by the student of the subject matter which the teacher wishes (or feels impelled) to impart. The student legitimated by this system is one who has a high grade-point average, which means that he scores high in delivering back to the teacher the knowledge which the teacher desires him to return. In one way or another, he has learned how to "con" the system to obtain the highest rewards which the system has to offer. For some time we have heard of parents who advise their capable children to take easy courses in high school so they can get good grades, achieve the honors which the school has to dispense, and gain admission to the prestigious institutions who consider entrance primarily on the arithmetic of grades gleaned from subjects or culture-bound tests of academic achievement. Having gained admission to these institutions, which are operated on the same basis as the lower schools, the students have the social credits which they need for later life regardless of how well they do from that point on.

The paradigm of the school today is not much different from the basic, ancient plan and reconfirmed by the medieval *trivium* and *quadrivium.* The model of the university has pressed itself down upon the lower schools regardless of its functionality for their purposes (or for the purposes of the university, for that matter). The proficiency of the teacher is determined primarily by the degree to which he can demonstrate his knowledge of a discipline. In the university, protestations to the contrary, publications are a key factor in promotion because they are presumed to demonstrate the scholarly proficiency of the practitioner. The transmission of knowledge to the immature is of lesser concern at all levels, with the possible exceptions of the elementary school, where ability to control pupils is more important than all other considerations. The curriculum itself is divided into separate streams of knowledge, to suit primarily the structure of academic disciplines and the scholarly achievements and ease of the teachers rather than either the learning of the students or the applicability of knowledge to human affairs. Each discipline must have some distinctive characteristics, including a methodological and theoretical base which is hard to acquire, the acquisition of which sets the elected apart from the untouchables, and gives the scholars in the field the criteria upon which they may select those from their ranks whom they will accord high honors and those who will be rejected as unworthy. A basic tenet of this system is that education is a process of screening out the unfit rather than helping to capacitate each youth to achieve his life's purposes.

Not only do we have the internal hierarchies and reward systems within each discipline, but they also exist among disciplines—and, in the lower schools, among the various other subjects admitted into the curriculum. Because of their rigorous method, high standards of admission, rigid selectivity, prolonged period of initiation, and ability to transcend the temporal and emerge into the irrelevant, the natural sciences and mathematics have been accorded the highest prestige in the academic community. The humanities have traditionally been held in high repute, and if they can gain the rigor of method through which they are striving to resemble the natural sciences in method, they may regain their former place. The social sciences (for two decades, at least, attempting to eliminate the term *social* in favor of the term *behavioral* to gain a more precise basis for operations) have also been searching for that methodological and theoretical sophistication which will enable them to turn all human thought to computers and the mathematics of statistics, evolving finally the basis for controlling, if not eliminating, idiosyncratic behavior through behavioral modification techniques. On the lowest rung of prestige, except for the ancient professions of law and medicine, are the professional schools which are essentially agencies for the training of students in the routine professional skills needed for the maintenance of human society.

To accommodate to this prestige ordering, the lower schools have attempted to develop a similar hierarchy of the importance of subjects and subject matter. The curriculum, either officially or in the almost too crass wisdom of the student culture, has been divided into "hard" and "soft" subjects—or to use similar terminology, "solids" and "non-solids," by the very terminology imposing a negative connotation. The "solid" subjects are of course those which should be included in the college preparatory curriculum.

Historically, the lower schools were in two tracks. The "dame" or "primary" schools were those designed merely to teach the children of the poor the basic tools of learning so that they would not be too hard to handle in the control systems of the establishment. If they could be trained to perform their routine jobs within this framework, they could render their services without getting out of line. The second track was the "preparatory" school, the traditional "prep" school avenue for entrance into higher education, the sanctuary of academia and the learned professions. The prep school psychosis still dominates American education, and all else is still peripheral to the main and prestigious objectives. Most schools boast of the academic honors and college achievements of their graduates. Most schools give their highest awards to those students who have done well in the academic (preparatory) program. Few, at least to this writer's knowledge, have justified their existence because of their contributions to good craftsmanship, responsive parenthood, creative homemaking, or the happiness of individuals.

These, then, are the essential characteristics of the paradigm upon which the present educational system is established: the primary goal is the transmission of knowledge; the primary measurable output is the acquisition of knowledge; the primary legitimation is scholarship as an end in itself; the primary function is to screen out of the system the academically unfit. The curriculum is organized into separate academic, subject-matter modules, each module being presumably self-contained and functionally unrelated to other modules. A prestige hierarchy is established in which the academic subjects are accorded high prestige and the vocational subjects are accorded low prestige. Applications to life and life problems are purely coincidental. The major emphasis is placed upon the logical organization of each subject-matter as a separate discipline rather than as a tool which can be used to solve the problems of living. Rigid requirements for graduation (or completion) are established in terms of courses taken and credits earned. Evaluation is a matter of giving eclectically determined grades based upon some arithmetic system to give the appearance that the numerical quantities reduce the amount of subjectivity involved. The reward system of the school is primarily for academic success, grades achieved, and the students' conformance to the requirements of the school. Tragically, the only real exception to the rule is found in the honor, prestige, and privileges accorded to athletes, which may at times exceed the recognition given to academic accomplishment.

In accordance with this model, each teacher works independently within his own classroom and determines the pattern of instructional activities which will be conducted within the classroom in accordance with a generalized curriculum plan provided for the entire school or system. Except for occasional supervision from administrative and supervisory personnel, the teacher is left virtually the sole arbiter of what transpires within the classroom, save when outside pressures may provide certain constraints upon his freedom.

The Anomalies of the Educational System

The question must be asked if despite all that has been accomplished within the framework of the paradigm, there are anomalies which recur and which cannot be resolved within the framework of the existing paradigm. The sense in which the term *anomaly* is used here is that it constitutes a deviation from the expected, anticipated or desired beyond a tolerable margin of error. It constitutes an incongruity for which the system cannot account and represents a pattern of deviation from the desired outcomes of the educational program.

Even the casual observer of the American educational scene must inevitably come to the conclusion that there are numerous anomalies within the system which seemingly cannot be resolved within the framework of the system. Some of these anomalies are of minor importance, but others are of such magnitude that they arouse doubts concerning the appropriateness of the entire system.

(1)   The schools have long faced the dilemma which results from the disparities between the basic objectives and programs of the schools and the concerns, problems, needs, and aspirations of the youth who are in attendance. The case for the problem has been well stated by Ralph Tyler:

> We currently fail to educate approximately one-third of the youth enrolled in high school. This is not due primarily to the inadequacies of the students but to the inappropriateness of the program to supply them with the kind of learning required. They are concerned with becoming independent adults, getting jobs, marrying, gaining status with their peers, and helping to solve the ills of the world. They perceive little or no connection between the educational content of the school and their own concerns. "What has algebra to do with me?" they ask. "Why should I try to remember the chief battles of the Revolutionary War?" Even the high school science laboratory appears to be a place for following directions of the laboratory manual to see if they can obtain the results reported in the textbook.[1]

The only question we can have about Tyler's statement is his estimate of the number of students whom the high schools fail to educate. U.S. Commissioner of Education Marland suggests that one-half of the high school population "are being offered what amounts to irrelevant, general educational pap."

Since the curriculum is handed down by tradition and relates to the structure of knowledge, not to the life needs of students, its function, one must presume, is not to be relevant to their needs and concerns. The schools are steeped in the academic traditions which emphasize scholarship, not effectiveness in performing one's roles. The stated objectives of the schools relative to human growth and development have become pure verbiage, for the curriculum of the school persists without a basic concern for them. The image of the student which the school seems to perpetuate is one of the scholar in his cloistered study, not the person deeply involved in and affected by the bitter, sometimes overwhelming problems of human and social existence. It is a rare school today that helps the student deal with the personal, social, economic, and moral problems which confront him. This is witnessed in the failure of education to deal effectively with the drug problem, the problems of youth alienation, the decay of standards relative to sexual conduct, the problems of the Pill, crime and delinquency, the disintegration of the family, the control of militarism, the burgeoning of welfare, and on and on. If the psychologists are correct that youth are seeking a sound basis for developing adequate coping behavior, then truly the schools with their core of "solid" subjects preparing them (presumably) for lives of disinterested scholarship are basically irrelevant to them.

(2)   Although presumably dedicated to the education of all children and youth, the instructional programs within the system are related specifically to the needs of the academically able students, and little deviation is provided for the needs of nonacademic students. Basically, the same requirements and expectations exist for all students regardless of whether their I.Q.'s are above 140 or less than 90. For those students who are extremely able, deviations are provided only in terms of more subject matter, more assignments, or more difficult exercises. For the less academically able students, the deviations permitted are for fewer subjects and possibly less difficult assignments. Remedial and corrective work is frequently provided for students who are not able to make the grade academically, but the purpose of this work is not to develop a curriculum uniquely suited to their needs, but rather to help them develop power to cope with the academic subject matter. Because of the standardization of the curriculum, students are frequently forced into subjects that require a degree of conceptual skill far beyond their level of ability. Consequently, the accumulated school experience is one of increasing inability to cope with the conceptual problems around which the school program is established. In the smaller high schools, practically the only curriculum is the college preparatory program in spite of the fact that few students from these schools go to college. In all high schools, whether large or small, the core of the curriculum is the composite of courses required for college entrance. The college preparatory program is justified in terms of its general educational values regardless of the extent to which it provides a conceptual base beyond the ability of numerous students to cope with it. Justification appears primarily to be that it is "good for them." Their inability to cope with the conceptual problems of these courses is looked upon as pathological.

(3)   Since the basic instructional program is unrelated to the developmental needs of the children who are subjected to it, expectations for accomplishment are extremely low, and children are permitted to move through the system without showing any substantial gains in knowledge or skill from the academic subject matter to which they are subjected. Examples are particularly evident in the so-called skill subjects. Every year that a child is in school, he is subjected to the study of language. Over a twelve-year span he engages in reading, studies good grammatical forms, studies the mechanics of writing including spelling, and is exposed to the appropriate forms of speech and oral communication. Yet at the end of the twelfth grade his skills of communication are generally no greater than would have been anticipated had he never studied language as a separate subject, but had interacted with fairly literate people. In fact, there is evidence to suggest that the communication patterns reflect more the expectations of the peer group than the standards which the school attempts to obtain. The research to account for this alarming phenomenon is sparse. It appears as though this condition results from the fact that having compartmentalized the study of language as a separate subject, students acquire the ability to demonstrate the minimal skills or perspectives required within that course but do not apply what they have learned to their everyday speech, writing, or communication in other subjects or in other experiences. Similar conclusions can be drawn about other skill areas of the curriculum as well.

It is hard to comprehend how this situation could be permitted to prevail, particularly in the light of the stated goals of education and the large outlay of resources which is made to the teaching of the core subjects. The answer can only be found in what Silberman refers to as the "mindlessness" of the educational practitioners. Recognizing, perhaps subconsciously, the irrelevance of the studies, and protected by college entrance requirements and graduation standards, the teachers of the academic subjects have been able to persist as though they were participating in a ritual. Why bother with standards of achievement when the system is mindless anyway?

(4)   The compartmentalized curriculum legitimates the acquisition of knowledge within the framework of the course but does not necessitate the student's application of the knowledge outside of the subject matter and particularly not to the behavioral problems which confront him outside the classroom. As Barker and Wright have demonstrated in their studies of psychological ecology, the roles of children become highly adapted to the particular needs of the social setting in which they are engaged. Students will show at least minimal conformity in role behavior to the requirements imposed within any particular behavioral setting, but unless there is some

training for carrying over or relating the learnings in one setting to other settings, it does not necessarily occur. Since the school constitutes something of a haven from the outside world, that which is acquired and legitimated within the school does not necessarily have to relate to the outside world. Presumably the school exists for the purpose of helping students become socially effective human beings, but since it has compartmentalized its entire program into self-legitimated modules there is no requirement that the student's life outside of the school give evidence of his having acquired knowledge and skill within the school setting. Hence, he may be forced to read Shakespeare in the English classroom, but if he reads at all outside of the requirements of the school, comic books may be his only fare. School assumes little, if any, responsibility for a carry-over effect.

(5) In spite of the philosophical goal of relating educational needs to all children and youth, educators have never succeeded in adapting curriculum and instruction to the socio-economic, cultural and ethnic differences of children. Until some of the consequences of this inability became the subject of political turmoil and social unrest, the problem, although well identified, stimulated little effort to study the ways in which adjustment could be made for these divergent characteristics. In spite of the disadvantages which result from the accumulation of disability and the lack of adaptability of programs, suggested remedies still seem to be based upon the assumption that there is nothing wrong with the existing paradigm or the curriculum and objectives that emanate from it. There is again the assumption that pathological conditions exist within these groups and new strategies are needed to accommodate these groups to the existing demands of the schools. That little progress is being made is evidence of the fact that more fundamental reform is needed than is now contemplated.

(6) Although statements of educational objectives have for most of this century concentrated attention upon a concern for individual growth and development, educators have failed to develop truly viable individualized programs and instructional strategies. Since methods of group instruction are more economical, since instructional materials for individualization are scarce, since most instructional strategies have not been adequately developed from a clinical perspective, and since teachers are basically not prepared to conduct a classroom in an individualized mode, the entire school system has been laggard in focusing upon the individual child and devising the means through which individualization can be accomplished. Dissimilar to the fields of social work and health, education does not consider its subjects as clients; consequently, attention is primarily focused on the maintenance of the system rather than services that can be rendered to individuals. Rather than displaying a tendency toward individualization, American education has been increasingly converted to a system

of mass education. The system is based upon the assumption that an individual can become a fully educated human being through mass education. Strategies of instruction and control have been developed to accommodate to the needs of the mass rather than to the individual. Even some of the current recommendations which purport to accomplish individualization— individual learning packages, teaching machines, computer-assisted instruction—are basically systems for better handling masses of students and spreading the effective control by the teacher over increasing numbers of pupils.

No greater argument prevails in local school administration than that involving class size. Obviously, class size is the single most important factor governing educational costs over which school authorities have any control. In the absence of conclusive, empirical evidence, and in spite of the weight of concern of specialists, school boards and superintendents find ready means for economizing by manipulating class size. The assumption is that the teacher can generally teach through mass techniques and strategies as many pupils as the room can hold. The whole structure of education, in fact, has been predicated upon the possibility that the school can mass-produce graduates, each of whom, like auto parts, is approximately replaceable by another. Because of mass emphasis, a broad range of tolerance for inability or indifference to learning is accepted. The measure of success is the mean score of a group on standardized achievement tests, and the use of averages, obviously, obscures the deviations that occur.

(7)   As has been noted by some observers of contemporary schools, as a result of mass education emphasis is placed upon the custodial functions of the school at the expense of its educational functions. Discipline and control are primary concerns. Teachers are more frequently evaluated upon their ability as disciplinarians than as instructors. Systems of rewards and penalties which dominate a great deal of the educational day assume exaggerated importance. Interest and creativity are of lesser concern than conformity to the system, and external requirements assume greater importance than internal motivation. As a consequence of the compulsory nature of school attendance, control mechanisms become of vital concern for the maintenance of order. Legal requirements for attendance have not been accompanied with corresponding measures to adapt programs and practices to all students. The recognition of this state of affairs has led some observers to compare schools with penal institutions. Behavioral problems of students are considered pathological manifestations rather than the consequences of boredom, lack of interest, or lack of motivation.

(8)   Finally, because of the rigidity of the paradigm within which educational programs are established, true legitimation has never been given to any educational programs other than the college preparatory. Since

the dominant philosophies of education stem from the conception of the school as a knowledge transmitting agency, the knowledge function of the school is the only truly legitimated one, and power within the school faculties is usurped by those who control the academic curriculum. There are those prominent in educational philosophy who maintain that preparation for the world of work, for active and satisfying involvement in avocations, for competent performance of family-related roles, has no place in the schools. For these activities, individuals should be trained, not educated. Training for these roles is considered a function of agencies other than the schools. Schools exist to teach subjects, to disseminate knowledge, and rude training for occupational skills is not a part of the knowledge disseminating business. As a consequence of the general application of this conceptual model, at least to a fairly high degree, the major resources of the schools are allocated to the college preparatory program. In small schools which cannot economically diversify programs, offerings are limited almost exclusively to the academic subjects which form the core of graduation requirements. A few courses such as "shop," typing, bookkeeping and homemaking may be offered for the students who hopelessly flounder in the academic curriculum. Even in the large high schools, priorities in the allocation of resources are given to the academic subjects, and the funds that are left over or "squeezed out" are allocated for the other areas.

This situation is particularly incongruous because much of the justification for compulsory education in this country has been based upon a vocationalism—a vocationalism with an absence of vocational preparation. The literature justifying compulsory attendance or strongly urging students to remain in school is based upon what schooling contributes to the earning power of the individual, how graduation from high school results in the ability to obtain and retain a job, and how greater career opportunities are opened to those who have completed this education. In spite of the rationales developed, vocational offerings in most schools are minimal, vocational training is considered inferior to academic or college preparatory programs, and the culture of the school leads students to conclude that those who are *able* enter the prestigious academic programs while those who can't make the grade are candidates for vocational programs.

There is nothing unique in the recognition of the existence of these anomalous situations. They have been identified not only by researchers within the educational profession, but by numerous non-educators who have carefully observed school programs. At the mid-point of the nineteenth century, Horace Mann's efforts toward educational reform were directed toward the remediation of many of these anomalous situations. John Dewey's studies of the American school system of the latter nineteenth and early twentieth centuries led him to develop an educational philosophy which he hoped would replace the existing paradigm, concentrate both on individual and societal needs, and result in an educational system aimed toward helping all youngsters acquire the power to deal effectively with their problems of living. Contrary to the popular wisdom, Dewey's theory did not eliminate the knowledge dissemination functions of the schools. He placed the knowledge disseminating functions in the perspective of the schools' responsibility for helping children become effective adults in a free society. To him, knowledge was an instrumental means through which the child acquired his capability for dealing effectively with the world about him. The necessity for schools' preparing children for a range of societal and human needs other than the academic was recognized by many people in the nineteenth century and resulted in the Congressional recognition that schools and universities were not providing for the total range of educational needs of the population. As a consequence, there was the enactment of the Smith-Hughes Acts stimulating the development of programs in vocational education and the Land-Grant College Acts which inaugurated the concern of universities for programs in agriculture, engineering, forestry, health and other practical arts.

That the legitimated objectives of education were narrow and incomplete was recognized in numerous studies by educators which resulted in new formulations such as: The Cardinal Principles of Secondary Education formulated by the Committee on the Reorganization of Secondary Education of the National Educational Association (N.E.A.) in 1911; the statements of objectives of various content areas developed by the Progressive Education Association in the 1930's; the *Purposes of Education in American Democracy* written by the Educational Policies Commission of the N.E.A. in 1938. The controversies which occupied a considerable amount of time over the reorganization of education for the post-World War II era were fanned into flame by publications such as that of the Educational Policies Commission entitled *Education of All American Youth* and *Education for All American Children,* the statement of the Harvard Commission on General Education entitled *General Education in a Free Society,* and Conant's response to both entitled *Education in a Divided World.*

There were extensive reactions among educators to all of these proposals for change. As a result of the work of early educational reformers, schools became more humane in their perspectives towards children. Significant adaptations of materials and content took place so that they were more directly related to children's interests and levels of conceptual ability. Diversification within school subjects took place and efforts were even made to provide tracks within the school program to accommodate to the needs of children with varying abilities. Programs of special education were introduced to provide means for children with learning disabilities to overcome their deficiencies so that they could participate in the normal activities of the school. Aesthetic and expressive activities were added to the schools. Arts and crafts became incorporated within the school curriculum. Home economics, industrial arts, agriculture, distributive education, typing, short-hand and bookkeeping were added in many high schools, particularly the large ones. An effort was made to provide for a range of vocational subjects, and in some communities following World War I, technical-vocational high schools were established to provide particularly for those students who were not successful in the academic program or were interested in specific occupational fields. The community college movement emerged into full bloom as a response to the high schools' deficiencies in vocational education following World War II.

More recently, attempts have been made to divert the thrust of the school away from routine lock-step programs and emphasis on control and discipline. Contemporary literature is filled with endeavors to relate materials to the needs of children, individualize instruction, utilize pupil and teacher time more creatively, and develop programs for helping children become active learners rather than passive recipients of instruction. New emphases were placed upon adapting instructional strategies to the needs and abilities of children who come from divergent socio-economic, cultural and ethnic groups.

But for all of these efforts one thing remained constant. The basic model of the school as a place for the dissemination of knowledge has not changed. The proposals for improvement have not removed the symptoms of failure which result from an educational program which does not have viable objectives and is still basically irrelevant to the lives of the children. The most significant of the anomalies in current educational practice have been with the schools for a long time, and despite the rhetoric about educational purposes and functions, they have not been resolved. A basic question arises as to whether they can be resolved within the paradigm upon which the existing educational system is based.

"Variations upon a Theme" is not the proper music today. A new theme is needed and must be tested to determine whether or not the deficiencies of the educational system in America can be removed. The new theme was suggested by John and Evelyn Dewey in their little book, *Schools for Tomorrow:*

> The academic education turns out future citizens with no sympathy for work done with the hands, and with absolutely no training for understanding the most serious of present-day social and political difficulties. The trade training will turn out future workers who may have greater immediate skill than they have had without their training, but who have no enlargement of mind, no insight into the scientific and social signifi-

cance of the work they do, no education which assists them in finding their way on or in making their own adjustments. A division of the public school system into one part which pursues traditional methods, with incidental improvement, and another which deals with those who are to go into manual labor means a plan of social predestination totally foreign to the spirit of democracy.

The democracy which proclaims equality of opportunity as its ideal requires an education in which learning and social application, ideas and practice, work and recognition of the meaning of what is done, are unified from the beginning and for all.[2]

What the Deweys said is that the true solution to our educational dilemma lies neither in the continuation of academic education *per se* nor in the development of a separate track for vocational training. They perceived what has actually happened. The separation of the two has been to the advantage of neither. Students have suffered from the division and the unbridgeable gap which has been created. The consequences have been that we have on the one hand provided an irrelevant education for those who might have the potential to advance to the more prestigious positions in the career ladder, and only low-level skills for the others. Both lead to consequences which are proving to be socially hazardous. The challenge of the Deweys is to bridge the gap and make education socially relevant and personally significant, a means of helping all children and youth find useful, self-fulfilled lives for themselves. Can their charge be accepted today?

There are those who believe it can. There are those who believe that sufficient evidence exists for the acceptance of a new set of presuppositions upon which the American educational system can be renewed and refurbished. The American educational system can be helped to resolve the anomalies which have been tearing it apart. The new concept has been termed *career education.* What it means, the presuppositions upon which it is based, the conceptual structure, the problems and the hopes are explicated in the articles which follow.

FOOTNOTES

[1]Ralph Tyler, "Schools Needed for the Seventies," in General Sub-Committee on Education of the Committee on Education and Labor of the House of Representatives, *Needs of Elementary and Secondary Education for the Seventies.* Washington, D.C.: U.S. Government Printing Office, 1970, pp. 794-95.

[2]From the book *Schools for Tomorrow* by John and Evelyn Dewey. Copyright 1915 by E. P. Dutton & Co., Inc. Renewal, 1943 by John Dewey and Evelyn Dewey. © 1962 by E. P. Dutton & Co., Inc., publishers, and used with their permission.

Part II CONCEPTS, ISSUES, PROBLEMS, AND TRENDS

One of the most influential voices to be raised in behalf of career education is that of the United States Commissioner of Education, Dr. Sidney P. Marland, Jr. In support of career education, Commissioner Marland brings both the authority of his office and the possibility of directing Federal resources for its development. The first speech of the Commissioner, "Career Education Now," was given before the National Association of Secondary School Principals at its 1971 convention in Houston, Texas. This document is the first announcement of the Commissioner's intention to place major emphasis upon the development of a new approach to career education.

The Commissioner calls upon educators to purge themselves of academic snobbery. He cites the failure of general education and calls for a unification of the academic and vocational programs into a broad, goal-directed career education. He states, "Contrary to all logic and all expediency, we continue to treat vocational training as education's poor cousin." He urges an end to the division of educational programs into "parochial enclaves," which has resulted in the social quarantine of vocational education. He calls for a career education program which, although solidly based in vocational education, is more than occupational training.

S. P. Marland, Jr.

CAREER
EDUCATION NOW

Since I intend to devote a major part of my remarks today to the subject of career education, it seems appropriate to begin by mentioning that I am finding my new job to be a richly rewarding learning experience.

Take the matter of the Commissioner's place in the Washington pecking order. I have always held the commissionership to be one of the great and auspicious positions in the Federal Government. So naturally, when I learned that a prominent Federal official is issued a brand new $30,000 bulletproof limousine each year, I immediately inquired into the nature of the transportation furnished to the Commissioner of Education.

It turned out to be rather basic—a small, misshapen, used Rebel. When I asked for an improvement, I was sent a slightly newer, small, misshapen, used Rambler.

I am not discouraged. I am merely chastened. It's really a very nice car. And, besides, I have been assured that the Commissioner hardly ever gets shot at.

This address was given at the 1971 Convention of the National Association of Secondary School Principals, Houston, Texas, January 23, 1971.

Career education is an absorbing topic at the Office of Education lately. In essence we are attempting to answer a very large question: what is right and what is wrong with vocational education in America today and what can be done to build on our strengths and eliminate our weaknesses?

I will indicate to you in a few moments the major points of our reply, the steps we believe should be taken by the Federal Government and particularly by the Office of Education to strengthen your hand in refashioning the vocational or career curriculum. For we are in wholehearted agreement that it is in serious need of reform and it is my firm intention that vocational education will be one of a very few major emphases of the U.S. Office, priority areas in which we intend to place the maximum weight of our concentrated resources to effect a thorough and permanent improvement.

But let me broaden the discussion a bit at this point to talk about career education not simply from the Federal point of view but from the point of view of you and me and of everyone who has committed his life's work to the proposition that education's prime task is to seek and to free the individual's precious potential. My concern with this vital area of education was with me long before I came into possession of my bent Rambler. It is the result of more than thirty years in school life, ample time to observe the vocational education problem in such diverse settings as New York City, Pittsburgh, and Winnetka, Illinois. For even in Winnetka, archetypal suburb, blessed in material things far above most communities in this country, there are many people who are worried about the logic and relevance of what is being taught their youngsters, particularly when considered in the light of the amazingly sophisticated, complex, and rapidly changing career situations they will face upon graduation from high school or from college.

Winnetkans, like most Americans, ask: "What are we educating our children for?"

Educators, it seems to me, have too often answered: "We simply are not sure."

Uncertainty is the hallmark of our era. And because many educators have been unsure as to how they could best discharge their dual responsibility to meet the student's needs on the one hand and to satisfy the country's infinite social and economic appetites on the other, they have often succumbed to the temptation to point a God-like finger at vocational educators and damn them for their failure to meet the nation's manpower requirements and doubly damn them for their failure to meet the youngster's career requirements, not to mention his personal fulfillment as a human being.

Most of you are secondary school administrators. You, like me, have been preoccupied most of the time with college entrance expectations.

Vocational-technical education has been a second-level concern. The vocational education teachers and administrators have been either scorned or condemned and we have been silent.

There is illogic here as well as a massive injustice. How can we blame vocational educators for the hundreds of thousands of pitifully incapable boys and girls who leave our high schools each year when the truth is that the vast majority of these youngsters have never seen the inside of a vocational classroom? They are the unfortunate inmates, in most instances, of a curriculum that is neither fish nor fowl, neither truly vocational nor truly academic. We call it general education. I suggest we get rid of it.

Whatever interest we represent, federal, state, or local, whether we teach or administer, we must perforce deny ourselves the sweet solace of knowing the other fellow is in the wrong. We share the guilt for the generalized failure of our public system of education to equip our people to get and hold decent jobs. And the remedy likewise depends upon all of us. As Dr. Grant Venn said in his book, *Man, Education, and Manpower:* "If we want an educational system designed to serve each individual and to develop his creative potential in a self-directing way, then we have work to do and attitudes to change."

The first attitude that we should change, I suggest, is our own. We must purge ourselves of academic snobbery. For education's most serious failing is its self-induced, voluntary fragmentation, the strong tendency of education's several parts to separate from one another, to divide the entire enterprise against itself. The most grievous example of these intramural class distinctions is, of course, the false dichotomy between things academic and things vocational. As a first step, I suggest we dispose of the term *vocational education,* and adopt the term *career education.* Every young person in school belongs in that category at some point, whether engaged in preparing to be a surgeon, a bricklayer, a mother, or a secretary.

How absurd to suggest that general knowledge for its own sake is somehow superior to *useful* knowledge. "Pedants sneer at an education that is useful," Alfred North Whitehead observed. "But if education is not useful," he went on to ask, "What is it?" The answer, of course, is that it is nothing. All education is career education, or should be. And all our efforts as educators must be bent on preparing students either to become properly, usefully employed immediately upon graduation from high school or to go on to further formal education. Anything else is dangerous nonsense. I propose that a universal goal of American education, starting now, be this: that every young person completing our school program at Grade 12 be ready to enter higher education or to enter useful and rewarding employment.

Contrary to all logic and all expediency, we continue to treat vocational training as education's poor cousin. We are thereby perpetuating the social quarantine it has been in since the days of the ancient Greeks, and, for all I know, before then. Since the original vocational fields were defined shortly before World War I as agriculture, industry, and homemaking, we have too often taught those skills grudgingly—dull courses in dull buildings for the benefit of what we all *knew* were young people somehow pre-judged not fit for college as though college were something better for everyone. What a pity and how foolish, particularly for a country as dependent upon her machines and her technology as America. The ancient Greeks could afford such snobbery at a time when a very short course would suffice to instruct a man how to imitate a beast of burden. We Americans might even have been able to afford it a half-century ago when a boy might observe the full range of his occupational expectations by walking beside his father at the time of plowing, by watching the farmers, blacksmiths, and tradesmen who did business in his home town.

But how different things are today and how grave our need to reshape our system of education to meet the career demands of the astonishingly complex technological society we live in. When we talk of today's career development, we are not talking about blacksmithing. We are talking about the capacity of our people to sustain and accelerate the pace of progress in this country in every respect during a lifetime of learning. And nothing less.

The question seems to be fairly simple, if we have the courage and creativity to face it: Shall we persevere in the traditional practices that are obviously *not* properly equipping fully half or more of our young people or shall we immediately undertake the reformation of our entire secondary education in order to position it properly for maximum contribution to our individual and national life?

I think our choice is apparent. Certainly continued indecision and preservation of the status quo can only result in additional millions of young men and women leaving our high schools, with or without benefit of diploma, unfitted for employment, unable or unwilling to go on to college, and carrying away little more than an enduring distaste for education in any form, unskilled and unschooled. Indeed, if we are to ponder thoughtfully the growing charge of "irrelevance" in our schools and colleges, let us look sharply at the abomination known as general education.

Of those students currently in high school, only three out of ten will go on to academic college-level work. One-third of those will drop out before getting a baccalaureate degree. That means that eight out of ten present high school students should be getting occupational training of some sort. But only about two of those eight students are, in fact, getting such training. Consequently, half our high school students, a total of approximately 1,500,000 a year, are being offered what amounts to irrelevant, general educational pap!

In pained puzzlement they toil at watered-down general algebra, they struggle to recollect the difference between adjectives and adverbs, and they juggle in their minds the atomic weight of potassium in non-college science. The liberal arts and sciences of our traditional college-preparatory curriculum are indeed desirable for those who want them and can use them. But there must be desire and receptivity, and for millions of our children, we must concede, such knowledge is neither useful nor joyful. They do not love it for its own sake and they cannot sell it in the career marketplace. Small wonder so many drop out, not because they have failed, but because we have failed them. Who would not at the earliest convenient and legal moment leave an environment that is neither satisfying, entertaining, nor productive? We properly deplore the large numbers of young men and women who leave high school before graduation. But, in simple truth, for most of them dropping out is the most sensible elective they can choose. At least they can substitute the excitement of the street corner for the more obscure charms of general mathematics.

I want to state my clear conviction that a properly effective career education requires a new educational unity. It requires a breaking down of the barriers that divide our educational system into parochial enclaves. Our answer is that we must blend our curricula and our students into a single strong secondary system. Let the academic preparation be balanced with the vocational or career program. Let one student take strength from another. And, for the future hope of education, let us end the divisive, snobbish, destructive distinctions in learning that do no service to the cause of knowledge, and do no honor to the name of American enterprise.

It is terribly important to teach a youngster the skills he needs to live, whether we call them academic or vocational, whether he intends to make his living with a wrench, or a slide rule, or folio editions of Shakespeare. But it is critically important to equip that youngster to live his life as a fulfilled human being. As Secretary Richardson said, "I remind you that this department of government more than anything else is concerned with humaneness."

Ted Bell, now Deputy Commissioner for School Systems in OE, made the point particularly well in a recent speech to a student government group. He was speculating on the steps a young person needs to take not just to get a diploma or a degree today, but to make reasonably sure he will continue to learn in the years ahead, to be an educated man or woman in terms of the future, a personal future. Dr. Bell said:

> Here the lesson is for each person to develop a personal plan for lifelong learning: learning about the world we live in, the people that inhabit it, the environment—physical and social—that we find around us; learning about the sciences, the arts, the literature we have inherited and are

creating; but most of all, learning the way the world's peoples are interacting with one another. If one educates himself in these things, he will have a pretty good chance of survival and of a good life.

In other words, life and how to live it is the primary vocation of all of us. And the ultimate test of our educational process, on any level, is how close it comes to preparing our people to be alive and active with their hearts, and their minds, and, for many, their hands as well.

True and complete reform of the high school, viewed as a major element of overall preparation for life, cannot be achieved until general education is completely done away with in favor of contemporary career development in a comprehensive secondary education environment. This is our ultimate goal and we realize that so sweeping a change cannot be accomplished overnight, involving as it does approximately thirty million students and billions of dollars in public funds. Until we can recommend a totally new system we believe an interim strategy can be developed entailing four major actions.

First we are planning major improvements in the vocational education program of the Office of Education. This program, as you know, involves the expenditure of nearly $500,000,000 annually, and our intention is to make the administrative and programmatic changes that will enable the states to use this money to make their vocational education efforts more relevant to the needs of the young people who will spend their lives in careers in business and industry. We intend to give the states new leadership and technical support to enable them to move present programs away from disproportionate enrollments in low-demand occupations to those where national shortages exist and where future national needs will be high.

Right now state training programs fill only half the jobs available each year. The other half are filled by job seekers with no occupational job training of any kind. We do better in some fields than others, of course, particularly production agriculture where we are able to come closer to meeting the total need because it is a relatively static job market with little growth projected. About 70 percent of the demand in farm jobs will be met with trained help this year compared with only about 38 percent in the health occupations and 35 percent in various technical fields. This is nice if you happen to own a farm, not so nice if you run a hospital or laboratory.

We obviously require greater emphasis on such new vocational fields as computer programmers and technicians, laser technicians, and jet mechanics. We particularly need qualified people in health occupations such as certified laboratory technologists, dental assistants, occupational therapists, and the like. And, of course, we badly need men and women to capably service the rapidly growing environmental industries. Though when we speak of new occupations it is always useful to remind ourselves that even some of the newest, such as computer programming, for example, will very likely be obsolete in twenty years or so, affirming once again the need for a sound educational base underlying *all* specific skill training.

Second—here I speak of all cooperating agencies of education and government—we must provide far more flexible options for high school graduates to continue on to higher education or to enter the world of work rather than forever sustain the anachronism that a youngster must make his career choice at age 14. This demands that we broaden today's relatively narrow vocational program into something approaching the true career education we would eventually hope to realize. Vocational students need much more than limited specific skills training if they are to go on to post-secondary education, whether at the community college or four-year level. And young people presently drifting in the general education waste-land need realistic exposure to the world of work, as well as to the option of general post-secondary schooling.

Third, we can effect substantial improvement in vocational education within current levels of expenditures by bringing people from business, industry, and organized labor, who know where the career opportunities are going to be and what the real world of work is like, into far closer collaboration with the schools. Eventually, further subsidies or other encouragement to industry to increase cooperative education and work-study could greatly enhance these programs. Efforts should be made by people in educational institutions offering occupational courses to get nearby employers to help in the training. This will not only aid the students but employers as well by providing these cooperating firms a ready supply of skilled workers well prepared for the specific demands of their particular fields. I would add only this caveat: that these work experience arrangements be accepted and operated as genuine educational opportunities, of a laboratory nature, not simply as a source of cheap help for the business and pocket money for the student. Youngsters should be given the opportunity to explore eight, ten, a dozen occupations before choosing the one pursued in depth, consistent with the individual's ambitions, skills, and interests.

Fourth, we must build at all levels—federal, state, and local—a new leadership and a new commitment to the concept of a career education system. For we require leaders willing to move our schools into more direct and closer relationships with society's problems, opportunities, and its ever-changing needs. I believe these leaders will come primarily from the ranks of organizations such as yours. Not only will the present vocational-technical education leaders be partners in change, but general educators, long dedicated to the old ways, must become new champions of the career program.

In closing, a word about two very promising OE efforts to help strengthen vocational-technical education in its most crucial aspect, personnel.

The teacher is by far the most important factor in the school environment. We all know this. And we also know that voc-ed teachers are in seriously short supply.

We are also keenly aware that vocational-technical education is starved for other critical personnel, especially those qualified to develop and administer productive programs.

The first effort, called Leadership Development Awards, is a doctoral fellowship program under the Education Professions Development Act. It seeks to identify and train a cadre of leaders for the vocational-technical career education field. As an initial move we have made the first group of awards to 160 experienced vocational educators to enable them to undertake full-time study at the doctoral level.

These men and women are attending eleven universities which share an emphasis on career education. These institutions pay special attention to the needs of the disadvantaged and handicapped; they cooperate closely with industry, the states, and the local districts; and they have established close working relationships with the surrounding communities.

Training lasts from two to three years. It is not tied to the campus but is essentially an intensive internship program with opportunities for research and exploration into the complexities of our constantly changing occupational structure.

We believe these doctoral candidates will make a very constructive imprint on the world of career education. But they will not be cast adrift upon graduation to search out their own niche in that world. Their home states will develop plans for the most strategic use of their skills—in colleges and universities which prepare career educators, in state departments of vocational education, in community colleges, and at the local level for development of the entirely new approach school systems must take to career education.

Our second effort is a program, already producing impressive results, to help the states attract and train teachers and administrators in vocational-technical education. The Leadership Development Awards I have described will produce the shapers and developers of the new career education; this second effort will produce the teachers to carry out the realistic and contemporary plans and programs they develop.

We are funding a variety of state plans. The money is helping to train personnel to work with the disadvantaged and the handicapped, to develop innovative and effective methods of exchange between teachers and businessmen, and to design and carry out more effective vocational guidance, a particularly crucial area. The funds are also being used to increase the number of trades and industry teachers in the emerging occupations that I spoke of a few moments ago.

The overriding purpose of this program is to encourage the states to develop their own capacities and their own resources to produce vocational-technical teachers in the numbers we need and of a quality we need. This new blood will energize career education, particularly in our city schools, whose revitalization is certainly education's first order of business.

President Nixon put the matter well when he said, "When educators, school boards and government officials alike admit that they have a great deal to learn about the way we teach, we will begin to climb up the staircase toward genuine reform."

We have, I believe, begun to climb that staircase. We have begun, at least in part, the difficult, continuing work of reform. These recent tumultuous years of challenge and strife and all-encompassing change have given us lessons to learn, especially lessons in humility. But they have also taught us to hope and to act. The actions in vocational education and teacher education that I have outlined to you today are but the first in a series of reforms which I intend to initiate and carry out within the U.S. Office of Education. I solicit your reactions to what I have said for I particularly want to bridge the gulf between the Federal Government and the education leaders in the states, in the communities, indeed, in all the classrooms of America.

With a guarantee of your tolerance and support I will return to Washington and my new duties confident that the absolute need to develop a strong new program of career education is well understood by you who must understand it, that you and I agree on the kind of action that must be taken and the urgency of taking it. I respect and salute your capacity to reform the secondary schools of the land. In sum, the schools are engaged in swift change because you the educators have chosen to change them. The schools, I conclude, are in good hands.

The second speech of Commissioner Marland was presented in Washington, D.C. to the annual meeting of State Directors of Vocational Education in 1971. (Some parts of the speech have been omitted because they dealt with matters of immediate concern rather than the long-range development of career education.)

The Commissioner indicates that his concern for the development of career education is based upon the failure of our present programs in vocational education to reach a sufficient number of students. He states that the new concept of career education is an effort to attune education to the realities of our times. In this presentation, the Commissioner outlined the general features of three model career education programs which are currently funded by the Federal Government.

S. P. Marland, Jr.

CAREER EDUCATION: MORE THAN A NAME

Speaking in Houston earlier this year, as you may have heard, I had occasion to urge that the term *vocational education* be dropped in favor of *career education.* Since that change would result in different job titles for you, not to mention a rather significant alteration in your professional lives, I think I owe you an explanation.

Let me say first of all that I was not indulging in an empty image-building exercise, the mania that leads us into such aberrations as renaming dog catchers canine administrators. A dog catcher by any other name will still catch dogs. But career education, as I envision it, will be, to mix my mammals, a horse of quite a different color. While it will necessarily and properly embrace many of vocational-technical education's skill-producing activities, it will also reach a large percentage of students now unexposed to the usual vocational education offerings. Instead of the slightly less than 25 percent of high school students now enrolled in some kind of vocational skills programs, for example, the career education concept could affect, and affect in a fundamental fashion, as high as 80 percent of those young people.

This address was given before the annual meeting of the State Directors of Vocational Education, Washington, D.C., May 4, 1971.

My motivation in suggesting *career education* is to acknowledge that the best of our vocational education is very good indeed but does not, under its present stereotype, serve enough students. Vocational courses, cooperative work experience, occupational training—by whatever name, this kind of education has provided millions of Americans with very usable skills. Equally important, it has given them a sense of the world that lies beyond the classroom. Too much of the rest of education fails significantly in this respect.

It is precisely vocational education's sense of continuity that should be extended to all education. The connection between education and a person's life work should be as obvious to others engaged in education as it is to you who are experts in the field. But the fact is that millions of children are processed through the classrooms of this nation every year in a kind of mindless shuffle that hardly deserves the name of education. How many of these young people, so many the victims of the general curriculum, will succeed in life, we can only guess at. But I suspect that those who do achieve some measure of success will be a very tiny minority of heroic types who can overcome the gross handicap of an inadequate public school preparation. For the rest, the great majority, personal failure patterned after and largely caused by the failure of those who sought to educate them is predictably certain.

I have spoken out against the secondary-level general track before and I feel impelled to do so again today. Almost all of the shockingly high number of unemployed youth are products of the general curriculum and we can expect small improvement until the general curriculum is completely done away with in favor of a system of high school education with but two exits—continued education or employment—and nothing else.

This is not to suggest that the concept of career education should be associated only with high school. Indeed, it is extremely dangerous, as we are finding out, to wait until the high school years to begin to acquaint the student with the idea of applying what he has learned, to teach him the purposes of education as distinct from the forms of education.

In Germany, Poland, and a number of other countries—some democratically governed, some not—the situation is quite different and, I would think, far more conducive to getting the youngster started toward making the difficult decisions of life: who and what each would want to be, and the kind of work or continued education necessary to accomplish the purpose. Work experience in these countries begins in the very earliest years of formal education. Here in the United States, by contrast, teachers encounter any number of nine-year-olds and ten-year-olds who have only the vaguest notion of what their fathers do for a living. It has even become a kind of upper-class ideal in this country for the boy or girl to put off thinking about a possible occupation until after completion of the baccalaureate degree which, by the time they receive it, may well be a surplus item. We have an excess of such degrees now in the aerospace industry and in certain parts of the teaching profession, and the National Planning Association predicts eventual excess of bachelor's degrees in every field except the health professions. The Department of Labor indicates that in the near future 80 percent of all jobs will be within the range of the high school diploma.

The consequences of isolation from the realities of the workaday world are painfully apparent in households everywhere. One distraught father, whose son like so many other sons and daughters these days dropped out of college for no apparent purpose, offered an explanation that seems as good as any. "A lot of kids," he said, "don't know what they want to do . . . because they've never done anything."

At the other end of the economic spectrum it is less a matter of indecision than inability. We daily witness the brutal rejection of untrained youngsters by our increasingly technological society because they cannot compete in the one area in which man is clearly superior to his machines —the ability to think. Consequently, we have in this country the highest youth unemployment rate in the world and the relentless advance of technology is making the situation explosively worse.

Of all the black girls under the age of 25, 30 percent are unemployed, a higher rate of joblessness than that suffered by this country during the Great Depression of the 1930's. The jobless rate among young black men stands at 25 percent. Even whites between the ages of 16 and 25 are unemployed at probably three times the rate of the labor force as a whole. And in the severe pockets of unemployment—the inner cities especially— the percentage of jobless youth balloons to many times these national averages I have been citing.

By 1975 we expect the unskilled to account for less than 5 percent of the labor force, or something in the neighborhood of 4.5 million jobs. Yet Bureau of Labor Statistics projections indicate that we will still have more than 3.5 million young people with no salable skills trying to squeeze themselves into this sad 5 percent category. For them there will literally be no room at the bottom.

This tragic situation clearly indicates that America's educational efforts are failing or at least that they are not attuned to the realities of our times. If we are to correct that failure and if education is to serve properly its national purpose, then we must bridge the gulf between man and his work. We in education must be actively concerned with the boys and girls in our charge not just until they receive a diploma but until they have made the transition from student to worker or are enrolled in post-secondary education. Our job is not done properly, in other words, until each and every one of those youngsters is capable of developing a clear sense of direction in life and is able to make a responsible career choice.

We must also be concerned and active on behalf of adults who cannot supply the skills and knowledge society now demands. Education must help upgrade the job skills of these men and women, and retrain them where necessary. I strongly believe that we must also make a particularly imaginative and energetic effort on behalf of the returning Vietnam veterans. The problem of readjustment to the requirements of civilian life, always severe, is far more difficult in their case because there is less enthusiasm in the country to receive and help them than there was for the veterans of World War II and Korea.

It is of course one thing to propose a new system of career education and quite another to attempt to answer the variety of questions that the proposition evokes. What would career education be like in actual operation? How would it differ from the skill training that some have seen as the province of vocational-technical education? What difficulties lie in the way of accomplishing the very broad and demanding objectives that career education implies at all levels in and out of school experience?

The importance of finding those answers cannot be overstated. It is flatly necessary to begin to construct a sound, systematized relationship between education and work, a system which will make it standard practice to teach every student about occupations and the economic enterprise, a system that will markedly increase career options open to each individual and enable us to do a better job than we have been doing of meeting the manpower needs of the country.

Because I am so convinced of the urgency of this matter, I have directed that the Office of Education research staff give major emphasis to this single area until we are successful in designing a workable system of career education.

The National Center for Educational Research and Development, under the direction of Harry Silberman, is at this moment concentrating much of its creative resources on the development of three model career education programs for use in schools, businesses, and homes. We believe these models, initially developed by Dr. Edwin Rumpf and the Division of Vocational and Technical Education, will provide useful alternatives to present practice. They represent to our knowledge the first comprehensive attempt to devise a career education system to serve virtually all Americans.

School-Based Model

The first model, oriented directly toward the school setting, would affect kindergarten through junior college, reshaping the curriculum so as to focus it directly on the concept of career development. It would tie the school closely to the activities of local community, local business, and local industry. Its principal objective would be to guide each student either to a job—a solid rewarding job, not dead-end labor—or to further formal education.

The essential elements in this model are coordination among the various grade levels and the establishment of practical relationships with those outside the school who strongly influence the student's choice of a career. Parents and counselors play a crucial role in guiding young people toward a career by encouraging them to set their own values and make their own decisions, not to have values and decisions imposed upon them. For this reason the school-based model should be combined with adult education efforts, especially among our more educationally disadvantaged population.

The school-based model will incorporate a number of the innovative concepts that are being developed in the vocational education programs that you represent. Specific skills training at the high school level is an important component of the school-based model. I certainly do not believe that general job information of some kind—the old industrial arts and vocational counselor apparatus—produces useful job skills. Under career education it would be the intention that every youth would leave the school system with a marketable skill. Otherwise career education would be no improvement over the present general curriculum.

Employer-Based Model

The second model career education system would be created, developed, operated, and supported primarily by business in companionship with the schools. The idea would be that a group of industrial, commercial, and other kinds of firms would collaborate in developing the program for the benefit of the 13–20 age group. These are the boys and girls who have left school without acquiring the kinds of understanding and competence they need to live fulfilled lives as free men and women in a free society.

This model would combine general education, vocational training, and work experiences carefully selected for their career development possibilities. Not just one but several part-time jobs would be open to each student to enable him to pick an occupational area he wants rather than accept the only thing he is offered.

We foresee the possibility that a firm of management specialists retained by the schools would operate this program and assume the principal responsibility for seeing to it that specific objectives were accomplished. We are also looking into the design of suitable incentives to encourage participation by businessmen, possibly through such arrangements as tax credits and performance contracts. And of course there would be the powerful built-in incentive for business to join this program in terms of the opportunity to find, train, and retain high-quality employees.

Home/Community Based Model

The final model, supportive of the first two, is a plan to use the home and community institutions as career education centers. Our purpose would be to reach and teach individuals with limited formal schooling or persons whose limited basic knowledge and restricted personal skills hold them back from job opportunities or job advancement. By combining effective adult education with vocational education we can open career opportunities to millions of adults who presently have little or no hope of advancement.

Women are a special target for this career education approach. Increasingly, women are going into the world of work, both for economic reasons and for reasons of personal fulfillment. They are held back by unfortunate stereotypes about so-called "appropriate" women's roles, by their own limited self-concepts, and by lack of preparation for effectively combining the occupational and homemaker roles. They need educational programs of the kind this home-based model can provide to broaden their vocational horizons and prepare them to be increasingly active in both domestic and commercial worlds.

We believe that occupational training of this sort can be effectively transmitted by television. The model would emulate the highly successful *Sesame Street* preschoolers' program, providing information in lively, entertaining, attention-getting style. Operating by means of educational TV and employing cassette techniques, the program would offer information on career options and general background for the viewer on what it would be like to work as a computer programmer, health occupations specialist, or whatever. The viewer would be motivated to enhance his employability and develop awareness of values associated with work. Given a career choice, he could then continue the cassette instruction by arrangement with the local schools, finally qualifying for examination and placement.

However these pilot efforts eventually work out, there is no question that putting a comprehensive program of career education together will demand all the imagination, energy, and good will that we can muster. And, as you may well be reflecting, it will also require money in generous amounts, much of it from the Federal treasury. In this connection we can be encouraged by the consistently strong record of the Congress in supporting vocational education since the time of the First World War. We are only beginning to feel the impact of the most recent major legislation, the Vocational Education Amendments of 1968, in the growth of total vocational enrollment to 8,780,000 in Fiscal Year 1970. And I particularly want to congratulate you on helping a million more high school students to receive vocational skills this year compared with the year before.

Post-secondary vocational enrollments in Fiscal Year 1970 topped the one-million level, an increase of more than 40 percent over 1969. The pattern of growth is also convincingly demonstrated in the areas of greatest need, with almost a million disadvantaged and handicapped youngsters enrolled in vocational training this year for the first time. State and local governments have responded admirably to the Federal initiatives, putting more than five dollars of their own money into vocational education for every dollar of Federal investment, an expenditure far exceeding the matching-funds requirements of the Federal programs.

Nevertheless, the picture is not entirely bright. While Congress has increased authorizations for vocational programs by more than 400 percent for the 1965–72 period, appropriations have been lagging. It is not unusual of course for appropriations to fail to match authorizations. But what troubles me—and, I suspect, you—is that the gap in terms of vocational education has widened considerably in recent years. The percentage of authorized funds that have been appropriated for vocational programs shows a decline from 88 percent in Fiscal 1965 to only 44 percent in the current fiscal year, a movement that must be reversed if we are to carry out the intention of Congress as well as covering the broader expectations implicit in career education.

I am distressed by this situation and I intend to use whatever influence I have to seek restoration of this percentage to a respectable level. In view of the critical unemployment situation among our young people, I would not think it unreasonable to ask for the full amount Congress has authorized —more than a billion dollars.

I am also distressed by the decision to reduce the request for vocational education funding in the Fiscal 1972 budget by 25 million dollars at a time when it should be increasing substantially. Again I am bound to say that I disagree and will argue for restoration of these and additional funds in Fiscal 1973 which will be my first year of budget influence. We have received reactions from the states to the proposed cut and their position, as you are aware, is uniformly and understandably in opposition to this budget treatment.

There is also the matter of staffing within the Office of Education, where the trend toward an ever lowered number of personnel has been of considerable concern throughout the entire vocational education field. In 1965, when the Division of Vocational and Technical Education program money stood at less than half the present level, the headquarters and field staff consisted of 141 positions. Despite the notable increase in funds and programs that has since taken place, the staff has sustained accelerating cuts until today it stands at approximately a third of its 1965 level.

I pledge to you today to do whatever I can within a very restricted personnel situation to restore the manpower levels for the future administration of our vocational-technical programs. For I want to make it clear that I have not cited these unfortunate personnel and funding trends for the purpose of belaboring the past. But since I am acutely conscious of your feelings about these matters, I wanted you to know that I am well aware of the situation and that I am not happy with it. I want to work with you, as we plan for our Fiscal 1973 budget, to seek substantially increased appropriations, to expand our vocational education staff, and to do whatever else seems necessary in order to provide you in the states with appropriate levels of financial and technical assistance.

Before we leave this matter of funding, I would like to comment briefly on prospects for vocational education under the Administration's planned revenue sharing program which is now before the Congress. Since the Federal money supporting vocational education is scattered through several pieces of legislation, it is not a simple task to lump all the programs together. Yet I believe that there is no reason to fear that the enactment of revenue sharing would have the effect of diminishing the total amount of that support. In fact, if revenue sharing were to go into effect in Fiscal 1972, it is clear that Federal support for vocational education would show a substantial increase.

In any case, it seems to me that the educational revenue sharing approach provides distinct advantages to the states and communities apart from any expansion of funds, as important a consideration as increased money unquestionably is.

First, the proposal—if enacted into law by the Congress, as I surely hope it will be—will greatly simplify the administration of Federal funds both in Washington and in the states and communities. Approximately twenty-eight legislative titles, and an even greater number of individual programs, would be consolidated, freeing government personnel at all levels from many of the complicated routines that now consume a significant portion of the staff's time. Relieved of much of this burden, both Federal and state personnel could devote far more of their knowledge and experience to the direct service of the children and adults who need their help. Our attention should be on education, not processing papers.

The second advantage that would accrue to the states from enactment of education revenue sharing would be greater flexibility. Those of you who work with the administration of Federal programs in the state offices would experience far more freedom in the use of vocational funds—freedom to select the applications that make the most sense to you, and freedom from obligatory adherence to a plan not necessarily a true reflection of local needs. Washington's intentions were good, as everyone would concede, in establishing the categorical approach of the 1960's, but the time has come when a shift to greater local direction and greater local responsibility is clearly necessary.

If a particular state so desired, for example, it would be free to transfer up to 30 percent of the funds allotted to any of four categories under education special revenue sharing—vocational education, aid to Federally impacted areas, aid to the handicapped, and general support services. The fifth category, aid to the disadvantaged, is properly exempt from the transfer clause. Under this arrangement, a state could transfer funds to vocational education. In fact its allotment could be increased to as much as twice the basic amount though such a major readjustment of priorities could only come about if you, as advocates of vocational education, could make a very strong and a very convincing case.

Indeed, your powers of persuasion will be a vital factor in determining how vocational education would fare under revenue sharing. The burden of leadership in strengthening your state's program would necessarily fall directly to you and to those educators, administrators, businessmen, and community leaders you call to your cause. It would be up to you to see that vocational education received its share not only of special revenue sharing funds but general revenue sharing funds as well. A solid combination of both can produce a far stronger, far more effective vocational program—career program—than the present system will allow. Of that I am confident.

In closing, let me offer you once again my congratulations on the achievements of vocational education and my personal pledge of support in the difficult and challenging days that lie ahead. If the Office of Education has faltered in the past with respect to your programs, I propose now to make career education one of five high priorities, along with aid to the disadvantaged, education of the handicapped, racial integration, and educational research and development. And I intend to give it more funds, more people, and a larger degree of national prestige than it has yet achieved.

In return I ask your help and the benefit of your counsel in the advancement of the career education concept that I have outlined to you this morning. These ideas are not fixed. Indeed, there is nothing we want or need more than suggestions and recommendations from you who have been deeply and professionally involved with every aspect of career education. Our efforts will come to little unless supported and enlivened by your thoughts and convictions. It is, in sum, our purpose to turn the world of vocational-technical education around to the point where it enjoys at least the level of concern, support, pride, and excellence now favoring the college-entrance program.

Oregon was one of the first states to develop an official policy for the implementation of career education in its schools. Dr. Dale Parnell, Oregon State Superintendent of Public Instruction, discusses the basis for the state's policy and the relationship of career education to other life roles, the occupational clusters, and the "zero-reject" philosophy. He calls for a totally integrated educational program which will implement an educational concept to meet the universal educational needs of children and youth.

Dale Parnell

THE CAREER-CLUSTER APPROACH IN SECONDARY EDUCATION

After listening to a great deal of esoteric talk about how curriculums should be constructed, what should and should not be done, and particularly about what is wrong with our high schools, one school board member leaned back in his chair and asked the most pertinent question of the entire board meeting. Thousands of students, and even teachers, are asking similar questions.

The board member's question was this: "You know, it took me three tries to pass English Composition in my first year of college, but since I was majoring in Business Administration, I took Business English and passed it on my first try with an *A* grade. Now, why do you suppose that happened?"

Why would an individual who barely made it through English Composition sail through Business English? This is the kind of fundamental question that must be answered before the great American experiment in universal education can be achieved.

A lot of questions are being asked about education and a lot of criticisms are being leveled at our schools. The American public is being deluged

This article was first published under the title, "The Oregon Way," in the December, 1969 issue of the *American Vocational Journal* and is reprinted by permission.

with fuzzy thinking on what the schools should and should not be doing, but few critics are coming up with workable solutions that will push the universal education experiment up the road.

What we need is a career-oriented curriculum with what former Associate U.S. Commissioner of Education Leon Lessinger has called a "zero-reject" philosophy of operation. As long ago as 1907, Teddy Roosevelt was preaching the idea of trained minds and trained bodies and advocating that all the children of all the people be educated to the fullest potential. He said: "Progress cannot discriminately exist in the abandonment of physical labor, but in the development of physical labor so that it shall represent more and more the work of the trained mind in the trained body."

Is It Really Universal?

Today, in a society oriented to higher education, one out of five Americans still does not finish high school, and only one in ten actually graduates from a four-year college. Yet, most of the school curriculum (high school in particular) has been structured as though everyone were preparing for a four-year college education.

Is it any wonder that schooling has been irrelevant—totally unlike life —for the majority of secondary-school students? There they sit in the classroom for eight, ten, or twelve years, perhaps for hour after hour of classroom experiences which are often unrelated and irrelevant. The school day is fragmented, students are passive rather than energetic and involved. Grades are the hard currency, critical thinking a major goal, yet grades don't generally seem to reflect even remote attainment of this goal.

Although Americans have called for universal education (every student has worth), schools have given them the bell-shaped curve which says that unless you receive an *A* or a *B* in algebra, geometry, physics, chemistry, etc., you're a terminal student, not advanced, and you don't really amount to much.

School life has by and large been separated from real life, from real work, and from real community service. Small wonder our present approach to universal education has tuned out many young people. Bored, restless, disenchanted, they seek alternate avenues to fulfill their innate desires to learn and to experience.

If there is one thing we have learned in recent years, it is that today's students and parents are career-oriented. They are looking to their schools for career-oriented education.

Speaking of his own son, A. A. Messer, internationally known psychiatrist and journalist, said: "Working has given our boy a sense of identity and of making a contribution. My own family experience is no different from what other parents of teenagers have told me from the very first day I began listening. When a youngster feels able to do a job—no matter what it is, so long as it is important to the child—he feels unique. He feels confident and assertive about himself, and when he is happy with himself, he feels more tolerant toward others; there is less need to find fault with and disparage those about him."

The Oregon Way

Oregon is embarking on a new approach to secondary education that will affect general as well as vocational programs. We are calling this new approach *The Oregon Way.* It is based upon two assumptions:

1. Secondary schools should be preparatory institutions for *all* students. For years we have been telling high school students, "If you want to go to college, then you must prepare in high school by taking this course, that course, and that course." When you boil this advice down to its common elements, what we have really been saying is: "If you want to enter any career that requires a bachelor's degree or more, then while in high school you need certain preparatory programs." Now this is perfectly sensible advice. Our only failing is that we have not generally structured our counseling or curriculums to give similar advice to students entering careers requiring less than a baccalaureate.

2. A secondary-school "preparatory" program should tie the curriculum to the goals of students in such a way that they are motivated while in school and also better equipped to choose from among many alternatives as they take that next step, whether it be on-the-job training, apprenticeship, community college, proprietary schools, or a four-year college.

In Oregon, we are building an approach aimed at the development of skills and understanding which relate to a family of occupational fields. To put it another way, a cluster of occupations is a logical group of selected occupations which are related because they include similar teachable skill and knowledge requirements.

Obviously, the implication is that most high school experiences will be centered upon the knowledge and skills common to the occupations which comprise a cluster, or family. This structure not only has a motivational effect but will prepare students for entry into a broad family of occupations rather than a specific occupation.

Major Change Implied

The career-cluster program will require five major changes in our school systems.

First, high schools must make a definite commitment to move from the present curricular tracking system which uses such terms as "advanced-college prep," "terminal-general" or "remedial-basic" to career-cluster tracks.

Instead of relating his program to a college-prep or terminal track, the high school student relates most of his high school experiences to one of the 18 or so career-cluster tracks. The long and short of it is that we are replacing the present counseling and guidance emphasis on academic ability with emphasis on "real life" goals.

Second, it will be necessary to give general education a massive infusion of illustrations from the world of work. The vast majority of students in our schools need to have academic subject-matter related to what concerns them in real life. Teachers at all levels must plow up their subject area fields and sow them with relevant materials. They must bring into the teaching process examples of how the concepts, symbols and language of their particular disciplines can be used in everyday life—and more particularly, in careers.

Third, high school curriculums will need to be rebuilt around the career-cluster or family-of-occupations concept so that students may select a career cluster at the beginning of their high school experience and then tie a majority of their high school experiences into this generalized goal. This will not involve so much a change in facilities or curriculum as a change in guidance and counseling patterns and a change in the way a secondary-school curriculum is outlined.

What we are really calling for here is a change in thinking so that preparation for a career becomes accepted as one of the clear and primary management objectives of the secondary school. Most of the 25,000 occupations listed in the Dictionary of Occupational Titles can be reduced to 18 clusters for purposes of secondary-school instruction and goal setting.

The new scheduling and student forecast sheet will likely include the following career-cluster options:

Accounting	Construction
Agriculture	Domestic & Custodial
Clerical	Electrical

Food Service	Metals
Graphic Arts	Secretarial
Health	Social Services
Marketing	Textiles
Managerial	Transportation
Mechanical & Repair	Wood Products

Fourth, specific training (as opposed to general occupational education) for those thousands of occupations that do not require a bachelor's degree will become largely the responsibility of post-high school institutions, i.e., community colleges, apprenticeship programs, on-the job training, or proprietary schools. If a student goes through a good career-cluster program in high school, he should be prepared for an entry-level job, but more likely, he will be prepared for specialized, post-secondary education and training.

We are urging community colleges and high schools to cooperate in planning an articulated educational program that will enable all students to achieve their career goals, regardless of where they live. Community colleges and high schools must cooperate in the planning of joint use of facilities, guidance and counseling programs (vocational as well as academic), and advance placement opportunities—and when feasible, share instructional staff.

Fifth, every school and community college must build highly integrated and greatly strengthened guidance and counseling programs. Elementary-school guidance must be slanted toward spotting problems and developing solutions to the problems of primary grade children—prevention now, rather than remedial action later on.

Secondary guidance and counseling is largely oriented toward helping students set goals and lifestyles. Schools must place heavy emphasis on services for normal students instead of limiting their services to those required by problem students. At present, guidance and counseling in many public schools is a fire-fighting operation rather than a service which reaches the majority of students who do not have highly deviant behavior patterns.

Students at the high school level should not be expected to set specific career goals. But they should choose a broad field of interest, and the guidance and counseling process should be so structured that if a student wants to change even the broad area in which he is studying, he can do so with minimal frustration.

Educators have probably worried excessively about the fact that students' goals change often. Let us plead guilty to that. Goals will change. But this does not alter the fact that all of us work better and are more highly motivated when we have goals. Aimlessness is one of the plagues of secondary and college students.

The beauty of the career-cluster approach is that students need not set a specific career goal but a general goal. It is still possible to connect most of the secondary-school experiences to the general goal without pinpointing specific careers.

Curricular Considerations

In addition to the changes necessary in the usual high school, we have made at least seven specific assumptions concerning the actual development of career-cluster curriculums at the senior high school level. These seven assumptions are:

1. Selection of a broad career-cluster goal will take place for all students at approximately the end of the eighth grade or beginning of the ninth. Because of differing desires and abilities, student schedules will differ widely even within career goals.

2. It is possible to develop families of occupations that will offer the necessary minimum skills, knowledge, and understanding for further training or minimal entry employment. A minimal program of occupational education for any high school of any size should consist of at least seven of the clusters. Schools will choose cluster curriculums based on student interests and needs, manpower needs and local employment opportunities.

(Obviously it would be impractical for every high school to offer complete preparatory programs for every cluster. Every high school will, however, be expected to offer complete curriculums covering the careers which the majority of its graduates will follow. Moreover, it is hoped that, through state and regional planning, students can find their desired program in a nearby high school, community college, or even business or industry.)

3. The most specific career education labs should be confined to the eleventh and twelfth grades. The minimum requirement to provide intensive and extensive instruction necessary for any effective entry-level performance will be ten hours per week—in addition, of course, to state or local general education requirements. (It is urged, however, that even the general education subjects be related to the career-cluster goal.)

4. A well-developed guidance and counseling program, particularly for the middle grades, is essential to the success of this program.

5. Exploratory experiences that allow students to develop a basic understanding of the various career families will be offered in the middle grades. Industrial arts, business education, home economics and social science will be broadened to include exploration in all career clusters for boys and girls.

6. Basic to all of this is solid achievement in the fundamental skills of communication and computation.

7. Some supervised work experience is a vital part of the cluster curriculums.

Not a Cure-All

Career education is not a panacea for all the ills of today's secondary schools. I do not even suggest that all young people are now going to get all the knowledge and skills we have heretofore been unable to give them in our so-called academic programs. What is suggested is a practical approach to making educational experience more relevant to the needs of youth and to relating the school program to what is going on in life. The changes suggested are not inclusive or exclusive, yet surely are seen as major innovations in the management objectives of the secondary schools.

What does career-related schooling mean for the American educational system? It suggests articulation of the educational enterprise through strong state-level planning and leadership. It means that the first major change should be a clear definition of what we can expect in the way of objectives for the educational system. I have suggested here that those objectives should be based upon life careers.

Taken into curricular consideration must be the career as family member, the career as citizen, the career having to do with a healthy personality and healthy body, the avocational-esthetic career, and finally, the vocational or economic career. It has been my observation that school curriculums have tended to concentrate on the other career objectives to the dilution of the vocational objectives.

First Commitment

If this article has focused on the vocational career, it in no way is intended to downgrade the importance of the other careers. If the American high school is to be truly comprehensive, if the needs of all students are to be met, the necessary changes must begin with a commitment to tie the curriculum to life careers.

Concomitantly, this means a move away from the caste system of college prep, advanced, terminal remedial, dropout. Students in a universal system of education must be able to move through the school programs proudly, energetically, and with purpose. It is fundamental to design our curriculum in such a way that every student sees something there that makes sense to him.

The field of guidance has long been concerned about the problem of career development. Issues related to how individuals choose careers, the personality characteristics of individuals who select specific careers, the influences of early experience, education, sociological variables, peer-group relationships, and parental influences, among others, have been the concern of researchers and scholars in this field. Although a large body of knowledge about these factors has existed for some time, the curriculum of the schools has been little influenced by the implications of such research. Dr. Edwin L. Herr, who is Professor of Education at The Pennsylvania State University, has brought together some of the research and related it to the problem of developing a total educational system which focuses primary attention upon the problems of career development. Dr. Herr points out that there is a considerable amount of evidence that such a unified educational system can successfully accomplish its objectives. He relates the research to specific aspects of such an educational system and shows the relationships of career education to the general educational development of students.

Edwin L. Herr

UNIFYING AN ENTIRE SYSTEM OF EDUCATION AROUND A CAREER DEVELOPMENT THEME

Introduction

The premise upon which this paper is based, that an entire system of education can be unified around a career development theme, may seem pretentious, but it is neither premature nor is it an impossibility. Such an expectation is not premature because, as the outcomes of education obtained by many young persons are appraised objectively, the irrelevance and the lack of specific purpose which results can be readily documented. For example, one study published by the U.S. Office of Education (Grant, 1965) indicated that for every 10 pupils in the fifth grade in 1957–58, 9.4 entered the ninth grade in 1961–62; 8.1 entered the eleventh grade in 1963–64; 7.1 graduated from high school in 1965; 3.8 were expected to enter college in the fall of 1965; 1.9 would likely earn baccalaureate degrees in 1969. Thus, approximately 30 percent of American children leave education before high school graduation. These statistics

This article was written for the Exemplary Programs Division of the United States Office of Education.

include young persons with above average intelligence who have found no meaning in school; who recognize that it is not designed for them. But needs for career development are not restricted to those who drop out. There is reflected in these statistics another 50 percent of the student population who, at the conclusion of high school, enter the labor market directly, and they, too, must come to terms with vocational choices and career considerations whether determined by purpose or by chance. Finally, if the college choice can be seen as something other than an end in itself, as an intermediate step in career development, then those who select this educational option also need help in facilitating their career development. Studies which examine whether career development and choice-making are really of concern to students in elementary and secondary school demonstrate repeatedly that students assert their interest in these areas but also that they are not getting from education assistance in planning the steps which will lead them to their goals, to personal clarification, or to a sense of the vocational and social contexts with which they must cope (Slocum and Bowles, 1967; Campbell, 1968).

It is not the purpose here to exhaust the documentation which supports the relevance of career development for pre-adolescents or adolescents. Rather, it is to acknowledge that the central purposes of education—to prepare the young to accept the reality of constructive pathways to adulthood, to help them engage these pathways successfully, and to assist them find personal relevance in the life options available to them—are not being effectively accomplished for a large number of persons. Because of the personal and societal deficiencies which obtain as a result of this reality, fundamental realignments must occur within the totality of the educational enterprise if the elements by which it discharges its responsibilities are to be made meaningful to all students, not just certain homogeneous strata.

One of the goals, then, toward which education must direct itself in a specific fashion is the provision for every student to acquire the skills which will allow him to make a livelihood; to be responsible economically for himself and for his future family; to be employable. Such skills are not confined to the manipulative skills—the ability to use some set of tools or knowledge to accomplish a specific task or function. While the attainment of such narrowly defined skills has validity in some isolated situations, the present dynamics of the occupational structure lend little credence to the generalized importance to education of such goals in responding to the future.

Rather, the skills necessary are those by which one can use his capabilities, whether limited or great, freely and responsibly in ego-involved activities which contribute both to individual fulfillment and to society's maintenance and progress. These types of skills precede and transcend task skills. They involve the personal values and attitudes which motivate one to gain task skills, to want to contribute, to be constructive. They are the foundation for goal-directed behavior which is vocationally effective. They involve knowledge not only of specific tasks but of the ways such tasks are combined interdependently in the occupational structure and in varied contexts as well as of the opportunities available by which one can use himself in shaping personal and social fulfillment. Such skills do not arise spontaneously, they must be developed in systematic ways.

Is a wedding of self-knowledge, knowledge of environmental options, the acquisition of requisite skills by which effective strategies of planning for, coping with, and mastering the diversity of opportunities which this society affords possible within the context of educational experience? The answer is a qualified Yes: qualified by the purpose and system which is applied as well as by a broadening of the lines by which education and the larger society relate.

In the past the goals of education have reflected a consciousness of the concerns expressed here. However, it has been assumed that all of the goals identified will result as by-products from general education. Little systematic attention has been given to the need to create experiences designed to foster the individual attitudes and skills which comprise such goals. In some instances, education has tried to meet the needs of individual groups within the society with emergency programs conceived in gross terms without responding to the variance, the heterogeneity, which is found in any group whether it be labeled disadvantaged, rural, pre-dropout, mentally retarded, specialty-oriented, or college bound. Further, education has often responded to the "whole child" by allowing the objectives of particular disciplines to define the boundaries within which educational experiences would be conceived, thus negating for the individual the possibilities for interrelating, articulating, sequencing, individualizing, differentiating, and integrating the deluge of experiences which constitute growth, learning, and the attainment of personal competence.

The purpose of this paper is to examine the efficacy of using career development as an organizing theme around which education can be unified and by which the relevance of education can be restored to a larger number of persons. To do this, the following will be considered.

1. Implications of a systems approach to education.
2. Career development.
3. Behavioral goals.
4. Relationships between career development and general education.
5. Relationships between career development and vocational education.

6.   Operational goals towards which exemplary programs and projects might be directed.

IMPLICATIONS OF A SYSTEMS APPROACH
TO EDUCATION

Before turning to some of the implications of career development *per se,* it is necessary to examine some implications inherent in a systems approach to education. A systems approach to the solution of educational problems requires a restatement of ends-and-means concerns of educational philosophy in terms of the application of resources (means) to the attainment of system objectives (ends) (Phillips, 1966). With regard to career development as a unifying theme, the questions become: Can it be accomplished within existing institutional forms? How? If not, why? What modifications to existing structures are necessary? What is required to arrange the educational environment of individual consumers so that particular types of behavioral change can take place? What are the management problems for which solutions must be found? Within the context of education, any system conceived must respond to the separate as well as the interdependent effects of at least the following:

1.   Learner Characteristics
2.   Resource Characteristics
3.   Teacher Characteristics
4.   Instructional Methodology
5.   Administrative Dimensions

The basic question which must be addressed is: "which resources or combination of resources (people, places, media) are appropriate for teaching what type of subject matter to what type of learner under what conditions (time, place, size of group and so on) to achieve what purposes" (Phillips, 1966). Implicit in this question are such realities as the different tempos by which learners can proceed through the system, the required translations of subject matter which will facilitate their progress, as well as a step-wise series of purposes or competencies to be achieved at different developmental points. Portions of knowledge and increasingly complex skill acquisition should be built one upon another according to the characteristics by which learner readiness is defined. It is necessary to define specifically and measurably the terms of competence students must demonstrate upon completion of a set of educational experiences. Abstract or global concepts are not sufficient for these purposes. They must be broken into their components in ways which diminish semantic effects and incremental goals so general as to be not susceptible to programming or measurement.

One of the thorniest problems of evaluation is the statement of expectations for students (Hull, 1967). It necessitates the making of value judgments of what the pupil ought to be able to achieve and it requires description of these activities in behavioral terms. If career development is to be individualized, then each student must be able to work on information or be exposed to experiences different from other students at any given time. This requires both an emphasis on diagnoses and on the availability of diverse learning experiences from which can flow prescriptions for individual progress. Thus, the individuality of pupils demands a set of expectations for each person because career choice, occupational interests, and other relevant variables are determined by each student's concept of occupations, are related closely to his concept of self, and are based to a great extent on his environmental development. Programmed efforts to facilitate career development must begin at the student's level of development and proceed on the basis of personal variables defined by experiences, aspirations, values, capacities, and a continuously spiraling series of success experiences within the career developmental objectives established.

Programmed instruction, as a technology, has made a valuable contribution to a systems process by defining at the outset the desired behavioral change in the student, then breaking down material to effect this change into a logical series of minute steps which the student can take. Through provision of continuous reinforcement and encouragement, immediate recognition of each increment of knowledge is provided and the learner is continuously tested to determine qualitatively whether or not the specific behavioral changes have occurred. If the intended changes have not occurred, one of the most important elements in programmed instruction is implemented—the system is redesigned until the desired results are obtained. There is no intent here to foster the use of teaching machines *per se* but rather to emphasize the importance of the philosophy of programmed learning to a systematic approach to the facilitation of career development. Indeed, in a systems approach to implementing career development, education cannot afford saturation with just one technique at a time, becoming hung-up on sub-systems, but rather available media must be orchestrated in ways which respond effectively to learner characteristics. The observations of Bruner (1964) about curriculum construction are of prime concern to a systems approach facilitating career development. He indicates that a curriculum reflects not only the nature of knowledge itself but also the nature of the knower and the process of acquiring knowledge. It is an enterprise within which the line between subject matter and method grows necessarily indistinct.

Goodlad (1964), Guba (1965) and Krathwohl (1965) have variously identified other factors which must be incorporated into curricular design and by analogy a systems approach to education. Among them are the needs for an explicit theoretical or logical framework; analysis of objectives at increasing levels of specificity, including broad and general statements necessary to program development, goals of sequences of lesson plans and of single lesson plans; curriculum sequences, which move from the bottom up, the elementary school forward; the development and testing of materials with children and youth representing divergent cultural groups; the testing of advantages and disadvantages of various learning styles; and, the implications of each of these for new styles of preparing teachers and counselors to implement and facilitate such systematic efforts to individualize development.

Career development offers the content and the objectives within which such a system can be conceived. The following section will provide an overview of career development and then, respectively, a concept of behavioral goals which might be evolved from career development.

Career Development

Work has always had the potential of meeting more than the economic needs of man. It also provides a means of meeting far broader social and psychological needs among which are needs for social interaction, personal dignity, identification and human relationships. In view of the prevalence of alienation, characterized by difficulties in seeing oneself surely and constructively as a part of the adult society, it seems apparent that many individuals have not been assisted to view work as having personal relevance, as being critical to the way of life they will exhibit, or as being a consistent vehicle for finding self-fulfillment.

The recent surge of findings and theoretical speculation from occupational sociology, developmental psychology, vocational psychology, decision theory and information theory have cast into increasingly bold relief the factors which facilitate or impede individual aspirations and plans of action which lead to placement in the labor market and to development of vocational identity. While career development theory is not yet addressed as completely or precisely to women or to the disadvantaged segment of society as is necessary, that which is presently known provides a sufficient context for programmatic approaches designed to spur the development of effective vocational behavior. The present state of career development is largely descriptive of what happens if no purposeful intervention is convened in the school or in the community to facilitate the process. Thus a systematic approach to such intervention will not only profit the individuals so exposed but will broaden the empirical base from which increasingly meaningful theory can flow.

Brayfield (Brayfield and Crites, 1964) has pointed out that the term *theory* as applied to vocational development is somewhat pretentious if used in the strictest sense. But, if one views the dominant approaches to career development with some objectivity, it is clear that even though no current approach yields the comprehensiveness of explanation desired, in a collective sense there exists a conceptual frame of reference which provides a set of constructs and propositions which serve to explain differential vocational behavior and decision-making as well to facilitate such developmental processes.

The approaches which describe career development or some piece of it can be classified in several ways. They have been classified by Hilton (1962) into the Attribute Matching Model, the Need Reduction Model, the Economic Men Model, the Social Men Model and the Complex Information Processing Model. Osipow (1968) has placed career-development theory into four categories: Trait-factor approaches, sociology and career choice, self-concept theory, and vocational choice and personality theories. The following discussion of career development will present a blend of these two approaches as they relate to a taxonomic structure of career development.

The most consistent approach to career development, at least in a historical sense, is that labeled *trait and factor*. The trait and factor approach to career development, because of its consistent partnership with the findings of psychometrics, has identified the importance of certain specific factors to choice behavior, job satisfaction, and job success. It has examined and identified the interaction of variables such as occupational aspirations, occupational stereotype and occupational prestige as they influence personal value systems and by which is delimited the occupational fields in which exploration will be focused; the importance of social status, socioeconomic background, parental influences and the existence or lack of existence of role models in creating the climate in which vocational development proceeds; the occupational limits prescribed by intelligence level and by the possession of specific aptitudes. It has demonstrated that most individuals have multipotentiality and, thus, the cliché that there is *one* right job for everyone has little foundation in reality. In addition, trait and factor approaches cast light on the range of ability and temperament found in and the latitude which is available to tolerate individual differences in most occupations.

Trait and factor theory has given impetus to an actuarial approach to vocational development in which are couched probability statements of success and failure in terms of specific tasks or jobs. The logic of trait and factor approaches is reflected in the assumptions that individual differences can be observed and classified in terms of certain variables; occupational requirements can be classified in analogous ways; and, thus the individual can be "matched" to the right occupation. Such assumptions represent both the strengths and the weaknesses of trait and factor approaches to career development. Trait and factor approaches have been primarily oriented to specific occupations or to specific tasks but career development is not concerned solely with the choice of an occupation *per se* but rather with a process by which such choices can be purposefully integrated in a patterning of decisions through which an individual plans and implements his measurable traits as well as their personal meaning to him. Further, trait and factor approaches are static in nature. They do not provide for or consider systematically the dynamics, the changing nature of the individual or the environmental characteristics to which he must relate himself.

An implicit derivation of trait and factor theory which pervades much of the thinking about career development is economic in origin. The assumption is made, based upon Keynesian economic theory, that one chooses a career or an occupational goal which will maximize his gain and minimize his loss. The gain or loss is, of course, not necessarily money but can be anything of value to a particular individual. Frequently, this approach assumes that all choice-making is positive. However, individuals frequently choose to escape from an undesirable situation by choosing a lesser evil rather than moving to a positive good. This approach does emphasize the importance of levels of investment—training, time, or energy —and of risk—the relative probability of outcomes—as these contribute to the ways by which different individuals approach choices.

A third approach to career development is *sociologically* based. It has become increasingly clear that the social structure of which one is a part has a great deal to do with the viability of the choices which are made. Thus, there are limitations placed upon career development by restricted social class horizons. Much floundering in decision-making is a result of limited avenues of career choice or limitations upon the knowledge of opportunities available to the individual so restricted. Indeed, such an approach also recognizes by implication the dilemma of a favored and gifted youngster who has so many choices that are relevant that he finds tremendous conflict operating as he chooses. However, the individual of restricted social support blunders in or finds himself in jobs without any purposeful selection on his part, because the only guideline he has is immediate gratification. Thus, the narrowness or the breadth of the individual's cultural or social class horizons has much to do with the choices he can make, can consider, or can implement. For example, the conditions of poverty produce a distinctive milieu that conditions the social responses, the educational attainment, the vocational ambition, and the general level of intellectual competence of many of those raised within its stifling precincts. And, each of these elements has important correspondence with the level and the meaningfulness of career development which can be expected.

A fourth approach is one which can be described as a complex information processing model. It suggests that the magnitude of the information, of the factors which need to be considered, in career development is so overwhelming that the individual prematurely selects a career, and supports his selection by rationalization, or by a process which Festinger (1957) calls cognitive dissonance, without sufficient thought to the implications of the choice. Although the chooser knows there are other options which might be more compatible with his needs and personal characteristics it is comforting to make a selection and suppress the costs of its unrealism by a variety of self-deceptive devices.

A fifth approach is based in need or personality theory. The major assumption of this approach is that because of differences in personality structure individuals develop certain need predispositions, the satisfaction of which are sought in occupational choices and ultimately through career development. This hierarchy or pattern of personal orientations directs the individual toward an environment within which can be found satisfaction or a reduction of needs. Such an approach gives more emphasis than the others cited to genetics, child-rearing practices, and early childhood experiences as these relate to later vocational behavior.

The sixth and final approach to be considered here is that which gives major emphasis to the importance of the self-concept. Self-concept approaches to decision-making and career development can be separated from personality or need approaches not because they reject the latter but because their emphases are more developmentally focused and the importance of the self-concept, as the integrating construct, is accentuated. The assumption is made that individual behavior is shaped by one's self-concept system, the pictures which one has of himself in different roles, which he attempts to implement through career development and in specific choice behavior. One learns through experience and by socialization what kind of person he is, that of which he is capable, what he values, his strengths and weaknesses, and the kinds of outlets which will be compatible with the pictures he has of himself. This is a dynamic model which provides for change in individual behavior, change in environmental expectations, and change in the interaction between the individual and the environment. Rather than espousing only the concept of compromise among options, or the "chance" variables expressed by error and accident, it emphasizes the importance of progressive synthesis in role clarification and in choice options.

The collective finding of these several approaches to career development is that career development like all human behavior is complex. Like other developmental processes, individuals will differ in their readiness level and in the ways by which they develop. Thus, not everyone will reach the same point at the same time. Career development is integral to the total fabric of personality development broadly conceived. It is characterized by progressive development within a network of impinging forces intrinsic and extrinsic to the individual. Career development and choice behavior develop through processes of growth and learning which extend from infancy through at least young adulthood. Choice behavior involves a series of interdependent decisions which are to some extent irreversible. The factors which interact with choice-making and which need to be developed include personal capacities, interests and values; the availability and the requirements of training; opportunities available in the occupational structure; and, the self-concept as it is cast against such relationships as self in institution, self and environment, and self-in-process.

Vocational behavior and career selection develop from less effective behavior and unrealistic or fantasy choices to more complex behavior, more specifically in selection and more realistic choosing. The dimensions of such convergence effects are seen in the work of Tiedeman and O'Hara (1963) who describe choice anticipation as involving substages of exploration, crystallization, choice and clarification; Super (1963) who describes the exploratory stage as involving substages entitled tentative, transition, and trial (little commitment) and the earlier work of Ginzberg, Ginsburg, Axelrod, and Herma (1951) in their choice paradigm involving fantasy, tentative and realistic progression. Specific choices and decisions are seen as intimately tied to one's personal history and personal perceptions of the future, to both antecedent experiences and future alternatives.

Career development theory indicates that individuals progress through life stages which place upon them different expectations in terms of the specificity and the realism of career choice and these are mediated to a large degree by the cultural strata and the socio-economic class of which one is a part. Thus, what one becomes as a person as well as in the vocational sense depends upon his mastery of an array of developmental tasks, including specific learning tasks, which find their genesis in the early years of the family.

Because of the importance of early childhood experiences in the family, the school and the community, intervention in career development needs to begin during the first decade of life. This is the nursery of human nature and the time when the attitudes are formed which ultimately are manifested in vocational commitment or rejection. Youngsters in elementary schools must be exposed to experiences which are meaningful in terms of their individual characteristics and to information which is accurate if they are not to carry residuals of exaggeration and over-romanticized occupational stereotypes into later decision-processing. Further, it is relatively futile to expect one in early or mid-adolescence to commit oneself to a specific occupational choice, except as he rejects the normal cultural expectation to involve himself in education, but it is possible and central to this life stage to wed occupational and educational information to vocational exploration. If career information is to be meaningful to students it must be cast in terms of the questions students are asking themselves and in a format which responds to the language system, readiness level, and stage of development at which they are located. To be effective career information should include not only objective factors like earning possibility, training requirements, and numbers of positions available but also the social and psychological conditions in which the work activity is performed.

Career development theory also emphasizes the importance of providing youngsters experiences which enable them to identify and try on suitable work roles. Probably the richest source of these opportunities for most young people is part-time work experience. But to receive maximum educational value, the stimuli which work provides must be analyzed in relation to the self. Work is not the only way to rest reality. Curricular experiences and extra-curricular experiences if used with purpose, analyzed, and placed into a context meaningful to the individual can serve this purpose well.

Career development theory also points out that decision-making involves action. Thus ways must be found to help students take responsibility for their own learning and increasingly for their own direction. They need to be more involved in planning. To learn to be responsible and to be involved you have to be given responsibility and involvement.

In sum, as the findings of career development have unfolded, the emphases attendant to guidance and the aspects of education which have vocational implications have shifted from a Parsonian model of matching man and job to a model more committed to the clarification of those aspects of self—e.g. interests, capacities, values—which need development for a lifelong process of planning and decision-making. Within the individual must be fostered a conscious awareness that he *does* have choices, he must be assisted to verbalize and make explicit those choices with which he is presented, and to translate these into action. The base of alternatives from which individuals conceptualize choice must be made broader than the dichotomy between work and college. The alternative plans of action which ensue must be tested against a clarified value system within which are recognized and implemented concepts related to the risk function as a basic and essential reality. The individual must be encouraged and assisted to determine at any given choice point what kind of decision is involved and the factors inherent in the decision that make a difference to him. Such expectations cannot be accomplished by any set of specialists alone but must pervade and be reinforced throughout the educational process.

Behavioral Goals

Vocational or career maturity is by definition the goal toward which career development is directed. Can such an abstraction be used to create unifying themes and behavioral descriptions which can serve to facilitate the steps leading to such a goal? In other words can vocational or career maturity be dissected into the elements which make it up and educational experiences built around these elements? In the discussion of career development theories it was noted that developmental tasks and stages of increasingly mature behavior have a strong partnership in these frames of reference. Several theorists, among them Havighurst (1953), Erikson (1950), Super (1957, 1963), Tiedeman and O'Hara (1963), Gribbons and Lohnes (1968) have discussed the presence of such phenomena in career development.

What utility might a development task concept or its sub-elements have in creating a unified system of education built around a career development theme? A developmental task has been defined by Havighurst (1953, p. 2) as "a task which arises at or about a certain period in life of the individual, successful achievement of which leads to happiness and success with later tasks, while failure leads to unhappiness in the individual, disapproval by society, and difficulty with later tasks." This definition has come to be accepted rather universally as the major interpretation of this concept. Those who are involved with developmental task formulations generally agree on the following statements:

1. Individual growth and development is continuous.
2. Individual growth can be divided into periods of life stages for descriptive purposes.
3. Individuals in each life stage can be characterized by certain general characteristics that they have in common.
4. Most individuals in a given culture pass through similar developmental stages.
5. The society makes certain demands upon individuals.
6. These demands are relatively uniform for all members of the society.

7. The demands differ from stage to stage as the individual goes through the development process.
8. Developmental crises occur when the individual perceives the demand to alter his present behavior and master new learnings.
9. In meeting and mastering developmental crises, the individual moves from one developmental stage of maturity to another developmental stage of maturity.
10. The task appears in its purest form at one stage.
11. Preparation for meeting the developmental crises or developmental tasks occurs in the life stage prior to the state in which it must be mastered.
12. The developmental task or crisis may arise again during a later phase in somewhat different form.
13. The crisis or task must be mastered before the individual can successfully move on to a subsequent developmental stage.
14. Meeting the crisis successfully by learning the required task leads to societal approval, happiness, and success with later crises and their correlative tasks.
15. Failing in meeting a task or crisis leads to disapproval by society (Zaccharia, 1965).

Thus, the developmental task concept can be used to describe a nomothetic or average set of demands or requirements with which individuals must cope as well as a way of looking at how a given individual is attaining such expectation, where he may be having difficulty, what specific experiences or competencies he needs to acquire, and what resources might be committed to his needs. Such a concept permits a sequential development of experiences which relate to emerging developmental tasks as well as an opportunity to prescribe on an individual base alternative strategies for coping successfully with the developmental task at which point specific difficulties obtain. Individual variation relative to the attainment of developmental tasks can be further considered in the sense that first, "a given task has a unique *meaning* to each individual. . . . secondly, individuals vary with respect to their *general approach* to developmental tasks. . . . the third idiographic dimension of developmental tasks is the *pattern of mastering* developmental tasks" (Zaccharia, 1965). In the latter dimension, LoCascio (1964) has identified three basic patterns for mastering developmental tasks: continuous developmental pattern, delayed developmental pattern, and impaired developmental pattern. Obviously, the individual differences which contribute to such differential patterns relate to such factors as values, attitudes, need systems, age, sex, temperament, and cultural factors such as socio-economic class.

Developmental tasks can be utilized also as short-range, intermediate-range, long-range or ultimate goals as they are translated into criteria by which individual progress can be monitored. It is of principal concern that the specific sub-tasks or sub-elements which contribute to the accomplishment of developmental tasks be analyzed, monitored, and related to the development of specific individuals.

As a framework for implementing this approach, Havighurst (1964, p. 216) has identified both broad and rather more specific developmental tasks in his analysis of the lifelong process of vocational development. The gross stages and more specific developmental tasks are as follows. Only the developmental tasks of the first and third stages will be identified.

I. Identification with a Worker. (Ages 5–10)
   Father, mother, other significant persons.
   The concept of working becomes an essential part of the ego-ideal.
   Principal Developmental Tasks of Middle Childhood:
   1. Developing fundamental skills in reading, writing and calculating.
   2. Learning physical skills necessary for ordinary games.
   3. Learning to get along with age-mates.
   4. Learning an appropriate masculine or feminine social role.
   5. Developing concepts for everyday living.
   6. Developing conscience, morality, and a scale of values.
   7. Achieving personal independence.

II. Acquiring the Basic Habits of Industry. (Ages 10–15)
   Learning to organize one's time and energy to get a piece of work done (school work, chores).
   Learning to put work ahead of play in appropriate situations.

III. Acquiring Identity As a Worker in the Occupational Structure. (Ages 15–25)
   Choosing and preparing for an occupation.
   Getting work experience as a basis for occupational choice and for assurance of economic independence.
   Principal Developmental Tasks of Adolescence:
   1. Achieving new and more mature relations with age mates of both sexes.
   2. Achieving a masculine or feminine social role.
   3. Achieving emotional independence of parents and other adults.
   4. Achieving assurance of economic independence.
   5. Selecting and preparing for an occupation.

   6. Acquiring a set of values and an ethical system as a guide to behavior.
   7. Preparing for marriage and selecting a mate.
   8. Starting a family.
   9. Getting started in an occupation.

IV. Becoming a Productive Person.   (Ages 25–40)
    Mastering the skills of one's occupation.
    Moving up the ladder within one's occupation.

 V. Maintaining a Productive Society.   (Ages 40–70)

VI. Contemplating a Productive Life.   (Ages 70+)

Although the developmental tasks identified by Havighurst in this illustration are too gross to be of much operational utility, several pertinent points are valuable. If one looks at the first gross stage, identification with a worker, what does this suggest for a student who comes from a home and a culture where there are no productive workers? If the achievement of later tasks is predicated upon the success of such identification, it requires education to respond to that lack in the case of this individual. In accordance with Havighurst's belief that one must repeat a missed stage before going on, what resources, what role models, what experiences can the school provide which will help this particular youngster acquire a concept of work as a part of his ego-ideal?

There is another implication here. If, for example, the development of fundamental skills in reading, writing, and calculating are critical to later developmental success, and there is no doubt that they are, and if developing a concept of work as a part of one's ego-ideal is also essential, can these concerns not be mutually addressed through materials and experiences which help children to learn to read, write, and calculate about work-oriented topics? The answer seems to be obviously affirmative.

One final point here. The developmental tasks of Stages I and III clearly indicate a process of increasing specificity through thema which become more intense as one ages. As examples, development of a value system, acquiring a sex-typed social role, achieving effective interpersonal relationships are each points along a fluid process which has specific manifestations at different points of time but has roots early in the life of the individual.

Another example of the longitudinal shaping of tasks which are relevant to ultimate vocational behavior is that provided in the work of Stratemeyer, Forkner, McKim, and Passow (1957, 208-214). In this illustration (See Table 1), a concept such as Using Effective Methods of Work,

TABLE 1

USING EFFECTIVE METHODS OF WORK

	Early Childhood	Later Childhood	Youth	Adulthood
Using Effective Methods of Work				
Planning Deciding on and clarifying purpose	Identifying immediate purposes in general terms	Determining major issues involved in achieving purposes	Extending ability to identify aspects and long time implications affecting purposes	Making the clarification of purposes needed to give effective direction in a variety of situations
Determining sequence of steps to achieve purpose	Planning immediate next steps	Making longer-range plans	Extending range and details of planning	Projecting appropriate sequence of steps to achieve a variety of purposes
Budgeting time and energy	Planning time allotments with the help of others	Developing the ability to make independent decisions as to use of time	Budgeting time in terms of a greater number of activities and a longer time span	Making the time allotments needed to carry out desired activities and to secure balance in activities
Evaluating steps taken	Deciding on the success of immediate steps	Considering the effectiveness of progress toward longer-range plans	Taking increased responsibility for evaluating progress toward goals	Using evaluation effectively and independently as an aid in planning

Using Appropriate Resources			
Locating and evaluating resources	Finding how people, books, and materials provide needed information	Learning how to use the more common resources effectively	Making increasingly critical use of resources	Making discriminating use of available resources
Using a Scientific Approach to the Study of Situations			
Solving practical problems	Applying simple tests in the solution of practical problems	Finding when and how to use simple research technique	Extending ability to use scientific methods appropriate to situations	Using a scientific approach effectively in the situations of daily living
Testing beliefs and attitudes	Learning to distinguish facts from opinions in situations of concern to one	Finding how to use facts to test opinions	Extending ability and inclination to examine beliefs and attitudes in the light of available evidence	Making unbiased use of available evidence to test present beliefs and attitudes

Reprinted by permission of the publisher from Stratemeyer, Forkner, McKim and Passow, *Developing a Curriculum for Modern Living*, "Using Effective Methods of Work," pp. 208-14. (New York: Teachers College Press, 1957; copyright 1947 by Teachers College, Columbia University).

is broken into pertinent subaspects or sublevels like Planning on and Clarifying Purpose and then extended longitudinally across ages and contexts in which they might operate. Such a procedure permits the elaboration of a conceptual scheme which is built from the bottom up and provides the opportunity for building experiences on experiences which flow toward and from common denominators. This scheme also permits a gross profile of the experiential background which one is expected or assumed to have but which may not be present in the personal history of a given individual. Thus, it can be used to show instrumental relationships between present and future levels of expectation, as well as for diagnostic purposes to determine what present experiences need to be acquired and what successes an individual might need to move from a particular developmental plateau to increasingly effective behavior.

Both of the illustrations cited provide a frame of reference from which to move in more specific operational terms. They both suffer from the gross nature of their content, the lack of current findings from career development research and theory, and behavioral descriptions which permit evaluation of the degree to which an individual student has accomplished the behavioral goals set for him. Hull (1967) has examined one approach to this latter requirement which is relevant here. He states that, "Behavioral objectives couched in descriptive expectations for individual performance enhance evaluation efforts." Hull used as a conceptual scheme the work of Bloom, Engelhardt, Furst, Hill, and Krathwohl (1956) in which the cognitive domain was divided into six classes: knowledge, comprehension, application, analysis, synthesis, and evaluation. These classes represent spiraling complexity of individual cognition. Hull applies this schema to the evaluation of pupil attainment in vocational tasks in each of six occupational fields. Most importantly, for the purposes here, he defined the tasks in behavioral descriptions, the attainment of which can be measured. His work is as follows:

Occupational Field	Objective Class	Operationally Defined Tasks in the Cognitive Domain
Office Occupations	Knowledge	To spell a list of fifty "most difficult" words correctly
Carpentry	Comprehension	To lay out a rafter cutting diagram for a gable roof with a 1/4 pitch
Food Service	Application	To serve a full-course dinner to a party of eight persons quickly, efficiently, and without disrupting conversations

Distribution	Analysis	To recognize unstated reasons for the customer's initial questions about a sales product
Production Agriculture	Synthesis	To plan a schedule of fertilizer application (time of year, type and amount of fertilizer, etc.) for a given crop rotation on a particular farm
Welding	Evaluation	To apply 60,000 pounds of pressure per square inch to a butt weld of 3/8 inch mild steel

Hull, of course, applies his example to vocational tasks which are more related to the acquisition of occupational skills than to the concepts of career development and his illustration represents a point in time rather than a longitudinal process. But the wedding of a cognitive concept to a specific behavior which can demonstrate the acquisition of the skills inherent in the concept is the major point. With some juxtaposing of time and space, without consideration of the occupational field labels in the first column, one can see how the concepts of knowledge, comprehension, application, analysis, synthesis, and evaluation could correspond to the developing characteristics of groups of children or particular children in a longitudinal schema for fitting experiences to the complexity of unfolding abilities.

Although Hull's framework used as a model the analysis of the cognitive domain by Bloom *et al,* there is a more recent companion piece dealing with the affective domain (Krathwohl, Bloom, and Masia, 1964). Stripped of their definitions, the category and subcategory titles which embrace the spiraling hierarchy of affective complexity are as follows:

1.0 Receiving (attending)

    1.1 Awareness
    1.2 Willingness to receive
    1.3 Controlled or selected attention

2.0 Responding

    2.1 Acquiescence in responding
    2.2 Willingness to respond
    2.3 Satisfaction in response

3.0 Valuing

    3.1 Acceptance of a value

3.2 Preference for a value

3.3 Commitment (conviction)

4.0 Organization

4.1 Conceptualization of a value

4.2 Organization of a value system

5.0 Characterization by a value or a value complex

5.1 Generalized set

5.2 Characterization

Krathwohl has stated (1965) "If the analysis of the cognitive and affective areas is correct, then a hierarchy of objectives dealing with the same subject matter concepts suggests a readiness relationship that exists between those objectives lower in the hierarchy and those higher." Thus, the taxonomies of the cognitive and the affective domains provide models which can be extended longitudinally, which can be used to represent nomothetic expectations, which can be translated into profiles of individual development, and to which can be related experiences designed to facilitate progress in particular categories of development.

The question now becomes, how can the input from current work in career development be placed in some specific way into a model which is longitudinally viable, which lends itself to behavioral description, and for which facilitative experiences might be designed? Two examples will be cited. Both contribute elements making up vocational maturity which fall principally within the cognitive domain. The first example comes from the longitudinal research of Gribbons and Lohnes (1968, 15-16). They have examined the concept of Readiness for Vocational Planning which has been cited as a measure of vocational maturity during adolescence. They have identified eight variables which in combination correlate to a high degree with readiness for vocational planning at the eighth grade and at postsecondary school levels. They are:

Variable I. Factors in Curriculum Choice

Awareness of relevant factors, including one's abilities, interests and values and their relation to curriculum choice; curricula available; courses within curricula; the relation of curriculum choice to occupational choice.

Variable II. Factors in Occupational Choice

Awareness of relevant factors, including abilities, interests, values; educational requirements for choice; relation of specific high school courses in choice; accuracy of description of occupation.

Variable III. Verbalized Strengths and Weaknesses

Ability to verbalize appropriately the relation of personal strengths and weaknesses to educational and vocational choices.

Variable IV. Accuracy of Self Appraisal

Comparison of subject's estimates of his general scholastic ability, verbal ability, and quantitative ability with his actual attainments on scholastic aptitude tests, English grades, and mathematics grades.

Variable V. Evidence of Self-Rating

Quality of evidence cited by subject in defense of his appraisal of his own abilities.

Variable VI. Interests

Awareness of interests and their relation to occupational choices.

Variable VII. Values

Awareness of values and their relation to occupational choices.

Variable VIII. Independence of Choice

Extent of subject's willingness to take personal responsibility for his choices.

The other example is from the work of the Career Pattern Study, a longitudinal study of career development directed by Super. The example used here is from the first of five gross vocational development tasks which are respectively: Crystallizing a vocational preference, Specifying a vocational preference, Implementing a vocational preference, Stabilizing in a vocation and Consolidating status and advancing in a vocation. Super and his colleagues have indicated that the first of these, crystallizing of a vocational preference, is the process of formulating a generalized vocational goal. It takes place in early and middle adolescence, and, it is essentially and, at its best, a cognitive process.

Attitudes and behaviors associated with the vocational development task, crystallizing a vocational preference, include the following: (Super, *et al.,* 1963, 84-86)

1.   *Awareness of the need to crystallize*—The behaviors which constitute this attitude are often verbal as illustrated by voluntary discussion of the need to choose a career, but they are also frequently instrumental, as in the case of going to the school library to read an occupational pamphlet, or seeking an appointment with the counselor.

2.   *Use of resources*—Relevant instrumental behaviors are consulting with counselors and other sources of occupational information and self-

understanding, reading occupational materials, seeking part-time or vacation jobs in one's field of interest.

3. *Awareness of factors to consider*—A cognitive process in which the individual takes into account self and situational factors which affect the wisdom of a preference: intellectual requirements, interests for which outlets are possible, accessibility, security, the timing of choices and the need for alternatives. Relevant behaviors are largely verbal and involve expressions of the importance of a given consideration, self-awareness, and knowledge of situational factors.

4. *Awareness of contingencies which may affect goals*—Seems more likely to assist in ruling out some possible preferences, in narrowing the field of preferences, and in providing a basis for greater stability of whatever preferences are crystallized. Relevant behaviors are largely verbal and include statements concerning the need for parental approval of preference and plans, and the need for continuing financial support may also be instrumental.

5. *Differentiation of interests and values*—Shown by depth and patterning as in inventoried interests and values, by the degree to which a person makes some low and some high scores, as contrasted with all average scores on an interest or values inventory. The behaviors in this instance are verbal behaviors recorded in inventories, but they could also be instrumental behaviors manifested in extracurricular activities, clubs and hobbies.

6. *Awareness of present-future relationships*—Consists of relating present prevocational activities to intermediate and ultimate vocational preferences. Relevant verbal and motor behaviors are illustrated by the mention of the fact that choosing algebra is essential to entering engineering school, and by taking blueprint reading in order to help qualify for advancement to skilled factory employment.

7. *Formulation of a generalized preference*—Self and situational awareness, crystallized interests and values, make possible the formulation of a generalized vocational preference. In many cases, this may seem to be a specific occupational preference, but it is in fact a more general occupational-type preference. In such cases, the occupational title serves as the symbol of a number of related activities for which liking is indicated.

8. *Consistency of preference*—Consistency of preference at this age is largely verbal, but it may also be instrumental, as in the consistent election of subjects relevant to a particular vocation.

9. *Possession of information concerning the preferred occupation*—Is manifested in verbal behavior, in which the subject reveals what he knows

about requirements, training, duties, conditions of work, and so forth in the occupation which he prefers.

10. *Planning for the preferred occupation*—Is a type of verbal behavior which can be characterized in the same way as possession of information. However, the focus is on decisions as to what to do and when and how to do it. The amount and specificity of planning like information, has been shown to be a measurable characteristic of vocational maturity in early adolescence.

11. *Wisdom of the vocational preferences*—Shown in verbal behavior.

The elements of the Gribbons and Lohnes and Super *et al* data can be condensed and blended in several ways. It is clear in both that students need a comprehensive body of information which links what they are doing educationally at particular points in time to future options which will be available to them within the context of education as well as within the context of work. Thus, they need to know what curricula will be available to them, what factors distinguish one curriculum from another, what components make up separate curricula pathways, what personal factors are relevant to success in different curricula, and how the various curricula are linked in an instrumental fashion to different field and level responsibilities in the occupational world.

Students also need self-knowledge. They need to be able to differentiate personal values and personal interests as these are related to personal strengths and weaknesses in the several manifestations of ability—verbal, quantitative, scholastic. They need to be able to assess these elements of the self, incorporate their meaning into the self-concept, and relate the relevance of self information to the choices with which they will be confronted.

Transcendant to this necessary base of knowledge is the motivation to use it in purposeful ways. Or as Clarke, Gelatt, and Levine (1965) observe, to develop "an effective strategy for analyzing, organizing, and synthesizing information in order to make a choice." There are in the making of decisions skills which can be learned. Once a person has made a plan for some segment of his life which he is content to live by, he is better able to make the next one intelligently and with less hesitation or conflict. As has been indicated previously, one cannot make vocational decisions without educational implications and vice versa. Nor can effective planning and choice-making occur without recognizing and assessing the psychosocial, emotional implications inherent in the choice.

Inherent in the studies of Gribbons and Lohnes and of Super and his colleagues is the need for an attitude of planfulness to be generated in students as well as recognition of possible alternative actions, possible outcomes of these actions, probable outcomes of these actions, and the desirability of the outcomes as defined by personal preferences and values. In this context, students can be helped to assess the sequence of outcomes —proximate, intermediate, ultimate—which lead from immediate choice, the factors which are personally relevant at each experimental branch point, the probabilities associated with those factors, and the personal desirability of the outcomes which make up the sequence. The facilitation of planfulness and of career development, then, involves not only knowledge, but opportunities to apply the knowledge to one's personal characteristics. It involves the student's willingness to commit to work a sense of value, ego-involvement, personal endeavor, and achievement related motives.

Education can equip students with accurate and relevant information which is translated in terms of the developmental level and state of readiness of individual children; it can encourage and assist them to formulate relevant hypotheses about themselves, the choice points which will lie in their future, and the environmental options available; it can help them use appropriate ways of testing these hypotheses against both past and new experiences; and it can help the student to come to terms with the educational relevance of what he already knows, or will learn, about himself and his future. In other words, students can be helped to see themselves in process and to acquire the tools and knowledge which will allow them to exploit this process in positive, constructive ways.

If expectations are to be met that education, or, more precisely, career education, will facilitate career development, it would seem important that there be designed descriptions of student behavior which would demonstrate the acquisition of different elements of career development. Such descriptions would need to be placed at appropriate developmental levels and related systematically to educational strategies which are likely to facilitate them. In substance, such an approach would create much of the structure for the implementation of career education.

Relationship Between Career Development and General Education

As one views general education it becomes quite clear that there is already operating a number of activities which are at least tangentially related to career development. In fact, all contacts with people, things, and ideas have potential for influencing career development (Roeber, 1965–66), if these are purposefully and systematically addressed to this expectation. The creation of the behavioral goals suggested previously as ways of bringing focus to the activities and experiences through which career development can be facilitated would be powerful means by which career development can be made to stand clearly as a central activity at all educational levels. The early work of Comenius and Dewey and the more recent work of Piaget and Bruner among others have supported the premise that success experiences and the realities of the adult society can be grasped and internalized by even very young children if these concepts are placed in a language system and an experiential framework which is attuned to the readiness level of the children being served.

It is important that general education be seen not just as an opportunity for the *expression* of certain personal characteristics which make up career development but rather that it be seen as devoted to *developing* these characteristics. Although this distinction is subtle, it represents the difference between purposeful, sequential development and development by chance and happenstance. Thus, a series of exposures to career development-oriented activities adapted to the developmental level of children and provided through different media will have an impact that isolated, compartmentalized experiences can never realize.

It is also important that any sequential development within general education recognize that if the present conditions of occupational illiteracy, lack of goal directedness, and nonemployability are to be overcome, a broader perception of the many types and degrees of talent necessary to the world of work must be fostered. If schools are in fact to develop the requisites of career development, emphasis must be given from the elementary school forward to the identification and facilitation of the positive elements, strengths, and talents, which for each individual represent the best coin for future career success. In addition, education must attend to the facts that support it in programmatic ways, that students will differ in their approach to career orientations and in their readiness for such thinking because of the high degree of interdependence between one's concept of self, his concept of occupations, and his environmental development. Educational practices must embody better and more comprehensive approaches to the diagnosis of where students are in their career development, in success with learning, in their interest and value formulations. Equally important, however, is the need to make available large numbers of learning experiences which can be related to individual needs and capacities. In the last analysis, the objective of education built around career development must be the development of the individual, not the needs of the labor market.

The discussion which follows is not intended to be exhaustive of the ways by which general education can facilitate career development but rather illustrative of some of the activities now underway at different educational levels from which systems to facilitate career development can flow.

The discussion does not center about the specific roles which teachers or counselors can play in their respective professional endeavors to facilitate career development although it is only by the application of their separate skills and their cooperative behavior that a unified system of education through career development can be brought to fruition.

The Elementary School Level

If Luchins Primacy Affect (1960) is a valid premise—that the information which is obtained first carries the most weight in ultimate decisions—significantly more attention must be concentrated at the elementary school in terms of attitude development, decision processing, self awareness as well as awareness of and knowledge about the broad characteristics and expectations of work. Frequently, unrealistic vocational plans are made at this level because of the emphases on parental and community attitudes as well as in textbooks upon "prestige fields," which obscure the existence and the significance of other fields that employ a large proportion of workers. The occupations and careers exhibited should cover the full range of alternatives from unskilled and semi-skilled worker to Ph.D. However, the greatest stress should be placed on those jobs which do not require a four-year college education, but probably involve continuing education beyond high school.

Increasingly rigid walls have been erected between the pre-adolescent, and for that matter the adolescent, and the vocational niches or educational options to which they must relate. In far too many instances, large segments of our student population—those from the culture of poverty and others—have no systematic models to which to relate or psychological support for the quest for behavior which is personally and socially relevant. These conditions occur at a time when attitude formation is in its seed stages. Consequently, the total educational process must support and reinforce those experiences which will generate attitudes and self-acceptance ultimately having a vocational manifestation. Vocational values and attitudes need attention prior to specific skill consideration although current levels of knowledge and procedures now incorporated in such areas as industrial arts could be placed in the elementary school with benefit to individual children. The integration of vocational values, attitudes, and facts, as well as the relationship between academic content and occupations as reflected in curriculum development, is a priority concern. Students must be helped to relate, in an instrumental way, what they are doing in the classroom to the expectations of varying work contexts. Teachers must be made sensitive to the fact that their attitudes toward work of various kinds make a significant impact on the attitudes of students as they develop personal perceptions of aspiration and prestige. It is in these gross ways that the objectives of guidance, career development, and general education must interface and infuse the formative experiences of children.

More specifically, through the creative use of curricular materials, films displays, role-playing, dramatizations, gaming and simulation, elementary school children can be introduced to career development concepts which are accurate and pertinent to their future development. This is not to suggest that elementary school children be robbed of their fantasies, but rather that their fantasies operate from a base of knowledge instead of overromanticism and stereotype. Almy (1955, p. 200) states that the six year old lives more in a world of reality and less in a world of fantasy. "He can understand a number of relationships in the physical world. . . . He knows his actions have consequences for other people and is more alert to their responses and feelings." Jersild (1951), too, has indicated that children have at an early age greater capacities for learning to meet, understand, and deal effectively with realities than has been assumed in psychological theories or in educational practice. Certain of the behavioral objectives discussed previously can be introduced in different stages of the elementary school and identification of those students requiring specific experiences to cope with the developmental tasks demanded of them can be placed in process.

Gross (1967) has suggested that preparation for work life involves four dimensions: (a) preparation for life in an organization, involving authority, security quests, impersonality, routine, conflict, mobility, and demotion; (b) preparation for a set of role relationships; (c) preparation for a level of consumption, involving a certain style of life, and (d) preparation for an occupational career, involving changes in the nature of jobs, and different types of jobs depending on the position in the life cycle. Such topical areas would seem to lend themselves to language arts, social studies, science, geography or, in fact, virtually any elementary school endeavor. Such themes are not confined to the elementary school population but could create organizing concepts which spiral in increasing complexity throughout the educational continuum. Blocher (1966), too, has discussed the importance of social roles as they relate to developing human effectiveness. Students could examine social roles as they relate to leadership, creative or original contributions, helping relationships, and unusual levels of accomplishment. The study of social roles could be extended to occupational fields and levels of responsibilities as well as to such areas as coping behaviors and their implications for growth and development.

Goff (1967) demonstrated in two socio-economically different elementary schools that measurable increments in vocational knowledge, level of occupational aspiration and realism of occupational choice can be attained through a planned vocational guidance program. Stress was placed upon developing a respect for all levels of human endeavor, toward gaining an understanding of personal strengths and limitations, and toward acquiring satisfaction in the task of learning itself. Children were asked to work through the making of occupational choices for the purposes of testing and discussion as well as to reinforce the idea that early and specific choices were not expected at the elementary school levels.

In an attempt to determine whether primary grade children could gain occupational awareness important to vocational attitude and value formation, Wellington and Olechowski (1966) found that eight year old youngsters could: develop a respect for other people, the work they do, and the contributions made by providing production and services for everyone; understand that occupations have advantages and disadvantages for the worker; understand some of the interdependent relationships of workers. The group of students with which Wellington and Olechowski worked was first exposed to a unit of study entitled "Shelter." The building industry and the variety of workers related to the industry were explored. Initial indications were that youngsters at the conclusion of the unit did not yet understand the workers' role and function. Follow-up discussions were then focused on methods for increasing the children's understanding. The students were assigned to interview a variety of workers. With the assistance of the teacher and the counselor, the students developed questions to be asked in the interviews. The interviews and the class discussions which followed were taped. After the children listened to the tapes and completed their discussions concerning the building industry and its workers, there was a significant increase in the students' understanding and awareness of working people and their work. The important point is that the initial lack of increased student awareness was a result of faulty techniques, not a lack of student ability to grasp the concept.

Vocational guidance or exploration at the elementary school level and later cannot be confined to an informational service although relevant, comprehensive information is vital. Arbuckle (1963) has suggested that the world of work be viewed at the elementary school level as a "world of people" thus emphasizing the importance of individual characteristics in shaping one's future work life and to diminish the remoteness, the outside-the-person focus, which work is perceived frequently as being.

Kabach (1966) has indicated that "the younger the child the greater the interest in the actual job performance itself. Most children are natural born actors; they want to act out in order to understand what it feels like to be a carpenter or a ball player." There are several important implications here. First, in terms of media or vocational exploration, in the elementary school particularly, the use of dramatizations, role-playing, simulation each has potential for allowing youngsters to try on possible occupational roles. Secondly, it is possible to facilitate student identification with attainable vocations represented in their immediate neighborhoods or community. Finally, if children base their occupational preferences on job performance itself this is a prime time to introduce them to the relationship between interests and occupational areas. An array of experiences can be built upon how interests develop and their importance in life. Interest themes can also be related to change as a process, to capacities, to values, to decision-making or any other process.

A set of materials encompassing these concepts specifically designed for use in grades five, six, and seven were developed by personnel of the Abington School District in Pennsylvania under a grant from the Pennsylvania Department of Public Instruction. The model they developed drew upon the resources of the school, home, and community. As one piece of this model, six sessions were developed so that they could be integrated in the language arts curriculum and, thus, contribute to student development in the area of spoken and written communications. The objectives for these sessions were met through:

1. A card game which demonstrated how interests develop.
2. Short stories based upon characters with whom students could readily identify.
3. An interest inventory designed to obtain a profile of the interests of students through media which were relevant to their age level.
4. An "open-ended" play illustrating the influence of interests on personal relationships which provided students the opportunity to write the second act showing the outcome of the situation.
5. A taped series of role-played interviews with various workers in which the students were to determine the occupation from the interests described by the person interviewed.

Similar experiences were created to facilitate awareness of change, values, educational and occupational relationships and similar pertinent concepts as these interacted with student development.

In a sense, many of the possibilities for influencing awareness of career development in the elementary school are built around the premise that at the base of later career differentiation and integration must be a foundation (O'Hara, 1968). And, this foundation has as a basic ingredient the development of a language of vocations, a base for personal imagery and symbolization. Through the acquisition of relevant words, children begin to accommodate to cues by which to differentiate and integrate both the world around them and themselves as part of this world.

Junior High School Level

Many of the concepts and methods introduced at the elementary school level can be reshaped and extended to the junior high school level. It must be remembered, however, that as a result of experience and growth students at this level have needs and abilities which are different from those of elementary school pupils and from secondary school pupils. Students of this age level are more able than elementary school pupils to comprehend relationships and to use abstract terms and symbols; they are in a period where they are preoccupied with belonging and conformity while they are also attempting to achieve independence from their families and sort themselves from the mass. They are enmeshed in the continued development, refinement, and strengthening of basic academic skills begun in the elementary school and they are beginning to converge on the more specialized experiences of the secondary school. Because specific choices of curricula or of the specific high school they will attend are rapidly approaching, however theoretical that might be, their sensitivity to work and its personal relevance to them as creatures who will "become" is accentuated. It is a period where intensive, almost frenetic, exploration can be expected. It is also a period where many students will absent themselves from formal education permanently. It is a period when such career development concepts as compromise become operational as realities and ideals are reality-tested through curricular and extracurricular experiences. Thus, experiences designed for these students must be timely and immediate to the questions which they are asking themselves. It is a time when student responsibilities through participation in planning can be related to the consequences of decisions made. It is a time when sex differences exert important influences in curriculum choice and when choice considerations become different in kind and value for males and females (Cass and Tiedeman, 1960). It is also a time when, because of the unevenness of development, there are wide ranges of maturity within the population and within individuals.

It is inevitable that the junior high school student will move toward a conception of self as seen against a background of work. For some youngsters at this level purely academic content holds no appeal at all unless its immediate relevance to salable skills can be made obvious. These students need access to a skill-centered curriculum, to vocational education if you will, at what is organizationally the seventh through ninth grades. If they do not receive this opportunity, the chances are that they will leave the school as unemployable. Some of these young people do not have the tolerance or the ego-strength to wade through a morass of personally meaningless experiences until the ninth, tenth, or eleventh grades when they can get their hands on the tangible and the concrete. This is not to imply that these students should not be provided the experiences which will facilitate career development beyond the narrowness of task skills. Indeed, it is within the context of skill development that they can be helped not only to see where they might go but prescriptions of the specific ways by which they can implement their goals can be created. For these persons for whom skill-centered learning is most relevant and the source of success experiences, training in decision-making and in planning which transcends job layouts can facilitate their self-understanding and their recognition of alternative goals to which they can respond. The concept of continuing to learn throughout one's work life through apprenticeships, on the job training, post-secondary vocational/technical schools and other experiences can be introduced and explored.

Integral to skill-centered access for some students, and different exploratory experiences for students not requiring skill emphases, is work itself. Work for many students will be the best of all try-out experience. For some students, organized work and study programs are ways of shortening the period of economic and psychological dependence under which so many youth chafe. To facilitate career development, however, such work experience should be more than casual, unsystematic ventures into whatever chance opportunity presents itself. Rather, the behavioral goals to be attained within the developmental task frame of reference previously elaborated are pertinent here also. They represent motivational as well as diagnostic possibilities to which work can be related. If such a possibility is to be realized, however, education and industry will need to come together in mutually creative exchanges in order to provide such opportunities systematically. This would seem to require that schools accept a placement responsibility for placing youth in jobs on a part-time or summer basis where they can make use of what they have learned.

If work as a try-out experience cannot be made available to all junior high school students or if it is not relevant for some individuals, one of the alternatives is the purposeful wedding of educational technology to career development. To this point, educational technology has been more concerned with how to communicate rather than what to communicate. It has, however, clear and powerful potential in simulating career development and decision-making processes, contingencies and outcomes, as well as a medium for translating informational retrieval in terms of individual needs. Many relevant projects already exist. Among these are the following:

1. The work of Loughary, Friesen, and Hurst (1966) in developing Autocon, a computer-based automatic counseling simulation system.

2. The development of a Man-Machine Counseling System (Cogswell, Donahue, Estavan, and Rosenquist, 1966) which among other things will track students through their school progress by computer to identify counseling problems and automate interviews to help students in the areas of course programming, post high school educational planning and vocational exploration.
3. The computerization of vocational information using Roe's field and level classification and relating student information to this classification for the purpose of conversation between computers and students about decision-making (Harris, 1968).
4. Life career games, in which students plan the life of a fictitious student within simulated environments and receive feedback on the possible consequences of their decision (Boocock, 1967).
5. The work of Gelatt and his associates in the Palo Alto public schools in which locally developed probability data as well as general probability data available from government and commercial sources were used in the group guidance program. A control group which received no probability data was also included. In an evaluative design integral to this project, it was found that the group which received local probability data scored significantly higher on knowledge about the process of decision-making, awareness of high school and college alternatives, and knowledge of the probabilities involved in these alternatives than did the group receiving general probability data or the control group which received no probability data (Yabroff, 1964).

These projects are not intended to supplant teachers or counselors, but it is probable that with increasing sophistication the outcomes of these projects will cause a reordering of the possible uses to which teachers and counselors can put their energies.

To return again to curriculum content *per se,* it is necessary that a body of content be identified which is relevant here. The concept of change as it relates to characteristics of the self and to environmental options has been mentioned as a thread which can complement career development. At the junior high school such a theme can be related to implications of accelerating application of new technological discoveries to the occupational structure. It can reinforce the validity of preparing oneself to be versatile and yet firmly grounded in the fundamental processes which undergird all occupations. Such a continuing concept can be related to work habits, mechanical principles, electrical principles, structural design and representation, chemical and biological principles, numerical operations and measurement, verbal communication as this is related to supervisor-subordinate relationships and human relationships. In this context, students can be increasingly encouraged to ask not only whether I like it? but What does it take? and Do I have what it takes? In addition to simulated and work experiences, these kind of questions can be tested in various courses. Students can be encouraged to ask such questions as Why am I taking chemistry or algebra or English and how can I use it? And, teachers must be encouraged to respond to this question as one for which there are fairly specific answers.

A relevant technique for synthesizing many of these suggestions is that used by Lockwood, Smith, and Trezise (1968). They took the position that if students are even to begin making meaningful vocational investigations they must first become more aware of the almost infinite possibilities that are open to them—their world must be enlarged. Students were, therefore, introduced to four worlds: the Natural, the Technological, the Aesthetic, and the Human world. In the Natural world, the students studied not only what nature has to offer men, both materially and spiritually, they also looked into man's preoccupation with the destruction of nature. In the Technological world, topics dealing with machines, mass production, automation, cybernetics, and computers were used to stimulate students to discuss not only how developing technology will affect jobs of the future, but more broadly, what will it do for man and society as a whole? In the Aesthetic world, students discussed the role of the arts in modern society and the place of the artist, contemporary trends of art, the "culture boom," and why the arts must have a vital place in any mature culture. In the Human world, students studied overpopulation, poverty, war and peace, social injustices and the individual in mass society. The important dimension here is that the students discussed career areas related to each world and the interrelationships among them.

Senior High School Level

The continuation of career development at the senior high school level must as at other levels be predicated upon individual needs, readiness, and motivations. In one sense the principal concern at this level is the intensity of the planning, individual readiness, and goal-directedness which characterizes the individuals to be served. Specific career development activities must take each student from where he is to the creation and the achievement of a set of specific goals. Here, perhaps more than at any other point in the educational continuum, activities must be individually prescribed and they must proceed with logic and system to permit the realization of future motivations whether these be immediate job acquisition, post-high school technical training, baccalaureate preparation, or a potential future mix of each.

If the architect's dictum that form should follow function is valid, then institutional shapes and organization will need to incorporate more flexibility, more interdisciplinary integration, variable time blocks, individualized programming, multi-media approaches, and self-teaching devices than is presently characteristic of most educational systems.

Because of the importance of fundamental cognitive skills—e.g., reading, writing, computing—to career development, many students will need renewed efforts to attain these skills through remedial or individualized methodology. But their acquisition can be facilitated by placing them in the context of vocational experiences. One of the exciting possibilities for doing this lies within the cluster concept which blends an interdisciplinary approach to academic learning with a family of skills or career clusters which are broadly applicable to many jobs. Through the ES 70 program, pilot projects are already underway in such places as Quincy, Massachusetts, and in the Richmond Pretechnical Program, San Francisco, to use students' occupational interests as a means of developing their general and academic skills. Lessons are not separated into such courses as physics, math, English or electromechanics; they are interwoven in ways which insure that students have attained skills which are salable but which permit students the opportunity to qualify for advanced training at the junior college level or in other post-secondary educational endeavors (Bushnell and Rubel, 1968). Thus curricula can be blended in ways which emphasize both the acquisition of technological principles and the personal skills which permit one to make use of the technical skills which are acquired. Theoretically at least, one can train a young person to be the finest machinist in town, but unless he is given the personal skills and attitudes which permit manifestation of the technical skills, e.g., be willing to be at work at 7:00 a.m. five days per week each week, he is still unemployable.

If career cluster curricula could be developed beginning at the ninth grade, this would not preclude the continuation of specific job training for some students. Not all vocationally oriented students are capable of or desire preparation for the skilled trades or for technical occupations. Specific programs must be developed for the low end as well as the high end of the intellectual continuum whether such preparation is to be a helper, a dishwasher, a waiter, a lawnmower repairman, an industrial landscape gardener or whatever. Indeed, low intellect aside as a rationale, pathways to constructive work must be broadened so that youth are not fitted to programs but programs fitted to youth. The existing lockstep of certain training durations and specified training experiences must be broken to exploit the enlarging opportunities in the occupational world to use the talents of individuals characterized by a wide range of capability. The specialty-oriented youngsters (Hoyt, 1963), who are not solely representative of those with limited intelligence, can be provided clusters of job skills in such areas as social and public services, transportation, management, finance, business communication, distribution—areas which are not mechanical or theoretical, if such dichotomies are viable, but are nevertheless tangible, concrete, and important outlets for a range of personal predispositions.

Integral to any of these conceptions of creating vocational experiences and tying them to academic learning in meaningful ways is the opportunity for individual and group problem-solving. These opportunities must span educational levels. Students can be helped to identify and define problems to be solved within the context of current vocational experience and ways can be identified to solve the problems. Students can participate in planning projects which exploit decision-making behavior and through which their own interests can surface.

At the senior high school level, the possibility of integrating work experience with schooling is a reality. The age and sex of the student are no longer the contingencies they are at the junior high school level. Blocks of time can be developed by which students will actually report to jobs instead of school for two or three weeks or perhaps a term at a time. While the economic appeal is obvious, the training and the exploratory potential needs to be fitted to individual needs. Hence, if a particular student is interested in business or in electronics, a program could be made available by which he can complete his high school work and simultaneously secure the on-the-job training available through part-time employment. For some students, this could be pretechnical training, for others it will be a permanent job, and for still others exploration prior to baccalaureate study.

All of this emphasis in the senior high school on vocational experience, career clusters, work is not to denigrate the continuing career development potential of the academic curriculum *per se.* The types of activities integral to curriculum but complemented by simulation devices and processes which have been indicated as possible at earlier educational levels are also important in modified form at the senior high school level. A continuing career development theme in courses designed to prepare students for college will serve to diminish the persistent assumption that college is an end in itself. It, too, is an intermediate vocational choice for the vast majority of students who enter college. With such an emphasis, college will be seen less as a way of deferring career thinking and more as one of the alternative ways to achieve particular vocational goals. Indeed, many of the students for whom college is the immediate step following high school will also profit from direct work experience or from access to vocational experience in the school itself in order to heighten the purpose with which college is approached.

Relationships of Career Development and Vocational Education

Vocational education has been called the Bridge Between Man and His Work (The General Report of the Advisory Council on Vocational Education, 1968). If a career development theme is to be viable, such an appellation must come to describe the total educational enterprise—not just a segment of it. If any one part or all of education is to deserve this label by bringing to reality in the lives of individual students the complex of experiences necessary to bridge education and work, more than narrowly defined job training is involved. It is this very specificity of trade or job training which has led to cries of obsolescence in vocational education and unresponsiveness to the dynamics of the occupational structure. As one evidence that these charges have some validity, the first nationwide study of the postgraduate employment experience of male graduates of trade and industry vocational courses shows that the majority of vocational course graduates do not, for their first job, enter the trade for which they trained in high school nor do many tend to enter the trade in later years (Eninger, 1965, p. 25). Thus, the intent and the patterning of vocational education as it is manifested in many current programs of education must be reshaped and reconstituted.

Virtually all of the relationships which have been suggested as pertaining between general education and career development, apply with equal force to vocational education. They will not be repeated here. Indeed, if such relationships are incorporated into a reshaping of the many thrusts of vocational education, the lines which presently separate or dichotomize vocational education and "general education" can be made to blur or vanish.

For too long vocational education has been seen as having validity only for a highly restricted sample of the total student population rather than for all students. Operationally, it has been seen as a second class alternative for those with low verbal skills or for those with technician interests. In the process, many of these students and many vocational educators have become defensive about their alleged inferior status, moved further into an isolationist stance, and tied themselves to training experiences rigidly defined by time and content. As a result, many students who desperately need what vocational education and vocational experiences can offer have been blocked from this access. Students have been arbitrarily separated into supposedly homogeneous categories of college-bound and non-college-bound, the experiences for each category being seen as mutually exclusive.

The alternative to releasing more of the potential contribution which vocational education has to make to career development lies not in assigning to or recruiting more students for a vocational education track, but in making vocational education an equal partner with all other activities which constitute the educational enterprise. This means that vocational education courses must be systematically structured to teach not only skills across families of jobs but to develop within students the elements of career development which will free them to conceptualize the alternative ways in which these skills can be used and to attain the personal competency to capitalize upon skill acquisition. Further, it means that more avenues must be created by which all students can move freely between "academic" and vocational education with the criteria for such movement being individual need, readiness, interest, motivation and the blend of academic and vocational experiences which can meet these criteria. As Moss (1968) has indicated, it is "the relative prevocational value of various patterns of preparation that is of prime educational significance." To aid students in patterning and mixing academic and vocational experiences, counselors will need probability as well as multiple discriminant data which compare the characteristics of the student contemplating a particular blend of experience with the characteristics of those individuals who have completed different sequences of experiences and the career outcomes they have attained. Such a procedure cannot be a once and done exercise but rather a complementary and continuing reinforcement of decision-making, value refinement, and personal planning as these occur not only in the selection of pertinent educational experiences but within the experiences themselves.

Higher Education

Although the place of higher education in a unified system or education built around a career development theme has not been made explicit in this paper, it is a necessary corollary to the goals discussed. Post-secondary vocational/technical schools, community and junior colleges, and private institutions providing specific skill training all have a contribution to make to the acquisition by late adolescents and adults of particular types of training. Many of the experiences which they can offer must include the types of experiences and content recommended at earlier educational levels. For some persons, post-secondary education will be the final step of specific skill acquisition before moving into a technician role or a skilled craft. These may be persons who have been exposed to broad prevocational and exploratory experiences before entering post-secondary opportunities. Other persons will seek post-secondary skill training who have not acquired a mastery of more fundamental skills in communications, mathematics, reading, other prerequisites to skill acquisition, or the attitudes necessary to making effective use of skills to be attained. Thus, post-secondary programs, much like secondary programs, will need to begin where the individual is and build in systematic ways the individual experiences necessary to meeting particular interests and goals. Other persons, because of possible displacement by changes in occupational activities, will need retraining or upgrading opportunities and these, too, need to be made available through the several possible combinations of post-secondary education.

In the last analysis, it is necessary that post-secondary vocational experiences be characterized by flexibility and diversity in order that individuals of divergent characteristics can be equipped with skills at the levels and in the fields consonant with their personal needs and the realities of the occupational structure.

Summary

This paper has examined some of the needs, conceptual elements and educational strategies which pertain to facilitating career development among students at different educational levels. It is contended that career education, as the term has been used in federal and state legislation, is the institutionalization in education of purposeful and systematic efforts to facilitate career development.

Career education can be seen as the synthesis of two streams of thought about educational purpose. One uses an occupational model as its stimulus; the other uses a career model. The occupational model has been concerned principally with insuring that some students, when they leave education, have highly developed skills in rather narrowly defined occupations. The career model, on the other hand, conceives of the individual as moving through the educational system along a number of pathways which have differing points of entrance to or implications for adjustment in the work system. This model emphasizes the importance of the individual having the skills which will permit him to choose as freely as possible among the multiple opportunities available to him.

Both the occupational and the career models are important inputs to the implementation of career education. The occupational model, which lays stress upon matching man with and preparing him for his work has been a central emphasis in vocational education. With the cluster concept emerging, this model has obviously been enlarged in scope and given renewed vitality in an era of rapid realignment within the occupational structure. Given the need for continuing refinement, the occupational or cluster model does represent the component of career education which is devoted principally to preparing students to engage successfully in the activity or process requirements of work. The career model is broader than the occupational model. It includes not only the acquisition of occupational or employability skills but also the factors—attitudes, knowledge, self-concepts—which motivate choice and decision-making styles. This model has to do with helping students develop preferences and execute plans by which they can implement these preferences. Thus, the implications for personal growth found in the career model are not confined only to young people going directly to work. It maintains that all students regardless of the ultimate goal they pursue beyond high school need to be helped to find purpose in what they are doing and considered ways for meeting these purposes.

The thoughts about career education identified in this paper are places to start. They are anchor points, however fragile, which add reality to the promise of this dynamic society that man not only has as a basic right an occupation to choose, but that he is entitled to the assistance and the preparation to choose well and to experience the dignity that such a condition permits.

BIBLIOGRAPHY

Advisory Council on Vocational Education. *Vocational Education—The Bridge Between Man and His Work,* Highlights and Recommendations from the General Report Publicational. Washington, D.C.: U.S. Office of Education, 1968.

Almy, Millie. *Child Development.* New York: Henry Holt and Co., 1955.

Arbuckle, Dugald S. "Occupational Information in the Elementary School." *Vocational Guidance Quarterly,* 1963, 12, 77-84.

Blocher, Donald R. "Wanted: A Science of Human Effectiveness." *Personnel and Guidance Journal,* March 1966, Vol. 44, No. 7, 729-733.

Bloom, B. S., M. D. Engelhart, E. J. Furst, W. H. Hill, and D. R. Krathwohl. *Taxonomy of Educational Objectives: The Classification of Educational Goals, Handbook I: Cognitive Domain.* New York: Longmons, Green and Co., 1956.

Boocock, Sarane S. "The Life Career Game." *Personnel and Guidance Journal,* December 1967, Vol. 46, No. 4, 328-334.

Brayfield, Arthur H. and John O. Crites. "Research on Vocational Guidance: Status and Prospect," *Man In a World of Work.* (Henry Borow, Ed.) Boston: Houghton Mifflin Company, 1964.

Bruner, Jerome S. "Some Theorems on Instruction Illustrated with Reference to Mathematics," *Theories of Learning and Instruction.* (Ernest R. Hilgard, Ed.) Sixty-Third Yearbook, Part I, National Society for the Study of Education. Chicago: University of Chicago Press, 1964, 306-335.

Bushnell, David S. and Roberta G. Rubel. "A Skill and A Choice." *American Vocational Journal,* September 1968, Vol. 43, No. 6, 31-33.

Campbell, Robert E. "Vocational Guidance In Secondary Education: Selected Findings of a National Survey Which Have Implications for State Program Development." Paper presented at the National Conference on Vocational Guidance: Development of State Programs. U.S. Office of Education, Washington, D.C., January 16–18, 1968.

Career Development Activities, Grades V, VI, VII. Abington School District, Abington, Pennsylvania, 1967–68. (Mimeo)

Cass, John C. and David V. Tiedeman. "Vocational Development and the Election of a High School Curriculum." *Personnel and Guidance Journal,* March 1960, Vol. 38, No. 7, 538-545.

Clarke, R., H. B. Gelatt and L. Levine. "A Decision-Making Paradigm for Local Guidance Research." *Personnel and Guidance Journal,* September 1965, Vol. 44, 40-51.

Cogswell, J. F., C. P. Donahue, D. P. Estavon, and B. A. Rosenquist. "The Design of a Man-Machine Counseling System." Paper presented at the American Psychological Association Convention, New York, N.Y., September 1966.

Eninger, Max W. "The Process and Product of T & I High School Level Vocational Education In the United States." Pittsburgh: American Institutes For Research, Institute for Performance Technology, September 1965. Ch. 5.

Erickson, E. H. *Childhood and Society.* New York: W. W. Norton & Company, Inc., 1950.

Festinger, L. *A Theory of Cognitive Dissonance.* Stanford, California: Stanford University Press, 1957.

Ginzberg, Eli, Sol W. Ginsberg, Sidney Axelrod, and John L. Herma. *Occupational Choice: An Approach to a General Theory.* New York: Columbia University Press, 1951.

Goff, William H. "Vocational Guidance in Elementary Schools, A Report of Project P.A.C.E." Paper presented at the American Vocational Association Convention, Cleveland, Ohio, December 6, 1967.

Goodlad, John I. *School Curriculum Reform in the United States.* New York: Fund for the Advancement of Education, 1964.

Grant, Vance W. "Statistic of the Month." *American Education,* July-August 1965, back cover.

Gribbons, Warren D. and Paul R. Lohnes. *Emerging Careers.* New York: Teachers College Press, Columbia University, 1968.

Gross, Edward. "A Sociological Approach to the Analysis of Preparation for Work Life." *Personnel and Guidance Journal,* January 1967, Vol. 45, No. 5, 416-423.

Guba, Egon G. "Methodological Strategies for Educational Change." Paper presented to the Conference on Strategies for Educational Change, Washington, D.C., November 8–10, 1965.

Harris, JoAnn. "The Computerization of Vocational Information." *Vocational Guidance Quarterly,* September 1968, Vol. 17, No. 1, 12-20.

Havighurst, R. J. *Human Development and Education.* New York: Longmons, Green and Co., 1953.

Havighurst, Robert J. "Youth in Exploration and Man Emergent," *Man in a World at Work.* (Henry Borow, Ed.) Boston: Houghton Mifflin Co., 1964, 215-236.

Hilton, T. L. "Career Decision-Making." *Journal of Counseling Psychology,* Winter 1962, Vol. 9, 291-298.

Hoyt, K. B. "The Specialty Oriented Student Research Program: A Five Year Report." *Vocational Guidance Quarterly,* 1968, Vol. 16, No. 3, 169-176.

Hull, William L. "Evaluating Pupil Attainment of Vocational Tasks." *American Vocational Journal,* December 1967, Vol. 42, No. 9, 15-16.

Jersild, Arthur T. "Self Understanding in Childhood and Adolescence." *American Psychologist,* 1951, 6, 122-126.

Kaback, Goldie Ruth. "Occupational Information for Groups of Elementary School Children." *Vocational Guidance Quarterly,* Spring 1966, Vol. 14, No. 3, 163-168.

Krathwohl, D. R., B. S. Bloom, B. B. Masia. *Taxonomy of Educational Objectives, The Classification of Educational Objectives, Handbook II: Affective Domain.* New York: David McKay Co., Inc., 1964.

Krathwohl, David R. "Stating Objectives Appropriately for Program, for Curriculum, and for Instructional Materials Development." *Journal of Teacher Education,* March 1965, Vol. 16, 83-92.

LoCascio, Ralph. "Delayed and Impaired Vocational Development: A Neglected Aspect of Vocational Development Theory." *Personnel and Guidance Journal,* 1964, Vol. 42, 885-887.

Lockwood, Ozelma, David B. Smith, and Robert Trezise. "Four Worlds: An Approach to Vocational Guidance." *Personnel and Guidance Journal,* March 1968, Vol. 46, No. 7, 641-643.

Loughary, John W., D. Friesen, and R. Hurst. "Autocon: A Computer-Based Automatic Simulation System." *Personnel and Guidance Journal,* September 1966, Vol. 45, No. 1, 6-15.

Luchins, A. S. "Influences of Experiences with Conflicting Information and Reactions to Subsequent Conflicting Information." *Journal of Social Psychology,* 1960, 5, 367-385.

Moss, Jerome. "The Prevocational Effectiveness of Industrial Arts." *Vocational Guidance Quarterly,* September 1968, Vol. 17, No. 1, 21-26.

O'Hara, Robert P. "A Theoretical Foundation For The Use of Occupational Information in Guidance." *Personnel and Guidance Journal,* March 1968, Vol. 46, No. 7, 636-640.

Osipow, Samuel H. *Theories of Career Development.* New York: Appleton-Century-Crofts, 1968.

Phillips, Murray G. "Learning Materials and Their Implementation." *Review of Education Research,* June 1966, Vol. 36, No. 3, 373-379.

Roeber, Edward C. "The School Curriculum and Vocational Development." *Vocational Guidance Quarterly,* Winter 1965–66, Vol. 14, No. 2, 87-91.

Slocum, Walter L. and Roy T. Bowles. *Educational and Occupational Aspirations and Expectations of High School Juniors and Seniors in the State of Washington,* Vocational-Technical Research and Development Project No. 1. Pullman, Washington: Washington State University, 1967.

Stratemeyer, F. B., Hamden L. Forkner, Margaret G. McKim, and A. Harry Passow. *Developing A Curriculum For Modern Living.* New York: Bureau of Publications, Teachers College, Columbia University, 1957.

Super, Donald E. *The Psychology of Careers.* New York: Harper, 1957.

Super, Donald E., Reuben Stariskevsky, Norman Mattin, and Jean Pierre Jordaan. *Career Development: Self Concept Theory.* New York: College Entrance Examination Board, 1963.

Tiedeman, David V. and Robert P. O'Hara. *Career Development: Choice and Adjustment.* New York: College Entrance Board, 1963.

Wellington, J. A. and N. Olechowski. "Attitudes Toward the World of Work in Elementary School." *Vocational Guidance Quarterly,* Vol. 14, No. 3, Spring 1966.

Yabroff, W. W. *An Experiment in Teaching Decision-Making.* Research Brief, California State Department of Education, 1964, 9, 1-6.

Zaccharia, Joseph S. "Developmental Tasks: Implications for the Goals of Guidance." *Personnel and Guidance Journal,* December 1965, Vol. 44, No. 4, 372-375.

In the spring of 1971, the United States Office of Education announced three grants to develop different models of career education programs. Model I, to which Gordon I. Swanson refers in his paper, is a school-based model. Model II is a career education program based in business and industry and associated with schools, while Model III is a home and community based career education program. Although Swanson's paper deals with a broader range of issues than those involved in a single model, he is primarily concerned with implications and developmental problems of the school-based model.

Tracing the antecedents of the present concern for career education, Swanson points out that the contemporary concern "appeals for the repair of the attendant damages to society." A relevant educational system must provide for the basic needs of the maturing population so that its members will not become victims of current social pathologies. From this discussion, Swanson analyzes various approaches to the definition of career education and the elements which must be incorporated within a comprehensive career education program. He presents an array of characteristics essential for schools which desire to install career education programs and concludes with a statement of problems which must be resolved if career education is to have a lasting impact upon education in this country. Dr. Swanson is Professor of Education and Coordinator for International Education in the College of Education, University of Minnesota.

Gordon I. Swanson

CAREER
EDUCATION

Introduction

This paper addresses itself to the concept of Career Education as it has evolved and culminated in several efforts toward implementation. Its primary focus will be toward school-based implementation as embraced by the U.S. Office of Education, but the examination of the concept will embrace other types of implementation.

This paper will not begin with a definition of "Career Education." At present, "Career Education" is merely a label for evolving concepts and the concepts are as elusive as the label. Career Education has been endorsed by many groups of educators whose endorsement is based on numerous caveats related to interpretation. A curious phenomenon in education is that professionals are often more loyal to labels than to the ideas presumably implied by them. The concept of Career Education is now in the process of being defined to accommodate proprietary interests among and within various groups; an effort to find an acceptable definition is often an exercise in arriving at a tolerable level of generality.

This paper will address itself to the following general topics:

(a) The emergence of the concept of career education
(b) Approaches to describing or defining career education

This paper was written for use in staff seminars at the Center for Vocational and Technical Education at The Ohio State University, September, 1971.

107

(c) Unique and essential elements of school-based career education
(d) Characteristics of schools with exemplary programs
(e) Educational assumptions which mitigate the influence of career education
(f) Problems of implementation
(g) Development needs

Career Education—
The Emergence of a Concept

The emergence of a concept of Career Education raises the question of antecedents. What stimuli gave rise to the acceptability of educational goals oriented to careers and career choice? Is Career Education another fashion or fad which will soon fall by the wayside? Is Career Education another in a series of educational gimmicks whose purpose is to serve bureaucratic or proprietory interests rather than educational goals? Are the antecedents of Career Education durable or fragile?

Vocational educators would contend that Career Education is another stage in the developmental history of Vocational Education. Beginning with Franklin's Academy, Career Education became rooted in the American educational enterprise, at least until the Academy gave way to the domination of colleges. Toward the end of the nineteenth century the concept of career-related education continued to emerge as industrial workers began to clamor for a larger share of the public educational goods.[1] The meager but important gains included an expansion of public secondary education as well as the passage of the Morrill Act whose amendments were clearly vocational and career oriented. In due course the Morrill legislation, too, gave way to dominant influences in higher education. Subsequent state and federal vocational legislation from 1906 to 1968 embraced more occupations, a greater age span of students and an interpretation of Vocational Education which included career choice, job training, and long-range planning to accommodate broader definitions of Career Education.

Other advocates would contend that Career Education now emerges as a natural consequence of concomitant advances in education's "state of the art." Advances in knowledge related to the developmental stages of children, the role of task-analysis in learning and the psychology of careers —all of these converge, it is argued, to provide a conceptual base for Career Education which did not exist previously.[2]

A third influence arose from the work of the National Advisory Council on Vocational Education. In a series of short, pungent and penetrating reports, the Advisory Council assumed a role which was both diagnostic and prescriptive. Their recommendations demanded a response. The third report, issued in July, 1970, called for a complete reform of the educational system to include Career Education, and it identified some essential elements of a career-oriented educational system.[3]

A fourth influence arose from the worldwide scene. Career Education, it is contended, is a pervasive international movement whose conceptual base is still not clear, but whose impact is being felt as strongly as the widespread phenomena of student activism and peasant revolts. The Career Education movement in Europe began in Sweden, the hotbed of European educational reform. Legislation in 1967 reformed the entire system and provided an exemplary pattern for the region.[4] The USSR established a comprehensive career development system in 1969 with elements which are home, school, and industry based. With assistance from UNICEF, the USSR sponsored an international invitational seminar on Career Education in October, 1970.[5]

A fifth explanation credits the U.S. Office of Education and State Education Agencies with strong leadership in identifying a defensible conceptual base for Career Education and encouraging implementation through grants for exemplary projects and further innovation.

As seen through the five influences described above, the movement now described as Career Education has a background of evolving concepts and numerous reinforcing elements. It is thoroughly imbedded in the developmental pattern of Vocational Education. It is not necessarily dependent upon the transitory nature of gimmick labels and fragile slogans. In a sense, it is reactionary; it reacts against an educational system which affords itself the luxury of an orientation toward status rather than an orientation toward tasks and it appeals for a repair of the disabling effects of the former to an economy. Most important, the concept has begun to develop its own momentum as a dynamic force. It is, however, still incomplete. The problems of implementation are still enormous and largely unsolved. These await further commitment and further action.

Approaches to Describing
or Defining Career Education

In the introduction to this paper, a deliberate decision was taken not to begin with a definition of Career Education. Yet the concept can be described, and perhaps defined, by discussing the various approaches to explicating the concept. It is the purpose of this section to examine the various approaches to describing the concept.

Career Education may be described as a *philosophical commitment* by the enterprise of public education to the values of a work-oriented society. These values are implemented through the instructive functions of the school by introducing career relevance into all instruction, by focusing on the decision functions of career choice at all grade levels and by providing occupational preparation to job-entry level for all school leavers or graduates.

A second approach is one of describing a set of *essential components* required for a functioning Career Education program. These components are as follows:

(a) A curriculum and instruction component in the academic curriculum which provides occupational relevance and career identification to all academic instruction in all grades,

(b) Vocational skill training up to job-entry levels in occupations chosen by students,

(c) Supplementary instruction to include observation, work-study and work-experience in selected occupations within the community,

(d) Specific instructional programs permitting students to develop awareness of self in relationship to careers and an opportunity to pursue exploratory and orientation activities in a number of occupations,

(e) A planned program of relating the instructional program to the community and its occupational structure, and

(f) A follow-up program which obligates the school to engage in placement and to improve the Career Education program through evaluation and feedback.

Career Education may be described, thirdly, as the utilization of an *educational delivery system.* This approach has the elements of clean and tidy accountability. The delivery system accommodates all of the resources available to the educative function—the time of students, the time of faculty, the materials (including the curriculum), the equipment and space in the school. The Career Education program utilizes all of these resources in varying amounts and with varying degrees of effectiveness. The delivery system may focus largely on guidance services, in-school instructional modes, or on field-trips and community activities. The delivery system for Career Education is the motion element of the program as viewed in its day-to-day operation. An important aspect is the curriculum and its orientation to the purposes of career goals. The delivery system is an important way to view any function of the school.

A fourth approach to the description of Career Education focuses on *educational levels* beginning with the elementary level and concluding with adult and continuing education. Each level has specific educational objectives and each contributes as a subsystem to the cumulating outcomes of the total system. Ordinarily the emphasis of Career Education at the elementary level involves educational objectives related to occupational awareness and career orientation. The middle level embraces educational objectives related to career exploration. The senior high school provides the opportunity to further exercise the options derived from previous levels including job-entry, further job preparation and/or other types of further education. A final level is adult and continuing education with objectives related to upgrading, updating, and retraining of those individuals holding jobs or preparing to change jobs.

A fifth approach to the description of Career Education is concerned with *outcomes.* It describes Career Education in terms of the qualifications of individuals who exit from the program, the congruency between qualifications and occupational or further education performance and, finally, the effectiveness of each level of Career Education contributing to objectives which are cumulative.

No single approach to the description or definition of Career Education is complete or adequate. All of the approaches mentioned above are mutually reinforcing. Unfortunately, schools are not always organized to permit a smooth flow of students from one level to the next nor do all students complete their education within a single educational jurisdiction. Career Education is cumulative and programmatic, it is not discrete and episodic. Schools whose structure or location does not easily accommodate Career Education will need the variety of approaches in order to add strength where needed in order to minimize the effect of gaps or weaknesses which may exist.

Finally, and most importantly, it should be emphasized that the word *career* in Career Education is grammatically and conceptually an adjective. Career Education is not synonymous with education; it is a special kind of education which affords parity of esteem to the values of work. It accepts work as an activity which rations the goods, services, and satisfactions available to mankind and its central feature, thus, is its endeavor to insure that all instruction includes occupational relevance and that all students may acquire job-entry skills in a career cluster of his choosing.

Unique and Essential Elements of the School Based Model

Adding to the complexity of Career Education, and specifically to the definition and the implementation of the school-based approach, are a series of essential elements or conditions. Without these elements or conditions, the Career Education emphasis can easily become an exercise in rhetoric or a mere expression of hope. Accordingly, these conditions should become measures of process and benchmarks for evaluation.

Transcending the entire career development emphasis is the important role of decision-making for career choice. Traditionally, teachers have urged students to keep their options open and to delay a choice of career as long as possible. Schools have been organized to minimize the opportunity for occupational choices except as delayed compromises after other options are diminished. Vocational preparation, for example, has been advanced along the educational time-line so that much of the institutional growth has been at the post-high school level. Career Education reverses the tendency to delay career choice. One of its essential features is the opportunity for students to engage themselves in decision alternatives in the early grades. This advancement of the decision context is not done to insure an earlier decision of an ultimate career choice. It is done to enable the student to employ career decision-making as an instructive aspect of his own growth and development and to insure that career choice can accommodate a rationale if undertaken soon enough but only a rationalization if delayed too long.

The introduction of career decision-making in the early grades adds numerous implications for instruction. Decision making implies alternative choices and the opportunity to reject as well as accept alternatives. The evidence that decisions have been made is not only the existence of a career choice; it is also the evidence that alternatives have been rejected. Whether accepted or rejected, career choices may be instrumental: they may exist as platforms or points of vantage from which to explore further decisions. The implications for instruction include the need to illuminate many career options and the need to understand the instructive function of decision-making.

As an instructional concept, career decision-making is not well-researched. Unlike the concepts of mastery or achievement, it does not have interchangeable parts which can be adjusted and fitted as students move from one school to another. Career decision-making is thought to be a cumulative phenomenon which results from a growing awareness of self and a growing awareness of career options. The instructional implications of this are not yet clear.

Another essential element of the school-based model is the need to integrate Career Education into the entire school curriculum, into science, reading, mathematics, and into every subject of the school. Career Education, it is proposed, will become the vehicle for carrying the load without diminishing the educational objectives of academic subjects. In return the academic subjects will serve as vehicles for providing occupational relevance and clarified decision options within the total curriculum of the school. This integration of Career Education into the total curriculum reduces the need to rely solely upon separate courses entitled "Career Education" or upon guidance services as the only delivery system for Career Education. Again, it is not clear how this curriculum integration may be accomplished or how its outcomes may be evaluated. It is essential, nevertheless, as a demonstration of the commitment of the school to the concept of Career Education and to the objectives which illuminate and facilitate career choice.

A third essential element is the adoption of some orderly system for comprehending the enormous number of occupations which may be examined in the process of accepting, rejecting, or otherwise considering an occupational choice. One of the ways to do this would be to move methodically and analytically through the Dictionary of Occupational Titles. Most would agree that such an approach would be dull and tedious. Another approach would be to examine career clusters or families of occupations in which there are a sufficient number of common elements to warrant being studied as a group of occupations. This approach has demonstrated its usefulness in Career Education. It permits a comparative view of occupational clusters and it allows students to start by examining the broad characteristics of various occupational families and to conclude with an intensive study of the job-entry requirements of a single occupation. Such an operational approach to the study of occupational clusters is essential to a program of Career Education. The occupational clusters commonly found in Career Education programs are the following:

> Business and Office Occupations
> Marketing and Distribution Occupations
> Communication and Media Occupations
> Construction Occupations
> Manufacturing Occupations
> Transportation Occupations
> Agri-Business and Natural Resource Occupations
> Marine Science Occupations
> Environmental Central Occupations
> Public Services Occupations
> Hospitality and Recreation Occupations
> Personal Services Occupations
> Fine Arts and Humanities Occupations
> Consumer and Homemaking Occupations

A fourth essential element in school-based Career Education is instruction for occupational proficiency to the job-entry level. This requires an expansion of vocational offerings in almost every school. The only alternative to this expansion is an exercise in colossal deception—of the students and the community. If schools attempt to expand Career Education programs without an expansion of their vocational offerings, students will be denied the opportunity for Career Education to lead toward career development. Nor is it sufficient for schools to rely on the job-entry skills available solely through work experience and cooperative programs. Such an approach would restrict students in Career Education programs to the least remunerative jobs in the occupational structure and to a very limited spectrum of career choice. Work experience, cooperative education, and vocational guidance may supplement the needed preparation in job-entry skills but they cannot serve as a substitute. Minimum job-entry training programs should include the opportunity to make occupational choices and to receive specific skill training in occupations contained within any one of the 15 occupational clusters identified by the U.S. Office of Education. Anything less than this minimum would not measure up to a complete program of Career Education.

As important and as essential as any characteristic of Career Education is its important linkage with the community. This linkage is so important and so essential that Career Education cannot exist without it. School-based Career Education can actually be closer to the community than employer or home-based Career Education. Linkages include advisory committees for each career cluster and school-community cooperative relationships with goals which include a development of the community environment as an instructive environment for career growth.

There are other essential and unique elements of school-based Career Education such as its applicability to all students and the obligation of the school to engage in placement and follow-up activities. These additional elements can be accommodated rather easily in most school systems.

Characteristics of Schools
With Exemplary School-Based
Programs

Sooner or later it is necessary to turn attention from educational concepts to the operation of educational programs. If Career Education is a durable concept, its durability must be demonstrated in educational settings. How do schools prepare themselves for this? What are the characteristics of schools which are prepared to implement Career

Education? Exemplary programs are in existence in many places. Following are some of the school characteristics regarded as important to Career Education:

(a) Faculty and administration acceptance of the concept of Career Education is an obvious need. This is demonstrated by a willingness to:

1. involve *all* students in Career Education,
2. make Career Education an integral part of the total curriculum,
3. accommodate work-experience, part-time employment, and work study as a part of the curriculum,
4. encourage the return of drop-outs into special programs and job preparation,
5. establish a close relationship with the community and its values related to the work ethic, and
6. engage in inservice training as necessary to increase the career education capability of faculty.

(b) A high research and development capability:

Exemplary schools should be active in creating curriculum materials for Career Education and alert to the possibility of utilizing materials created elsewhere. The faculty should be active in experimenting with different approaches to instruction and the school should be perceptive and penetrating in its approach to evaluation.

(c) A willingness to reclaim its casualties including its drop-outs, unemployed graduates and college drop-outs. The reclaiming of casualties includes the need to concentrate on programs of prevention and a continuous concern for placement.

(d) An expanded program of vocational offerings available within career clusters to all students at all levels including those in adult or continuing education.

(e) A willingness to make adjustment in the organization and structure of the school in order to accommodate Career Education. Some schools are not organized or equipped to provide Career Education. They will need to rely on services available from intermediate districts or on similar types of area-wide service. Other schools will need to reorganize schedules and calendars. Adjustments in organization and structure will be a characteristic of almost every school with exemplary Career Education.

Educational Assumptions
Which Mitigate the Influence
of Career Education

Even under the most desirable or exemplary circumstances, Career Education is likely to win its way slowly into general educational practice. Certain conventions have captured institutionalized forms of education and have mitigated the impact of such programs as Career Education.

One is the insistent preoccupation of educators with individual behavior and the neglect of concern for group behavior or with variation among groups. One of the most important research findings of the last decade was the discovery that education is not culturally irrelevant; that there are observable differences from subculture to subculture.[6] Yet this discovery has not resulted in any improvements in the approaches to educating groups in conditions of obvious disadvantage. Could it be that we are educationally influenced too strongly by a Judeo-Christian heritage wherein salvation is available to an individual but not to a group? Is it possible that education is best organized when it can focus only on competitive individual achievement?

Competitive values often become instilled by motives which have little to do with the instructional functions of the school. Individual academic achievement is the pathway to further education, status, and to social mobility. It is a system which places much emphasis on the *relative* value of individuals. What is less obvious and less understood is that this same system cannot avoid ascribing *relative* values to groups! Most particularly it ascribes a hierarchical value system to occupational groups. If the ascribed value is low, it is most difficult to encourage students to consider the occupation as a career option.

The educative process begins in individuals at the moment of birth. The sole purpose of the educative process at this early stage is to initiate communication and to link the identity of the child with the family as a group. The separation of identity begins in the school. By the time the child reaches the middle school, the entire system becomes rigorously competitive. Here the individual variations in intelligence become known but the school does very little except to measure them. Often the result is the segregation of the clever and the dull just as society segregates its criminals. Competitive values are instilled which suggest to students that schools are most concerned with the elimination of the unworthy and, alternatively, to stimulation of those whose worthiness is a highly individualized achievement.

Most communities provide a great many opportunities for an individual to merge his identity with a group. School drop-outs are often drop-ins; they opt out of the insecure environment requiring individual competition and they drop-in to some group wherein membership does not dispossess them of the feeling of security. The family, firm, church, the trade union, and the neighborhood gang—all of these provide individuals an opportunity to submerge his "I" into a collective "we" and gain more confidence in doing so. Paradoxically, a great deal of educational effort appears aimed in the opposite direction. Group guidance is avoided, for example, if time is available for individual guidance. Career Education may introduce occupationally based group identity into school systems where individual identity is the prevailing mode. It may be a difficult accommodation.

A second assumption which may mitigate the influence of Career Education is related to the assumed demise of the work ethic. The increase of leisure, it is claimed, will diminish the importance of the work ethic. Yet, it is almost impossible to describe leisure time. It is not time used to rest, vacation, sleep, or relax. All of these are preparatory to work. If it is none of these, what is it? Who has it? It is likely that the importance of the work ethic has nothing to do with the amount or the utilization of leisure time. Unemployment, it is agreed, is not a maldistribution of leisure. The assumption remains, however, that the work ethic will be diminished, somehow, by increased leisure time.[7]

Problems for Implementing Career Education

The problems of implementing Career Education on a nationwide basis are numerous and complex. The first, and perhaps the most obvious, problem is school size. Career Education is most easily implemented in large school systems and most difficult in small districts. More than half of the school districts in the United States are in jurisdictions whose populations are less than 50,000 persons. School districts with such limited enrollments have difficulty finding opportunities for a wide range of work experience and additional difficulties in obtaining coverage in all of the occupational clusters. Adaptations are possible as mentioned previously in this paper, but implementation will be difficult, nevertheless, for most schools.

The problems of implementing Career Education at the elementary level and in the middle school are likely to be most perplexing. The concept of careers is remote for elementary school children and a curricular emphasis on career decisions is subject to superficiality. The development of meaning on the experience level of elementary school children is a specialized skill not possessed by many who advocate Career Education at this level. Moreover, the school-based model of Career Education includes the presumption that elementary school children will move inductively through all of the career clusters by the time they reach the 6th grade. This may be an impossible expectation or it may involve more developmental effort than has been contemplated.

The middle school has special problems of implementation—problems related to the Career Education model, to the school itself, and to students at this level. The school based model literally pivots on the middle school. Instruction in Career Education begins at the kindergarten level and extends through grade six with emphasis on career awareness. During the middle school years, the students begin a series of career choices. The middle school is thus a pivot point for the entire program. From this point onward, the decision choices are expected to narrow and interest is expected to intensify. Unless a good job of implementation is done at the middle-school level, the entire program is weakened.

Implementation also encounters the problem of expanding vocational offerings in areas where vocational personnel are not now available. Teacher education institutions have not had lead-time to prepare teachers nor are they well prepared to offer inservice training. Implementation of the cluster concept requires trained personnel and, at least for the present, the supply is meager and the flow is almost non-existent.

Perhaps the most serious problem in implementation can be described as a need for guidelines which permit local education agencies to plan a smooth and orderly entrance into career development programs and a way of anticipating the costs of doing so. Such guidelines might propose organizational and structural alternatives available to schools, personnel requirements for installing and implementing programs, space and equipment requirements for various program components and the degree to which Career Education may develop interchangeable parts for use within or among local education agencies. The need is for a guide to sequencing the process of installing a Career Education program. What components should be installed first and which ones can be delayed?

Development Needs

From the very beginning of the focus toward Career Education, development needs have been underestimated. Thus far, Career Education has been assisted through exemplary grants and small research and development contracts. If the concept of Career Education is to embrace the entire school system, and if Career Education is to be integrated with the total curriculum, a developmental thrust of career development must find its way into every level of education including the university level. It must become a central focus for federal allocations to educational research and a central focus for educational planning. Such a scope for developmental costs has not been contemplated. Meanwhile, the meager resources for Career Education must be mobilized toward providing assistance to states and to local education agencies for planning, staff development, creating instructional materials, and evaluation. Career Education can easily become associated with educational gimmickry and its life can become as tenuous as other slogans which have preceded it. Its durability will depend on the willingness to invest in the needs for development or the willingness to bear the long-run costs of not doing so.

FOOTNOTES

[1]Wirth, Arthur G., "The Vocational-Liberal Studies Controversy Between John Dewey and Others, (1900–1917)," Final Report, Project No. 7-0305, USOE Washington University, St. Louis, Mo., September, 1970, p. 346.

[2]The argument for a convergence theory advanced by John Coster, Director—Center for Occupational Education, North Carolina State University.

[3]Third Report of the National Advisory Council on Vocational Education, Washington, D.C., July 10, 1970.

[4]Laroplaner For Yrkesutbildningen Samt Vissa Pedogogiska och Methodiska Fragor, Ecklesiastikdepartementet, Stockholm, 1967.

[5]USSR–UNICEF Seminar on Pre-Vocational Training, Education, and Vocational Orientation Within and Outside Schools, Moscow, October 12–31, 1970. (29 working papers)

[6]This conclusion was highlighted in the work of James Coleman in studies surrounding his work on equality of educational opportunity.

[7]Smith, Timothy L., *Work and Human Worth,* Congressional Record, House of Representatives, Vol. 113, No. 147, September 19, 1967.

Keith Goldhammer conceives of a careers education curriculum which is broader than an emphasis upon the occupational career, and which, in effect, constitutes a whole new paradigm upon which the curriculum of the school can be based. He uses the plural, *careers,* to designate the breadth of roles in which an individual must engage throughout his life. He holds that a relevant educational program must help to capacitate all children so that they can be effective in the performance of all their life activities. He concludes with a rough outline of how the careers curriculum might affect children with different levels of career aspirations.

Dr. Goldhammer is Dean of the School of Education, Oregon State University.

Keith Goldhammer

A CAREERS
CURRICULUM

The Academic Tradition

At least since Aristotle, we have been aware that man is a social animal. No one can well define the life of man separate from the social roles which he has to play. These roles are not numerous, but their identification is critical to the analysis of the functions of education. Although there are those critics of contemporary life who maintain that society is a prison in which man is confined, there are also those scholars who recognize that society and culture provide the enabling environment in which the full realization of man's humanity is made possible. Nihilistic existentialism to the contrary, there can be a dynamic interaction between man and his society, the result of which is the creative improvement of both. However, the dynamic tensions that give rise to that creative interaction result from the breadth of knowledge and skill which men have in the performance of their social roles.

This paper was written for use in staff seminars at The Center for Vocational and Technical Education at The Ohio State University, June, 1971.

Important as it is, the sociological concept of role is a fairly static one. A role is something which an individual performs throughout the course of his life. A role is defined by the expectations which an individual and others have for it, as well as by certain ideal norms which society in general attaches to it. Roles may be modified by the personality, aspirations and interpretation of the actor. To be successful in the performance of his roles, an individual must be knowledgeable of the societal norms and the expectations of relevant others, which prescribe the zone of tolerance within which his socially acceptable behaviors must fall.

This zone of tolerance may define only the traditional norms. The degree of openness of society may provide either a broad or a narrow latitude to the role incumbent. The more rigid the prescription, the more controls established, the more the performance of the role becomes little more than the ritualistic engagement of the individual in his social activities. The more the performance of the role becomes ritualistic, the less opportunity will be present for arousing the dynamic tensions necessary for the creative inter-relationship between the individual and his culture. In the technocratic society, there are strong influences to attempt to reduce human behavior to that of the clock-work mechanism. The more regularized performance becomes, the greater will be the predictability of human behavior, the less variation from established norms will be tolerated, the less conflict can be expected, the easier it will be for managers or leaders to govern the behaviors of the governed, and the more decadent and ritualistic social life will become. The highly bureaucratized society tends to establish the prescribed ritualism of role norms to increase predictability, establish the template upon which all behaviors can become uniformly patterned, and assure that variability will be restricted within desired tolerances. This basically is the new "Skinnerian" theme, which seems to suggest that the human problems of this age can be resolved only by conditioning the young to behave within the limits of toleration proposed by whatever central committee of the establishment gets to make the decision.

The problem for modern society has become that of helping every individual achieve a desirable balance in his role performance. On the one hand each person needs to achieve a requisite level of acceptability in the performance of his roles so he can live with his fellow men. On the other hand, he must engage his personality, his aspirations, his own insights and competence to act upon the role in such a fashion that he changes it to achieve a higher degree of personal self-fulfillment.

Classically, the concept of vocation fulfilled this requirement. One dictionary definition of the term *vocation* indicates that it is a "summons from God to an individual or group, to undertake the obligation and perform the duties of a particular task in accordance with the Divine plan."

It later came to be defined as the position into which God had placed a person. Although the term is sometimes used today to indicate a "strong inclination toward a particular type of work," it is more frequently used as a designation of a person's membership in a particular occupational class. Today, the term *vocation* generally has come to mean the job category in which one performs, and it is generally set off from the concept of the profession, which is felt to have a higher and more prestigious connotation. As Anderson has pointed out, the German word for profession is *Beruf,* which has come to relate to vocations and treats them in the nature of a calling and has implications of the social class designation as well as the use of one's innate capabilities.[1] In the most crass form, a vocation today bears with it the designation of a job which lies along the continuum from no particular training requirements to that which involves a high degree of technical skill. A profession, on the other hand, lies on the continuum beyond that of the vocation, and not only does it involve a prolonged period of academic and professional training, but it is also in the nature of a calling, a dedication, and a utilization of mental capacities along with certain highly refined manual or intellectual skills.

The placement of vocational education in the school curriculum is further evidence of the denigration that has taken place with respect to the term. The school curriculum is generally divided between the academic and the vocational, and the vocational is generally considered a form of training which is provided as an alternative for those students who through native ability or interest cannot perform satisfactorily in the academic. An important school of contemporary educational philosophy has held that the vocational has no place in the schools; that the term *education* relates to the development of the intellectual skills; while the preparation for a manual job should be considered training and offered in lesser types of institutions for those who will become the drones of society. This school of thought derives its philosophy from Plato, who claimed that only that man could be considered educated who has been trained to pursue "the ideal perfection of citizenship" and to distinguish how to rule and how to obey. Socrates concluded:

> This is the only education which, upon our view, deserves the name; that other sort of training which aims at the acquisition of wealth or bodily strength, or mere cleverness apart from intelligence or justice, is mean and illiberal, and is not worthy to be called education at all.[2]

Although educators have resisted the overt and negative connotations of the Hutchins' brand of perennialism, they have still fallen into the trap which Hutchins set for them through their concurrence with him that the main business of education is knowledge dissemination. The establishment of a public school system in the United States based upon the Platonic intellectual tradition has tended toward an elitist conception of its functions, has emphasized its selective characteristics, and has at least partially abrogated its responsibilities for the 75 to 80 percent of its students who by native ability, interest, and aspiration are identifiable with the practical affairs of our culture rather than inclined toward the more abstract and conceptual activities of the academic disciplines.

Vocational educators themselves have been victimized by the tradition and have inclined to think of their field in terms of narrow occupational training and as an alternative to college attendance. The false dichotomy between job and college has helped to perpetuate an aristocratic elitism in American education which is incompatible with democratic beliefs. What has been lacking, but sorely needed, is a conception of education which stresses the role of the school in helping each individual become capacitated so that he can develop his potential both for his own self-fulfillment and his contributing to the maintenance and healthy functioning of society.

That which is needed in today's world is neither a new brand of academicism nor a new style of vocationalism, but a fusion of the two. The emerging conception which may obliterate the false dichotomy between the academic and the vocational is that of *careers education.*

A definition of career comes close to being a secularization of the classical concept of vocation. The dictionary suggests that a career is an occupation or a profession for which one undertakes special training and in which one is engaged as a life work. The psychological aura surrounding career suggests the relevance to it of such terms as commitment, dedication, internalization, life-styles, service, the use of knowledge, perspective toward life, human relationships, and life goals. If the central mission of the school is to assist all students to become so capacitated that they can perform their life responsibilities competently, then there need be no false distinctions between various curricula within the school. All human beings are involved in career activities; all human beings must develop the competence, the skills, the personal understandings, and the knowledges essential for the successful performance of their roles, to serve the interests both of their fellow men and themselves. The concept of the careers curriculum involves a centrality of concern for the range of life careers in which the individual will engage. These careers constitute the scope of the curriculum, and all content of the curriculum can be formulated to produce the range of skills, knowledges and understandings essential for maximizing the individual student's potential both to perform and to become self-fulfilled.

EDUCATIONAL PURPOSE IN THE CAREERS CURRICULUM

The purposes of education must be stated in terms of the individual learner and what he does as a result of his engagement in the educational enterprise. From this point of view, *the primary purpose of education is to assist the student to become a fully capacitated, self-motivating, self-fulfilled, contributing member of society.* This definition of educational purpose encompasses four essential concepts which become the basic criteria for determining the breadth or scope of the curriculum and what happens in the instructional programs of the school.

1. *Fully capacitated* means that the school shall assist the student to perform all of his life roles with the skill, knowledge, and understanding necessary for his acquiring the competence necessary to be successful in all of them. If, as previously indicated, a man's life is divided into the roles which he performs, then each role suggests a basic career pattern. Each person must make his contribution to the economic life of society through his being a *producer of goods or a renderer of services.* The greatest failure of the schools is seen in the number of individuals who have not been *capacitated* to perform this role successfully. As a consequence, the economic burden placed upon those who can contribute to the wealth of the nation for the support of those who cannot is quickly becoming intolerable. As President Johnson indicated, a primary function of education is to help all individuals become tax-payers rather than tax-consumers.

Each person, regardless of his age, performs a career as a *member of a family group.* A key factor which constitutes either a means of facilitation or a barrier to an individual's capacitation in all his roles is the degree to which he can perform the responsibilities in his family careers effectively. To a large degree, alienation in our society is the outgrowth of the problems emanating from the deterioration of the American family as a primary social unit. The career as a member of a family meshes with that of the individual's participation in the economic life of society. It is through his participation in the economic life that he is able to sustain his role in the family, or it is as the provider of the services essential for maintaining the family that a woman in our culture may still make her greatest economic contribution. The primacy of the family is well recognized by virtue of the fact that it is considered the "home" of the individual or, colloquially, it is the place in which he lives.

The third basic career area in which the individual engages is that of a *participant in the life of the community.* The community is defined as the composite of the human beings who live within it. Regardless of whether the model is authoritarian or democratic, an individual must engage himself in the affairs of the community, even by the mere fact of existence if by no more positive means. The well-being of each community depends upon the active involvement of its citizens. The manner in which the affairs of the community are conducted also becomes a facilitative or impeding factor in an individual's self-fulfillment. To perform adequately the responsibilities of one's roles within the community demands knowledges and skills of citizenship as well as a commitment to values which extend the individual beyond himself and into associational activities with others.

A fourth career in which an individual must become capacitated is that of *a participant in the avocational activities of society.* Every human being is faced with two conditions of his existence which require his participation in these types of absorbing, self-renewal activities. In the first instance, to maintain his capacity for action, an individual has to relieve the monotony of sameness or of the use of his time without personal meanings or satisfactions to him. In a highly technological society, it is inevitable that a large percentage of the population engage in productive or service activities which are monotonous drudgery. For many individuals, the personal meanings necessary for self-fulfillment can never be acquired through the activities in which they engage in order to earn a living. For these individuals the primary source of personal meanings depends upon the avocational pursuits in which they may engage. Secondly, the human organism wears itself through activity which requires long periods of concentrated physical or mental endeavor; it renews itself, however, by engaging in other types of physical or mental endeavor which necessitate the use of different muscles, a variety of skills, or in concentration upon different cognitive or affective pursuits. The extent to which an individual can become absorbed and derive meanings from his avocational activities is related to the degree of competence that he acquires in the performance of those activities. This career, too, can be a powerful factor in meshing with the other careers in that it enables an individual to live a part of his life in shared activities with members of his family or his community even though his economic pursuits may keep him apart from them.

Finally, a person also has an obligation to relate himself and achieve competence in those activities of the community which regulate the behaviors of its members and give meaning to the activities in which the citizens of the community engage. This area may be described as that of the *aesthetic, religious and moral life careers* within the community. Neither society nor civilization can persist without its having a well defined sense of the beautiful, the good, the true, the legitimate. Failure in these areas may have as significant consequences in the disruption of the life of the individual as in any other of the career areas. No society can afford to fail to assist its members in developing the knowledges and skills essential for its own perpetuation and the maintenance of its regulatory functions.

2. *Self-Motivating* means that the individual has the inner strength and drives to perform his career roles as effectively as possible. It also means that he sees the necessity for exerting himself to perform his roles effectively and that he has well-defined personal aspirations related to the adequacy with which he engages in his life activities. The person who lacks motivation

is unquestionably alienated from his fellow men and from himself. It is through his motivations that he is able to develop a self-identity and feelings of adequacy and worth. There is more to motivation than merely having a well-defined set of values and aspirations with regard to one's careers. Performance necessitates sacrifice and disciplined perspective. Participation involves having to cope with difficulties and crises as well as the pleasant and agreeable. The individual who is not self-disciplined is frequently the one who finds it hard to cope with the unexpected, to acquire a degree of self-mastery that is essential for overcoming adversity, or to attain the degree of mental health that is basic for continuing self-actualization. To be self-actualized involves an understanding of self, of others, of society and the personal control necessary for dealing with the range of problems that occur in life.

3. To be *self-fulfilled* means that one has gained the ability to secure satisfactions and personal meanings from his life work and activities. Those activities and the aspirations which he has with respect to them become an internalized part of him. An individual then has integrated his entire personality around his unified perception of the totality of his life activities. He secures his *raison d'etre* within them. Self-fulfillment may be looked upon both as an end product and as an attitudinal relationship with one's careers. Although it is the end toward which one strives, there are no essential techniques which one can use to get there. The goal of self-fulfillment necessitates an attitude on the part of educators as well as on the part of learners. It focuses attention upon the human being and his needs for growth and development rather than upon a content to be mastered or a curriculum to be maintained. A school which is dedicated to the self-fulfillment of its students focuses its attention upon the evolving individual, his purposes in life, the degree to which he develops cumulative competence in his ability to cope with all of the things in his environment with which he has to deal. The curriculum for such a school must be flexible and adaptable to individual needs.

4. Finally, *contributing* means that what an individual does in his life roles is a constructive force for the maintenance and improvement of the social body of which he is a part. As he helps to provide for the well-being and satisfactions of others, he does the same for himself. A society which is built exclusively upon a selfish self-identification atomizes itself, and, in consequence, it fails to develop the basis upon which the effective, cooperative relationships of its parts can be established.

The concept of *full capacitation* relates to individuals who can effectively perform their careers. The concept of *self-motivation* relates to individuals who are self-actualized in their ability to cope with the problems of their existence. The concept of *self-fulfillment* relates to the establishment of the healthy personality, while the concept of *contribution* relates to the cumulation of healthy personalities within a healthy, purposive society. The degree to which the school achieves these ends for all students is the measure of society's ability to perform its functions satisfactorily.

Characteristics of the Careers Curriculum

OBJECTIVES

There are four basic objectives to the careers curriculum. These are:

1. *Social effectiveness.* Every individual needs to have the skills, knowledges and understandings essential for conducting his affairs within his community and in relationship to his fellow men effectively. This goal implies that the individual will have extensive knowledge about social organizations and social processes and the skills which are necessary for him to work effectively with both.

2. *Economic productivity.* Every individual in contemporary society needs to have the skills, knowledges and understandings essential for his maximizing his potentialities as a producer of goods or a renderer of services. The school has the basic responsibility to help each student make wise choices about his career as a producer and to gain the knowledge and skills essential for his later entry into a specific preparatory program for his completion of the entry requirements. No individual, either male or female, is free from the possibility of having to earn his own livelihood or support others during the course of his life. The school cannot have fulfilled its obligation to youth unless it has helped every young person, regardless of what his future potentialities may be, learn some salable skills before he leaves school. The responsibility of the school to teach salable skills is associated with the obligation of each individual to acquire the means, through his own efforts, of helping to support and maintain the society of which he is a part.

3. *Self-realization.* The school has an obligation to help each individual recognize his own worth and develop a feeling of self integrity while it helps him build respect for his fellow men and achieve the knowledge and skills needed to perform his life careers effectively. There is no more fundamental need in our society than for the development of that inner strength and sense of belonging which enables all citizens to cope with the realities of life and perform effectively in spite of the difficulties or vicissitudes which may confront them. The school cannot avoid the responsibility for helping to develop skills and attitudes necessary not only for successful working

relationships but also for those that are associated with an individual's total perspective toward life, including both his aesthetic and his avocational participation and appreciations.

4. *Moral responsibility.* Without an understanding by every individual of the core of basic values essential for the maintenance of civilization and the regulation of human behavior in accordance with the needs of a democratic society, the fabric of society is weakened and may eventually disintegrate. To develop a sense of moral responsibility which enables an individual to be a self-actualized and self-disciplined individual capable of making his own decisions about right and wrong and participating in those activities that emanate from a high sense of moral responsibility is an essential obligation of the schools.

SCOPE OF THE CURRICULUM

The scope of the careers curriculum is the various "life careers" in which individuals engage as members of society. As previously indicated, there are at least five such careers which should constitute the framework within which all content of the curriculum is organized. These careers are:

1. A producer of goods or a renderer of services.
2. A member of a family group.
3. A participant in social and political life of society.
4. A participant in avocational pursuits.
5. A participant in the regulatory functions involved in aesthetic, moral and religious concerns.

There are several essential aspects of each of these careers with which the school must be concerned. First, an individual must make significant decisions relative to each of these careers. Each decision involves a selection not only between alternatives that exist within the career itself, but also about the total life style in which he will live. Each decision establishes the zone within which choices relative to other careers may be made. Consequently, helping each student develop increased power to make rational choices which affect his present and future patterns of living is of importance in building self-activated and self-realized human personalities.

Second, these life careers do not exist totally in the future but to varying degrees are part of the life activities of every person at every stage of his life. Each person needs knowledge and skill to participate effectively in his social roles in the present as well as to gain increased effectiveness in his participation in his social roles in the future. To gain the knowledge and skill necessary for making relevant choices in the future necessitates that he experience effective participation in the present, both as the foundation upon which successful choices can be made and as the means through which a strong personality can be developed. Applicative knowledge is certainly the basis upon which skills and attitudes are formed. All areas of knowledge, the basic disciplines and the so-called academic skill areas, are needed by children to help them acquire the ability for living effectively and rationally today as well as in the future. Knowledge is needed to understand the breadth of available choices and to provide means through which the child can both vicariously and experientially determine the consequences that ensue from the decisions he has to make about his life. In the careers curriculum, knowledge needs to be functionally related toward the scope of the curriculum, namely the range of social careers in which the individual will participate. The areas of knowledge, therefore, do not need to be taught as separate and unrelated domains but rather as supportive and implementive means, helping to build the competence for actual involvement as well as the wisdom needed for effective choice. Harry Broudy has made the very useful distinction between applicative and interpretive knowledge. Applicative knowledge may be defined as that which an individual can apply to the solution of a particular problem about which he has to make a decision. It helps him understand the variables with which he has to deal and to forecast the consequences of his decisions. Interpretive knowledge helps to describe or interpret the structure, process or correlations which exist but cannot necessarily be used for other ends. Basically, the dilemma of the schools has resulted from their failure to use knowledge as a means to the students' ends rather than as an end-in-itself. English is valuable as a means of building communicative skills, not for achieving sophistication in literary analysis and criticism. History is valuable as it points the student toward the future rather than the past—and so on. In this curriculum, the criterion of content is *use* and the manner in which it helps to build the individual's power to make decisions and to deal effectively with his life's problems.

Learning experiences in the schools today must have a cumulative effect upon the students' performing their social roles effectively and gaining the basis for making responsible choices. Learning is not an exercise that can be measured by simple achievement tests. Rather it is the basis upon which one determines how he will act, in what contexts he will act, what ends he will seek to achieve, what means he will use to achieve his ends, what control he will exercise over his life activities.

To provide for the cumulative effect, the sequence of learning experiences may proceed through six steps:

1. The first step is that of *discovery*. The learner should discover the varieties of existing possibilities, the elements or ingredients involved in each of the possibilities, the range of ways in which individuals meet their needs in various cultures or settings and the consequences ensuing from each of the possibilities.

2. The second step involves the individual's endeavor to *identify with* or gain *internalized familiarity with* the various possibilities. The process of discovery may be considered primarily on the level of cognition, while the process of *identification* involves the affective domain as well. The process of identification involves the determination of attitudes and values and helps to lay the basis upon which an individual can understand himself with respect to the factors involved in the world external to him.

3. The third step is the individual's *selection or rejection* of those alternatives that appear to have some relevance for his own participation in his social roles. The process of selection proceeds from the general or broad area of concern to the more refined elements therein and leads to the fourth step in the learning chain.

4. The *refinement* of the field so that the individual can increasingly discriminate its elements is a continuing process throughout the entire educational experience. Refinement involves the determination of the patterns of organization of elements within a broader field and the understanding of alternatives on a more microscopic level than the student had been able to identify while he was in the process of discovering the elements contained in the total universe.

5. As an individual is being helped to refine his choices, he must also gain increasing knowledge and skill about the activity in *preparation* for his ability to participate in it. The complexity of life today necessitates the acquisition of some skill and knowledge for most social roles in which we engage. Hopefully, in the process of acquiring that skill and knowledge, the school will not only "train" the individual but will also involve him in the process of rational choice and evaluation, helping him to become both skillful and reflective as he engages in his life activities.

6. The school not only prepares the individual for effective performance of his careers, but it also provides him with some opportunity to *experience* the elements of the careers so that he can establish a stronger basis for increasingly acquiring the more highly refined knowledge and skill he needs for the modification of previous choices and decisions. Actual experience in role participation and on-the-job participation are essential methods of careers education.

THE CENTRAL FOCUS OF THE CAREERS CURRICULUM

Can there be a central unifying focus in the careers curriculum or are all of the elements contained therein of equal merit or value? Certainly, none of the five careers identified can be eliminated without doing violence to some aspects of the school's responsibility for assisting the student to become effective in all of his life endeavors. The issue of what may become most central is controversial, and in today's world there are arguments that would lead one to the conclusion that that which we select as most central may be becoming a less dominating factor in the individual's life pattern. We have selected the *vocational career* as that which is most central to the life of the individual and which is most significant in determining the life style of the individual. There are a variety of reasons why we think this career must be central to the school curriculum.

First, other things to the contrary notwithstanding, a person is primarily known for the occupation or profession in which he is engaged. This is not just a preoccupation of a capitalist society but is equally evident in all other societies. The occupation in which one is engaged is the primary determinant of the amount of money he has to spend; the pattern of consumer activities in which he is engaged; his social class status; the manner in which he rears his children; the manner in which he participates in the social life of the community; the manner in which he engages in cultural, aesthetic and avocational pursuits. Man's associational life with his fellows is primarily determined by his work orientation, and even though the amount of time man spends in work may be declining for the major portion of the population, it still remains the largest single block of time allocated to any one career for the vast majority of people on the face of the earth.

Second, all other factors taken into consideration, it is at the point at which an individual becomes economically self-sufficient and an earner of money and a payer of taxes in support of his governments that he achieves recognition of his adult status. To achieve adult status is a primary goal of the child. Being an adult means to be able to achieve independence through self-supporting activities. The value system of our society still puts primary emphasis during the formative years of an individual's life upon his making a decision about his adult, occupational role. From earliest childhood the individual is faced with the question asked by the adults in his environment "What do you want to be when you are grown up?" A remarkable *rite de passage* is experienced at the point when an individual starts to formulate other significant decisions affecting his existence in the light of his occupational choice.

Third, it is possible to build a functionally relevant curriculum for each learner, helping him acquire the depth of knowledge about culture, society, the physical world, and man within it, by centralizing the focus on man's vocational career. A central issue in a modern school curriculum is that of giving it a direction which indicates a point in time toward which the educational experience is heading. That point in time is the one at which the individual becomes fully engaged in a vocation of his choice. All realms of knowledge can be brought into the curriculum with respect to this unified theme and perspective.

Fourth, we must also face the reality of the present economic and psychological crises which confront our nation. The economic crisis arises, at least in part, because increasing numbers of individuals are alienated in our society from the work experience. Not being able to earn their own living through the skills which they have acquired, a large segment of our society seems doomed to a life-time on welfare. Many of these are also rearing their children for a similar fate. A large part of the population, the young and the disaffected, has not been helped to an association of their concerns about social service and individual identity with work identity. Their alienation from the work experience has led to both a social and a vocational disorientation, which, in turn, has led to the augmentation of violence, the increase in social incapacitation and the disintegration of basic social norms. The American school has failed both groups. In its failure it has augmented an economic and psychological alienation, both of which could probably be remedied by an orientation to vocation.

There is considerable controversy today relative to the place of work in our emerging society. Many jobs have been replaced by machines. Whole factories are being operated with only a few supervisory operatives, their jobs being to observe the gauges on machines rather than the expenditure of labor by workers. Computers make systematized decisions and even regulate the work flow. Does this mean that the concept of man as worker is obsolete? Dennis Gabor paints a gloomy picture of what has happened to the need for labor. He points out that at the turn of the nineteenth century, in European countries 80% of the population worked on the land and could produce just enough food for the people in those countries to survive, but in the United States and Canada today, 8% of the working force is producing more than enough food for the populations of those countries. Within a few years, he asserts, it will soon be able to produce all of the goods required by 2% of the population. However, even if this happens, he contends that the work culture will not be materially altered:

> Until a new kind of generation grows up, which is not yet in view, I believe we can take it for granted that work will remain a prime necessity of life; it makes people feel socially useful. For a long time to come, work will have to stay with us—to a diminishing extent as an economic necessity, to a growing extent as occupational therapy. We shall have to invent work which makes people feel socially useful and even creative.[3]

In spite of Gabor's forecast, there are elements of the current scene which tend to deny the forecast that work will become merely occupational therapy, important as that aspect of work may become. As one type of work diminishes, other types of work emerge and are enlarged upon. As Arensberg has pointed out, society has not as yet found a means for even minimally tapping all of man's creative and inventive resources as they can relate to his work activities.[4] As productive work decreases, the demand for greater numbers of service, professional, semi-professional, and managerial workers emerge. New jobs are defined along with technological advances, and new divisions of labor are established.

Both from sociological and psychological points of view, there has yet been found no substitute for work and the social and personal functions which work performs. Friedmann and Havighurst have pointed out that work is a conditioner of social purpose. In all cultures it has the function of distributing income, regulating life activities, establishing a basis for social identification, providing meaningful life experiences, and creating the social sub-systems for associational activities.[5] They also concluded from their studies that non-economic benefits appeared to be as strong or stronger motivations for work for a majority of the workers than the economic gains. Anderson, too, concluded that the range of satisfactions derived from work made work experience central to and the most significant aspect of an individual's social and personal identification.[6]

The evidence points strongly to the conclusion that work will remain the central, identifying characteristic of a human being's life, that work relationships will occupy the majority of one's time while awake, that one's status and role in society will be largely determined by the career in which he is engaged, and that the main purpose of education will continue to be preparation for one's life roles, with central concern focused upon the development of employability and career entry qualifications for 100% of the youth population.

Functions of the Careers Curriculum

The scope and functions of the careers curriculum, based upon the assumption of the vocational career as central to the educative process, is seen in Table I.

ELEMENTARY GRADES

In this plan, there are five functions which the elementary school must fulfill:

1. It must teach children the basic skills of learning and of social involvement. Participation in a technological society necessitates that an individual learn to read, write, and understand number relationships. These skills are necessary not only for participation as a citizen but also for conducting one's own affairs and for participation in the vocational life of the community. In addition to these basic skills of learning, there are a large number of skills associated with an individual's involvement in social activi-

TABLE I

The Scope and Functions of the Careers Curriculum

OBJECTIVES	Social Effectiveness	Economic Productivity	Personal Self-fulfillment	Moral Responsibility

FUNCTIONS

Elementary
1. Basic skills of learning and social involvement.
2. Examination of essential functions pertaining to life and the individual and social activities of human beings.
3. Examination of the basic characteristics of man's life in various societies.
4. Exploration of the environment and nature and how man has learned about them and uses them.
5. Exploration of basic interests and potentialities of each child.

Middle Grades
1. Continued growth and increased competence in the use of basic skills.
2. Examination of a broad range of vocational, avocational, family life, citizenship and cultural career alternatives.
3. Exploration of several potential personal career opportunities.
4. Developing skills and attitudes toward career choices.
5. Preliminary selection of general areas for future vocational careers.
6. Gaining knowledge of personal and educational requirements involved in various careers.
7. Examination of man's value and belief systems.

Senior High School
1. Emphasis upon continuous refinement, use and the application of basic skills.
2. Development of specific knowledge and skills needed for family life, avocational, citizenship and cultural careers.
3. Exploration and personal testing of vocational career opportunities within a specific cluster or area.
4. Selection of specific career and initial preparation and exploration of post-high school preparation potentials.
5. Development of some salable skills.

SCOPE				
Producer of goods & services	Member of family life	Participant in social & political life of society	Participant in avocational pursuits	Participant in regulatory functions of aesthetic, moral & religious concerns

135

ties with his fellow men. These have sometimes been characterized as the skills of socialization and are fundamental for an individual's accepting the limitations placed upon him and his independence of action if he is to associate effectively with his fellow men.

2. The second function of the elementary school is to help students examine the essential functions that pertain to life and the individual and social activities of human beings. One reason for the organization of the elementary school is to help the life of the child become expanded away from the centrality of the family to the broader social communities. Narrow or broad as the child's pre-school experiences may be, the school provides an opportunity for him to explore systematically the basic social organizations, processes, activities, and functions, all of which are necessary for the maintenance of human social life. It is through the examination of the essential functions pertaining to life and the individual and social activities of human beings that the child becomes fully aware of the range of potentialities for vocational careers that are available to him.

3. Central as the vocational career may be, it is imperative that the child becomes sensitive to the other types of social roles in which he will engage. This is accomplished in the elementary school through the study of his own society and culture as well as the societies and cultures of other peoples. By examination of the basic characteristics of man's life in various societies, he becomes aware of a broader range of alternatives, the consequences of each, the inter-relationships of the social, geographic and biological worlds, and the manner in which man adapts to varying conditions as a matter of his physical needs and social preferences.

4. As the elementary school is centered in the social activities of men, it helps the child understand both the limitations and the potentialities inherent in his environment. Man's vocational and cultural existence is as much a part of the environment as is his physical existence. The elementary school helps children understand the characteristics of the environment and nature and how man has learned about them and uses them.

5. While the child is exploring the social and physical worlds about him, he is also coming to know more about himself, his basic interests and his own potentialities. A basic function of each elementary school is that of helping each child become his own unique self, learning how to make relevant choices to gain the satisfactions he needs and to cope with the problems of his existence.

MIDDLE GRADES

In the middle grades the child engages in further exploration and discovery and the refinement of the knowledge and skills needed for effective participation and for making the choices about his careers.

1. The school emphasizes continued growth and increased competence in the use of basic skills. Basic skills have become tools for him to use in achieving his purposes and improving his ability to participate in social activities.

2. In these grades there is greater emphasis upon the examination of a broad range of career potentialities in all areas of life. This examination involves both general and specialized studies, skill building activities, and an opportunity for students to determine their perspectives toward basic issues involved in determining the life styles associated with each.

3. In beginning to narrow the range of potentialities for himself, the student selects certain specific elements for specific exploration in order to explore, from the total parameter of possibilities, those that have most relevance to his own interests and most potential for his own involvement.

4. In the process of exploration, an effort will also be made to help him acquire the skills necessary for making selection on the basis of pertinent criteria.

5. It is in the middle grades that the specific attention will be directed toward the selection of one's own vocational career potentialities. It is in the middle grades that the total curriculum in which the child is engaged can become centered upon and determined by his potential vocational career choices.

6. It is also in these years that the child's attention must be focused upon what it takes to become involved in specific types of careers or to be able meaningfully to engage in specific life activities. Hopefully, through these explorations, the child will realistically face decisions about future educational requirements needed to achieve his career aspirations.

7. With the growth in the conceptual skills of the middle school child, emphasis will be placed upon the exploration of man's value and belief systems. Characteristics of various value and belief systems will be studied with a particular emphasis upon the functionality and consequences of belief systems as well as upon the different ways in which man has been able to interpret his relationships and derive meanings for his existence.

SENIOR HIGH SCHOOL

In the senior high school, the student further refines his choices and begins a higher level of specialization in preparation for immediate job entry or post-high school technical training.

1. Some emphasis will be placed upon the continuous refinement and application of basic skills as well as the remediation for those skills in which the student may be deficient.

2. Emphasis will also be placed upon the development of the specific knowledge and skills needed for family life, avocational, citizenship and

cultural careers. Students will learn how to deal with specific kinds of problems associated with these careers and will develop the specific skills and knowledges that they need to become effective in their performance of their adult responsibilities associated with these careers.

3. By the time the student has passed from the middle grades to the senior high school, he should have selected some specific cluster areas in which he hopes to find his future vocational career. In the senior high school, he will have an opportunity to explore and personally test the vocational career opportunities within a specific cluster or area.

4. He will, in the course of his senior high school, have an opportunity to select a specific career for which he will need further preparation.

5. In the selection of a specific career, he will also have an opportunity to engage in the initial preparatory knowledge and skill building experiences while he explores the post-high school preparatory potentials which will enable him to achieve his goals.

6. At least three factors in our society necessitate that the senior high school help every youngster acquire some salable skills before graduation. The first factor is that no one can prevent vicissitudes or emergencies which will require that he earn his living or even possibly become responsible economically for the sustenance of another. Although the salable skills which an individual acquires in high school may not become his life-long vocational career, they nevertheless constitute an insurance policy against his becoming destitute or a ward of the state.

A second factor in the senior high schools' emphasis upon acquiring salable skills arises from the adolescent's need to become increasingly economically independent. Adult self-sufficiency cannot be achieved if the adolescent remains entirely dependent upon another person's willingness to share his earnings with him. Adolescents experience varying degrees of need for independence, and to help them become less dependent upon the whim or tyranny of adults, the school must aid them in developing salable skills upon which they can rely.

A third factor in the high school's insistence upon the student's acquiring salable skills lies in the need for an increasingly large number of students to pay for their own post-high school education. The costs of post-high school education are shared by the individual to such an extent in American society that a new caste system based upon economic privilege could emerge. To assure accessibility to post-high school opportunities for youth from all segments of society, their earning power must be increased.

This statement of the curriculum functions emphasizes a career choice pattern which is seen in Table II. The design of the curriculum is intended to help students become increasingly aware of the possibilities which confront them so that they eventually can "zero in" on their potentialities, arrive at choices which result in their discovering the situations in life which are most gratifying to them.

TABLE II

CAREER SELECTION PATTERN

Elementary	Middle Grades & Jr. High	Senior High	Post High
Exploration of what the world and the society in which one lives has to offer — Learning basic skills and what individuals do to become workers in various fields	Exploration of various career possibilities consistent with the potentialities of the individual child — actual involvement in activities performed in certain careers and learning some basic skills needed for success in these areas. Studying the styles of life and conditions under which people engaged in various careers live and work.	Narrowing the choice of a career to a few limited possibilities. Studying background knowledge and acquiring background and fundamental skills. Narrowing field of choice to increasingly fewer options. Learning more about self and training requirements for selected career areas.	Basic occupational or skilled or professional preparations

Vocational Career Education
in Elementary School Grades

An essential part of helping elementary school children become aware of and able to develop competence for entering a self-fulfilling vocation is their learning about work relationships within the community and the activities, social importance, and qualifications of workers in various occupations. Career education, in this narrower sense, becomes an effort to help children learn about the world of work in order to establish a foundation which helps them to emerge out of the world of fantasy about work and into the reality of understanding themselves and what their future life work might be.

In the elementary school grades, career education does not have to be a separate thread of the curriculum, since the learnings are consistent with the objectives of other areas of the curriculum, such as social studies. Table II schematically represents a possible career selection pattern from elementary through post high school. It starts with the exploratory efforts in the lower grades to achieve awareness of the functions and nature of work, the social contributions, and the patterns of preparation of workers in various fields. It emerges into the more extensive and more individualized explorations in the middle school grades, focusing increasing attention upon the understanding of self in relation to occupational and professional potentialities. It involves testing and application to determine individual relevancy in the high school grades, culminating in entry-level training in both the upper years of high school and the post-high school period.

The essential rationale underlying this pattern is that to the degree students become aware of the world of work, understand the requirements for involvement in various occupations, and realize their own capabilities and possibilities, they will be able to make rational choices through which most students will arrive at entry positions which are most appropriate for them. Dubin points out that, like marriage, the occupational commitment is an overriding consideration in one's life history which has consequences for his total life. It can readily be concluded that a decision of such magnitude should not be left to chance, as is now largely the case.[7] Instead of selection being left to chance, career choice will be a matter of rational decision-making involving careful assessment of the personal and technical variables that should be considered. Human decisions are never totally rational, but to the extent that students can be assisted in the making of rational decisions, the possibility of satisfactions and self-fulfillment should be greatly enhanced.

This process should begin in the elementary school grades, in accordance with an instructional plan, as indicated in Table III. The stage of development for his work has been indicated as "awareness," implying that this is the stage in which the child will be helped to discover and learn in some depth about the world of work in which relevant adults in his environment are engaged and which he will someday enter.

Three possible approaches to achieving the stated objectives and learning outcomes are indicated. Each of the approaches suggests a pattern through which content can be organized and dealt with by children. It is debatable whether or not one pattern is in any way superior to any other. The essential point is that through any of these patterns, pupils can be helped to organize relevant information about the world of work, the social importance of work, and their own attitudes and aspirations with respect to fields of endeavor. Hopefully, through these associations, children will be gaining increased power to differentiate between occupations, determining their own attitudes and aspirations with respect to certain types of jobs.

Curriculum Plan for the Secondary Schools

A possible curricular plan for secondary schools is schematically presented in Table IV. There are four areas to the curriculum.

BASIC STUDIES

The basic studies are those studies which help an individual build continuing competence in the use of basic skills and the acquisition of the basic knowledge and understandings essential for his careers as a citizen, as a member of a family, and as a participant in the regulatory, religious and moral activities of society. These are areas which emphasize the common learnings which all individuals need to participate effectively in society. Basic learnings may be taught in various ways depending upon the degrees of latitude for experimentation with the curriculum desired by local communities and educators. It is conceivable that this area could be handled through a regular course structure, through a combined core area, through individualized instruction relying heavily upon programmed learning devices, through team teaching efforts, or any other pattern which is comfortable to the community, consistent with the general philosophy of education which prevails in the schools, and centered upon the needs, interests and aspirations of the students. Certainly in this area, there should be a decided emphasis upon the skills of communication, the basic mathematical and scientific concepts required for understanding man's role in a technological society, the basic social studies materials essential for develop-

TABLE III

ALTERNATIVE CAREER INSTRUCTIONAL PLANS FOR ELEMENTARY SCHOOLS

Age and Level	Objectives	Learning Outcomes	Strategies for Instruction or Content Presentation
K–6	To help each child become aware of: 1) How people perform services, grow and prepare food and produce goods for human use. 2) The social importance of work. 3) The personal significance of work. 4) The styles of living of workers engaged in various occupations in our own and other cultures.	1) The pupils will be able to identify a large number of occupations in the community and differentiate the levels of training required in each. 2) The pupils will be able to distinguish characteristics of various levels of work in the job hierarchy. 3) The pupils will develop attitudes of respect and appreciation for all work that contributes to social well-being.	Approach No. 1 What is the range of occupations involved in the performance of a service or the production of articles? a) building a house b) keeping school open c) making and distributing items of food d) protecting health Approach No. 2 What are the occupations involved in a particular industry or social function?

5) The personal and training requirements for involvement in various occupations.

6) Some of his own expectations and potentials for engaging in the world of work.

4) The pupils will gain an understanding of and appreciation for the kinds of satisfactions people obtain from their work experience.

5) The pupils will gain understanding and appreciation for life styles associated with occupations in various cultures.

6) The pupils will gain understanding and appreciation for the preparation which is necessary for entering various fields of endeavor.

7) The pupils will gain in ability to assess their own interests and potentialities for work.

a) the automobile industry
b) the clothing industry
c) the construction industry
d) running the city
e) operating schools
f) maintaining streets and highways

Approach No. 3

What are the occupations involved in maintaining social functions?

1) producing goods
2) growing and processing food
3) distribution of goods
4) protecting health
5) regulating and governing human conduct
6) providing recreation
7) educating
8) communicating and transporting
9) providing for aesthetic needs
10) providing for religious needs

143

TABLE IV
CURRICULAR PLAN

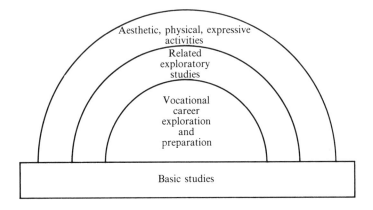

ing knowledge and skills for effective citizenship, and the personal living components related to the identification of personal potentialities, life needs, and the skills for fulfilling life roles.

THE VOCATIONAL CAREER EXPLORATION
AND PREPARATION AREAS

The central focus of the balance of the curriculum will be in the area of vocational career exploration and preparation. In this area the entire curriculum will be individualized in accordance with the areas selected for exploration and preparation by the student with the assistance of his parents and the counseling-teaching teams.

The basic plan for this area in the middle or junior high school grades will be to explore general areas of vocational careers. In this exploratory area, the students will select general fields for exploration. Their studies will involve an understanding of the general nature of employment within these fields, the general organization of work relationships within the fields, the social contributions made by the various occupations in the fields, the various types of vocations that are involved in each general field, the manner in which careers in the general field relate to other careers in other fields, the preparatory requirements for participation in the various jobs available within the fields, the personal qualifications associated with an individual's involvement in various occupational possibilities within the fields, the life styles of individuals involved in various occupations within the fields, the associational life related to the various occupations within the fields, factors related to working settings and compensation within the fields, career ladder opportunities within the fields, tools, equipment or other kinds of objects used by individuals working in the fields, and so on. An essential aspect of each exploration should be the attainment of certain fundamental skills and knowledges which would be required of a worker involved in some occupations within the fields. Although these skills and knowledges might be on a relatively simple level, nevertheless, they are essential for an individual's having experiences which help him to gain a reality orientation toward the requirements within each field and to test himself to determine whether or not he is suited for participation in the field.

The plan of the curriculum is based upon the assumption that either in the latter part of the junior high school years or the early stages of the senior high school years the student will have started to narrow his career choices to a specific field. The progression will be from exploration of a general field, to the exploration of a cluster area, to the exploration of specific occupational potentials within a cluster area. Finally, at some stage in the senior high school plan, the student will, hopefully, "zero in" on a specific occupation for which he will receive his initial preparation, while he develops his plan for further preparation in post-high school education.

RELATED EXPLORATORY STUDIES

The third area of the curriculum is that of related exploratory studies. These are studies which are particularly related to the choices made by the student with respect to his vocational career exploration and as related to his exploration of other life needs in relationship to his vocational career choices. This area of studies might also include fields of interest to the student which he may want to pursue exclusively for extending his general knowledge or developing knowledges and skills desired in areas of avocational interest to him. The areas selected for study will be based upon the individual student's choices and his plan for his continuing education.

What actually might be included in this area would depend to a considerable extent upon the basic needs of students as they select specific fields of vocational interest or wish to extend their explorations into other fields. For example, a student whose vocational career choices tend toward engineering, with high probability of his extending his vocational career preparation into the university, would be encouraged to accumulate some math and science as areas of knowledge needed for an engineering career or required for admission to the university. A student interested in exploring the world of construction might select some courses in draftsmanship to begin his formation of related skills essential for success in one of the construction occupations. A student interested in interior decoration would certainly be encouraged to acquire a background in art and general chemistry.

A flexible curriculum design would enable students to engage in related exploratory studies of varying length or intensity depending upon interests and needs. In this area, too, the school could provide the essential learnings and experiences either in a fairly structured or flexible curricular program.

THE AVOCATIONAL, AESTHETIC, PHYSICAL, EXPRESSIVE ACTIVITIES

In this area the student will explore his avocational interests along with fulfilling his needs for developing skill in physical and expressive activities. Again, this area should be highly individualized, related to student interests and needs, and provide the student with understandings and skills which have carry-over value for his establishing life long interests and patterns of activity. In the life of every person now living, greater emphasis will have to be placed upon avocational interests as occupying, potentially, increasing percentages of the individual's time. It is also essential for each individual to find some means for self-expression through channels other than through his occupation. This area of the curriculum will provide for a large area of interests and will be designed to meet the needs of students for present satisfactions as well as for later participation. It must also be kept in mind that a field which begins for the student as an avocational interest might become a vocational career for him and vice versa. Efforts must be made to help him explore the possibilities of careers in these fields.

One word is needed about the area of physical development. Along with other advances in technology, the human requirements involve far more sedentary occupation of man's time than has previously been the case. Larger numbers of individuals will find that although their jobs exploit their intellectual and nervous energies, they do not drain off the surplus of physical energies. For man to maintain a state of physical health, it will be essential for him to engage in non-work physical exercise. It is the role of the school to help him develop skills and knowledges which will help him maintain his physical health throughout his life.

TIME SCHEMATIC

Table V suggests a general, schematic plan for the distribution of the time in which students may engage in the various areas of the curriculum. These suggestions are very general and designed merely to illustrate a pattern of relationships. Any curriculum plan should be so flexible that time allocations can depend upon students' needs and interests rather than upon a rigid schedule of relationships which dominates the educational planning.

The curriculum suggested here can be accomplished either through a partially traditional type of curriculum or through an experimental program which allows for maximum flexibility. Although I prefer a flexible

TABLE V

Schematic of Possible Curricular Time Allocations

MIDDLE & JUNIOR HIGH	SENIOR HIGH
Basic Studies Areas 40% of time	Basic Studies Areas 15% to 33% of time
Vocational Career Explorations 20% of time	Vocational Career Preparation 33% to 50% of time
General, Related Exploratory Areas 20% of time	General Exploratory Areas 15% of time
Avocational, Physical, Aesthetic and Expressive Activities 20% of time	Avocational, Physical, Aesthetic, and Expressive Activities 20% of time

curriculum, I do not think the program has to rise or fall on some of the aspects of flexibility which characterize modern experimentation. What is essential, however, regardless of the degree of flexibility in programming, is flexibility in the attitudes of educators and the willingness to build a program of studies around the needs, interests, and potentialities of each student. The rest can be accomplished through the manner in which traditional studies are oriented toward the applicative knowledge needs of students and achieve functionality related to the total range of careers engaged in by the individual.

Case Studies

What might be the patterns of student programs under such a curricular plan? Although it is obviously difficult to establish all the specifics theoretically under which such a program would operate, within the general framework provided it should be possible to identify the nature of the program provided for students with varying interests and career potentialities. Seven such case studies are presented with some attempt made to discuss the characteristics of each.

CASE 1: A CAREERS PROGRAM FOR A MALE STUDENT WITH HIGH ACADEMIC POTENTIAL

Data Derived From Elementary School Records.   Both father and mother of this student were college graduates. The father is an accountant, and the mother is actively involved in women's civic activities. The home is a stimulating, intellectual environment. Dinners are characterized by lively discussions which involve both parents and the three children, of which this student is oldest. The family encyclopedia is kept in the dining room so it will be close at hand to research questions when new facts are needed.

This student knew how to read when he came to school and showed quick mastery of the fundamentals. He displayed continuing excitement about new learning tasks. Teachers encouraged him to engage in numerous special projects upon which he reported for the benefit of his fellow students. In appropriate units he explored professional fields of endeavor and the roles and career patterns of individuals engaged in professional fields which seemed most to interest him.

He was judged on the basis of tests and observations of teachers, as well as on the basis of his academic performance, to have a critical mind. He conceptualized readily. He was fond of dealing with broad issues and, later, filling in the details. He disliked precise memoriter activities although he had a high retention capacity. He had some difficulty with refined motor activities involving the use of his hands, although he engaged well but not outstandingly in athletic activities. He was particularly fond of those athletic activities which stressed individual performance, for he did not adapt well to team performance. He had great capacity for organization of materials either intellectually, verbally, or visually. He enjoyed writing reports, but he had difficulty with assignments which called for imaginative or fictitious writing. He liked to illustrate his reports with pictures clipped from magazines, drawings, charts, and diagrams. He was more favorably disposed toward history and geography than toward science and mechanics, but mathematics was easy and absorbing to him.

The elementary school teachers and counselors noted that his future vocational career might well take a number of different routes, but if his academic interests were to continue, he would certainly find fulfillment in a professional career. They emphasized, however, that his elementary school experience would suggest that this would probably not be in either scientific or engineering fields.

Junior High School Program.

A. *Vocational Career Explorations.* The school which he attended required that each pupil explore nine career patterns in the course of the junior high school. His selections, worked out with parents and members of the professional staff, were as follows:

7th Grade
a. The professions—law, medicine, and government
b. The educational professions
c. The scientific professions

8th Grade
a. Professions in higher education
b. Engineering
c. The visual and graphic arts

9th Grade
a. Professional, managerial and skilled occupations in the construction industry
b. Architecture
c. Electrical power

B. *General Exploratory Areas.* The student took advanced courses which emphasized mathematics, history, human relations, a foreign language, some science (although he was not excited about this area), literature and speech.

C. *Avocational, Physical, Aesthetic and Expressive Areas.* In formal courses the student enrolled in orchestra, debate and dramatics. In informal activities, he enrolled in the swimming and photography clubs.

D. *Pre-High School Vocational Career Choices.* In the junior high school the student was expected to indicate before completion of the 9th grade what he considered might be the three possible careers which he would most like to further explore in the senior high school. This student selected (a) professional photography; (b) law; (c) history as a career.

Senior High School.   Because of the academic interests of the student, the career and general exploratory areas were considered together. After considerable discussion and study of the records among his teachers, counselors, and parents, the student agreed to the following program:

1. To continue with his foreign languages.
2. To secure as much mathematics as possible.
3. To explore chemistry and physics which would be desirable if he intended to follow through with the possibility of entering photography.
4. Work in the academic basic block, which would include language arts, history, social problems, humanities and human relations.
5. To explore the academic social science as well as the advanced history.
6. To include in his program speech, debate and dramatics.

In the avocational areas, the student decided to include in his studies additional work in photography and to participate in the debating and dramatics clubs while engaging in a program which emphasized individual sports. As a further exploratory exercise, the school assisted him to obtain a part-time job during summer vacations in a local law office, where he ran errands, assisted the attorneys with clerical chores, running down references and preparing files for court.

Discussion.   The junior high school program was designed to give this student an opportunity to explore vocational career opportunities which were of interest to him and compatible with his potentiality. Further than this, the staff was concerned not only about his exploring areas which had the highest potential interest for him, but also other areas which might help him either to discover alternative career potentialities which he had neglected to consider, or by contrast, to enable him to firm up his interests in those areas to which he had already given consideration. Because the student's home life tended to legitimate his exploration of the academic professions, the effort was made to have him explore a different type of professional field which also would be a challenge to his native ability. Hence, the staff and parents agreed with the student that exploration of professional possibilities within the construction industry would be desirable. This is also the reason for incorporating architecture within that area.

Visual and graphic arts were incorporated in the student's exploration because the student had displayed a great deal of interest in visual presentations of his material and had demonstrated both in elementary and junior high school grades his interest and insights into aesthetic materials. He had shown a considerable interest in an instamatic camera which had been given to him and which he used tirelessly in his report activities. Electrical power was included as a cluster area in his ninth grade program so that he could explore at least one field which would determine his interest and aptitude for a field involving some mechanical competence.

The junior high school staff was interested in the evaluation of this student's program from two points of view. First, was the school helping this student with high academic potential explore the range of career possibilities within which he could be successful, while at the same time, opening up to him some fields which could place less emphasis upon the conceptual and more upon the technical or mechanical aspects of the vocational career while still challenging his academic potential?

Second, was the school helping the student identify some areas which in the senior high school would give him the basis for acquiring some salable knowledges and skills? This was provided for in his further pursuit of photography and the exploration of the field of electrical power, which could lay the foundation for developing a carry-over interest in the senior high school.

It should also be noted that the staff was concerned about a program which helped this student identify a range of potential avocational pursuits all of which might result in permanent interests throughout his life.

The senior high school built upon the program in the junior high school. It provided additional, more specific and more technical preparation in each of the three choice areas. Since at least two of the choices lay in college preparatory fields, a heavy emphasis on college preparatory courses was made. Gaining technical knowledge in photography, the staff thought, gave him an area of employability. The staff was certain this student would enter and be successful in college.

CASE 2: A CAREERS PROGRAM FOR A FEMALE STUDENT FOR WHOM HIGH SCHOOL WILL BE TERMINAL

Data Secured From Elementary School Records. This student's father was killed while on military duty in Korea. Her mother never remarried and had a job as a hostess in a large, downtown restaurant. The child was reared primarily by her grandparents, who devoted a great deal of attention to her and involved her in their church-related activities. They were very conservative, fundamentalist people who were understanding but somewhat restrictive.

The girl was slow to read and to learn basic skills. Her primary interest in elementary school was shown in either expressive or routine types of activities. She did not attempt to excel but did just barely enough to get by. She was socially alert and actively involved in the planning of social events, from which she derived a great deal of satisfaction. She usually volunteered and seemed to enjoy doing things around the room and was the teacher's pride and joy as a "room helper." She participated in class discussions only when called upon.

Teachers described her as a student who would always get by in school without displaying much interest in the studies. Her primary interests were in people and in doing things involving people. She displayed a high level of manual dexterity even in those activities involving fine muscle dexterity. She formed friendships quickly and formed close affective relationships with people. In units on community workers she wanted to explore waitresses, teachers, and social workers.

Junior High School Program.

A. *Vocational Career Explorations (nine required).*

7th Grade
a. Airline occupations for women.
b. Office occupations.
c. Occupations in the food service industry.

8th Grade
a. The cosmetic and beauty field.
b. Careers in merchandising.
c. Opportunities in child care.

9th Grade
a. Opportunities in education.
b. Homemaking as an occupation.
c. Careers in consumer homemaking.

B. *General Exploratory Areas.* The student elected experiences which involved her particularly in the areas of homemaking, typing, basic business, literature, humanities and arts and crafts.

C. *Avocational, Physical, Aesthetic and Expressive Areas.* The student elected future homemaking and a school service club. She did not elect any special area in physical education and took a routine physical education class.

D. *Pre-High School Vocational Career Choice.* The student had no decided preferences. She thought she might become a secretary although she wanted to get married and have a family soon after high school. She thought she might work at some time but could learn the skills necessary either on-the-job or at a later date.

Senior High School.   The student enrolled in the general basic studies block. In the general exploratory areas she chose all of the homemaking sequences available, reluctantly agreed to the general science sequences, and took some literature.

In the vocational area, she enrolled in the general business program, and she also took some work in the secretarial sciences and distributive education. In the latter program she participated in a work-experience program, through which she had part-time employment in a local women's apparel shop.

Avocationally, she developed a slight interest in tennis, was active in the Future Homemakers Association and joined a crafts club.

She was married in her senior year to a young man who had graduated the previous year and was working in a local filling station. She graduated from high school, took a job as a clerk in a small neighborhood department store until her first child was born.

Discussion.   The culture in which this student was reared did not place heavy emphasis upon a vocational career outside of the home. One can assume that the mother had frequently lamented the fact that as a widow she had to work to support her youngster when her fundamental interests would have been in the home. The grandmother certainly devoted all of her energies to her home and family and replaced the mother insofar as homemaking chores were concerned.

In junior high school the girl's vocational explorations were primarily routine academic exercises from which the girl received modest stimulation. Her junior high school program was designed primarily to help her identify a vocational career interest which would include the possibility of that as homemaker as an area of enterprise as well as to explore the possibility of areas which might help the youngster identify a program in the senior high school leading to salable knowledges or skills. Through secondary school it was becoming increasingly apparent that the consuming interest of the student was in human relationships and homemaking as a career. The avocational interests tended to settle in closely related fields.

The junior high school explorations in careers in merchandising and office occupations led to the student's developing some salable skills and knowledges in the areas of business and distributive education. Following graduation from high school, she was, therefore, able to get a job and contribute to the economic needs of her young family.

School programs contributed greatly to her vocational and other career roles through its provision of as much homemaking education as possible for the student, giving her at least some avocational interests related to her vocational career and also providing her with some salable skills through which she could make a contribution, when necessary, to her family economy. One might assume that this girl with her basic interests in the home would not seek any type of post high school educational experiences. She could, however, build an extended career in the fields to which she was introduced in school.

CASE 3: A MALE STUDENT WHO LACKS CULTURAL CONGRUITY WITH THE PURPOSES OF THE SCHOOL

Data From Elementary School.   This student's mother was deserted by his father when he was a small child. During the elementary school grades he did not know his father, except through pictures and the bitter comments which he heard his mother make about him. The mother was on welfare, although she almost always earned some money through part-time efforts to supplement the meagre welfare allotments. There were four older children in the household. One of the older brothers was drafted into the army after dropping out of high school. A second older brother was placed in a juvenile detention home after repeated convictions for petty robbery. The older sisters were in school but not highly motivated. The family was not closely knit. The mother attended church regularly and wanted her children to do so, too, but they generally went their own ways as soon as they were able to resist her demands. The flat in which they lived was cluttered and disorganized. The mother spent most of her time caring for the family clothes, cooking, or visiting with neighbors. She expressed affection for her family, but she complained a lot to them because they were almost always on the streets and did not do the things she wanted them to do. She rarely did things with them, and even meals were "catch-as-catch-can," with the children coming in when they wanted to help themselves to the soup or stew, one of which was invariably on the stove.

The pupil had language difficulties when entering the school, and he was given some assistance in a special class designed to improve verbal communication. In spite of the special education, he learned to read with difficulty and attained only a low level of skill. He was no discipline problem, according to the teachers, but he appeared to be listless in class, and had difficulty staying awake and paying attention. He liked mechanical things, but seemed fearful of doing more than unimaginatively playing with them. His art work was unintelligible, with no perceptible form emerging. He was generally reluctant to participate in class activities. In units on community workers he was finally urged to express an interest in firemen, cowboys, and soldiers. The family had a radio but no television, and he usually looked at television at a neighboring apartment or in the barber shop on the street.

As he gained greater language power in school, his performance levels seemed to display wide variations. In subjects which were routinely taught, he showed disinterest and had difficulty completing the work. On some topics, however, which seemed within the range of his experience and in some ways to arouse his interest, he displayed some mature ability to work with the materials and conceptual capability to interpret their significance.

The elementary school teachers had difficulty forecasting what might lie ahead for him or to make suggestions for his future educational programs. They thought he needed a broader range of experiences and more motivation from home. Although the composite scores on standardized tests were low, close scrutiny of items showed considerable variability. They felt that this indicated that there was more innate ability and potentiality than ever showed on the surface. They thought that with proper assistance it might be possible to interest him in some area so that he would eventually complete school.

Junior High School. In the spring of the year preceding the transfer of students from the elementary school to the junior high school, guidance personnel from the junior high school reviewed cases carefully with guidance personnel in the elementary schools. Social workers from the area school district also provided additional information for the guidance workers. After careful assessment of the child's problems and needs, it was decided that several related efforts would be made. First, an effort would be made to obtain a summer day-camp program, if his mother and he consented, with at least a two-week resident camp to supplement it. During this period of time guidance personnel would also work closely with the neighborhood community center to attract the boy's interest and help him become involved in its activities.

Second, the guidance personnel thought it would be desirable to help this student obtain some part-time work as soon as his summer camping experiences were completed and to see if they could build some of his educational program in the fall around the experiences of his continuing part-time job. In cooperation with community agencies, they were able to obtain a subsidized job for him as an errand boy in a printing shop, the job to start in the fall immediately before the opening of school.

Third, a young, male guidance worker in the junior high school was able to relate effectively to the boy. He lived in the same neighborhood and had developed effective working relationships with the community center. He accepted the responsibility for becoming the "communicator" in both in- and out-of-school activities with the child and his family. It was hoped that at best he might become a father surrogate or at least a relevant male who could provide a favorable male image and companionship.

The camping experience was particularly designed to accomplish three things. First, it contained a number of experiences which would help the participants identify interests and develop some competence in the pursuit thereof. Second, it provided a range of personnel, counsellors, hobby specialists, counsellors-in-training, and some special guidance personnel, whose function it was to establish close, helper relationships with the children. Through these relationships it was hoped that the needs and concerns of these children could be identified and something tangible could be done about them. Third, through its hobby, special interest, and physical activities programs, the camp was equipped to provide a contextual basis for working on the scholastic deficiencies of the children. Reading circles, discussion groups, show-and-tell responsibilities for demonstrating hobby and special projects, etc., were a part of the experience in order to develop, in particular, increased language power.

When school started in the fall, the student was already known to some of the counsellors and teachers. He had established a face-to-face relationship with some confidence in the counsellor assigned specifically to work with him. The school program was discussed with the student and his mother, and they finally agreed that the program would include the following elements to begin with:

1) He would enroll in a learning skills center which would help him acquire greater competence in the basic skills of communication with particular emphasis upon the skills he needed to retain and improve himself in his part-time job.

2) He would work in the graphics laboratory in the junior high school in order to explore the world of work in the areas related to the shop for which he ran errands.

3) He would begin work in the job training center on employability skills in order to develop the skills for holding his present job and preparing himself for obtaining one on a higher skill level as soon as he was old enough to qualify.

4) He would participate in the joint program with the community center and the junior high school in discovering more about the recreational and cultural opportunities within the community, and engaging particularly in its physical development and recreational programs.

Discussion.   What happens after this point in the student's program depends upon the degree to which he becomes motivated, the school and community center can maintain their adaptability and responsiveness to his needs, and what he and his counsellor-teacher advisors identify as elements which will help him develop along lines most meaningful to him. An adequate career education program must be flexible and resources must be present to assist students in the development of the skills, understandings, and appreciations they need for their self-development and improvement. This case assumes that the traditional pattern of the school will not be sufficient to help this student achieve the self-understanding and skill development he needs for participation and self-fulfillment in adult society.

Special assistance must be given to meet his unique requirements. Without this special assistance in breaking through institutional molds, the learning disabilities of the student will accumulate until he can no longer tolerate them. Once he drops out of school, there is little likelihood that he will return, except in a custodial institution. Tailoring a program to his needs, giving him some adult guidance and companionship (particularly male) which will help him secure an affective relationship and develop self-assurance, giving him the recognition and responsibility of a job which will enable him to put some self-earned coins in his pocket, helping him to realize that the school cares about him and has a program to assist him, giving him a future rather than a blind-alley—all of these elements should enable the student to make the necessary adjustment, develop the power to understand himself and the requirements of the world about him, and pursue what amounts to an increasingly "normal" educational pattern as he advances through secondary school. Through such a program as described here, it does not seem unrealistic to predict that this young man can become a self-fulfilled, productive, and contributing member of society. To achieve this end, a program adapted for him and considerable personal attention are essential.

If this sounds too expensive a process, let us be mindful of the fact that if the schools succeed with him, his tax-paying power will far exceed the costs of the program itself, let alone what might become the excessive costs of custodial care and the far greater tragedy—the misery of a wasted life. In the background of this student lies the potentiality not only of a productive career as a skilled worker, but the possibility that if the school can help him develop to his fuller potentiality, a professional career, which has been achieved by many individuals coming from similar circumstances.

The resolution of the problems of this pupil's development can not be achieved solely through the schools, and neither can they be solved through exclusively cognitive interventions. A coordinated effort by both school and community agencies is essential. The structuring of affective relationships to demonstrate that there is concern for him and that he can build an adequate image of himself as an effective human being is also of primary importance.

CASE 4: THE MALE STUDENT WHO DROPS OUT OF HIGH SCHOOL AND EVENTUALLY ATTENDS A COMMUNITY COLLEGE

Data From Elementary School.   This student's father was a logger, and his mother worked part-time at odd jobs. The father was a domineering person and spent most of his free time in outdoor activities, such as hunting and fishing. The mother was left alone with the three children a considerable amount of the time. She was a disorganized person who had difficulty maintaining any kind of schedule, but she did display a great deal of affection for her children. The father's affection was sporadic, and he did not involve his children in his own activities, either vocationally or avocationally.

The elementary school teachers considered this boy as shy, somewhat frightened, and insecure. He acquired a modest level of skills in the basic studies rather rapidly, and, then, he seemed to stay on a plateau without going on from there. He did not react enthusiastically to any of his school experiences. He was socially insecure, but physically well-developed, yet he did not respond well to efforts to involve him in athletic ventures. He was generally on the fringe of a group rather than in the central part of it. He seemed to like, or at least not resist, physical activity, but he did not demonstrate good general physical coordination.

In its recommendation to the junior high school, the elementary school staff stated that he was no trouble maker, no bother to have around; he was just rather listless or indifferent. His academic ability, when tested, seemed average or even slightly above, but his achievement was low. He did not conceptualize well, seemed to dislike language and literature activities, and demonstrated his greatest interest in mechanical or scientific fields. If the expectations were not too great, arithmetic was his best subject, but higher mathematical processes left him cold.

Junior High School.

A. *Vocational Career Explorations (nine required).*

7th Grade
a. Construction industry.
b. Manufacturing industry.
c. The appliance repair industry.

8th Grade
a. Farming and related employment.
b. Auto mechanics.
c. The forest products industry.

9th Grade
a. Aviation.
b. Metalwork.
c. Electricity and electronics.

B. *General Exploratory Areas.* He elected to engage in experiences involving basic business, metal crafts, woodworking, home repair, typing and biology.

C. *Avocational, Physical, Aesthetic and Expressive Areas.* He elected chorus, photography club and nature study, chose swimming as a sport, was encouraged to go out for athletics but did not continue with it.

   D. *Pre-High School Vocational Career Choices.* He thought he would like to work with cars but he was not sure about a career in mechanics.

Senior High School.   He elected the general basic studies block, and in the general exploratory areas he chose to take extended general science sequences, the general industrial education program, the work-experience program, getting part-time employment in a service station.

   Vocationally, he entered the metal working program.

   He continued with his chorus and swimming but without a great deal of enthusiasm. He continued basic interest in nature study and participated in an outdoor hiking club.

   His attendance was sporadic. In his junior year in high school he entered the learning skills program designed to assist students in finding their basic interests, but he still didn't feel he was getting ahead in school. At the end of his junior year he dropped out, getting part-time employment in an auto wrecking yard where he tore cars apart. After two years at several jobs he was employed in a sporting goods store. He became interested in guns and decided to take a course in gunsmithing at an evening education program in the local community college. He entered a counseling program and was advised to take courses necessary for receiving a high school equivalency diploma.

   Following his completion of his high school equivalency program, he continued full-time in the gunsmithing course until completion. In this program he finally found himself. He went to work in a local gun repair shop, at a good salary, and had hopes someday of owning his own small business.

Discussion.   This might be characterized as a case of a student who has difficulty achieving his identity because of the failure of his father to assist him in that development. The school might be considered to have at least partially failed with this student, except that it did assist him in developing some salable skills which enabled him to receive employment when he dropped out of school. It also laid a foundation for his eventual discovering himself through the extensive post-high school educational opportunities available in his community. His avocational interests were directed out of an area of longing but deprivation in his childhood, which also related to his eventual discovery of his vocational career pattern.

CASE 5: MALE STUDENT WHO COULD GO TO COLLEGE BUT CHOSE A COMMUNITY COLLEGE INSTEAD

Elementary School Data.   The student came from a middle-class home. His father was a salesman, and his mother worked in a large office in the central city. He had two younger sisters, and during his elementary school years he had responsibilities in taking care of them, although the parents hired a neighbor to supervise the children after school hours. The parents were interested in many things outside of the home and generally did not involve the student in their activities except for an occasional weekend outing.

He was an average student. He had a desire to do better, but he had so many interests that he had difficulty in settling down to any one. Generally speaking, he was somewhat motivated by all of his studies but not highly disciplined in any of them. He learned his basic skills at a normal rate and achieved and maintained grade level expectations. He displayed no behavioral problems. He always did what was expected of him and seemed to maintain a cheerful and cooperative outlook on life.

Basically, he liked to work with objects more than ideas. His conceptualizing tended to be on the level of the concrete rather than the abstract. His home demonstrated traditional values which he seemed both to reflect and to accept. He was particularly interested in things that moved—trains, boats, airplanes, cars. His vocationally-oriented projects tended to be directed toward operatives such as truck drivers, heavy equipment drivers, pilots, policemen, and firemen.

His best subjects were math and science. His poorest subject was history, with language a close second. He seemed to like geography and geology as long as they involved the concrete and avoided the abstract.

Junior High School.

A. *Vocational Career Explorations.*

7th Grade
a. Transportation.
b. Communication.
c. Power motors.

8th Grade
a. Science as a profession.
b. Electricity and electronics.
c. Manufacturing.

9th Grade
a. Airplane construction and mechanics.
b. Public safety.
c. Business occupations.

B. *General Exploratory Areas.* The student elected to have experiences in industrial education, the general science sequences and the general math sequences which led to algebra.

C. *Avocational, Physical, Aesthetic and Expressive Area.* The student took work in arts and crafts, became very much interested in boat construction and boating and developed a continuing interest in the school's hiking club.

D. *Pre-High School Vocational Career Choices.* The student said that, although he was not sure, he was thinking in terms of either a scientific technician, mechanic, or automotive engineer.

Senior High School.   With encouragement, the student elected to take the academic basic block, but in the middle of the tenth grade he transferred to the general basic block. He continued his interest in math and science and did average or slightly better work in these areas.

In his vocational program, he elected machine shop with an emphasis upon automotive mechanics. He also elected some course work in electronics but did not continue with it.

He went out for athletics, made the football team, and even though he was on the varsity, did not excel. He had a continued interest in outdoor sports, particularly fishing, hunting, and hiking. He had built his own boat and continued to engage in a boat building activity.

He was graduated from high school with a g.p.a. high enough to be admitted to the state university, to which he was accepted. However, he decided in the summer following graduation to go to a community college, and although he would take some transfer courses he would enter the program in aviation mechanics.

Discussion.   Here is a student who has the ability to be successful in a college program and a professional career but whose interests tend more toward the concrete than the conceptual. School attempted to have him explore some of the less conceptual professional fields as well as at least one of the more highly conceptual. It would be expected that with his background he might not respond to these studies and would find his orientation even in an academic field on a level that is more concrete. Through both his junior and senior high school years, he develops a program that increases his skills and knowledges looking toward a vocational career choice. His choices still present some alternatives to him as he graduates from high school. After graduation, as might be expected, he elects an applied field. The door is still open to pursue other possibilities, however. One might well assume that his avocational interests developed in the secondary school program will become a life-long and compelling interest for him.

CASE 6: A FEMALE STUDENT WITH AVERAGE ACADEMIC POTENTIAL

Data Derived From Elementary School Records.   This girl's father was a businessman who operated a small general merchandise store. The mother was primarily interested in her home and the care of her two children, although she did help out in the store during periods of pressure. The family had no great interests. The parents spent a great deal of time playing cards with friends and watching television. Family activities involved little more than television and an occasional weekend outing. The parents were interested in their children and had modest expectations for them.

The student learned her basic skills at an average rate. She was highly motivated only in work relating to art, music, and sports. She did complete all of her assigned work with average ability, but rarely went beyond minimal expectations. She occasionally had difficulties with teachers who attributed her behavioral problems to a "high-strung" personality.

She related well to people, and was a leader in some of her groups. She enjoyed her work in the school chorus. She displayed imagination primarily in her art projects. Although she had relatively well-developed conceptual abilities, these tended more toward the aesthetic and expressive than toward abstract thought. She had a great deal of ability in the organization of materials. In units on community workers she wanted to study architects, artists and newspapermen.

Junior High School.

A. *Vocational career explorations.*

7th Grade
a. Careers in art.
b. Careers in music.
c. Opportunities in child care services.

8th Grade
a. Careers in consumer homemaking.
b. Careers in business occupations.
c. Careers in interior design.

9th Grade
a. Careers in recreation.
b. Careers in graphic arts.
c. Careers in merchandising.

B. *General Exploratory Areas.* The student elected to take work in the areas of typing, arts and crafts, humanities, a foreign language and general science.

C. *Avocational, Physical, Aesthetic and Expressive Areas.* The student enjoyed work in art, art appreciation, Glee Club, the Homemaking Club. In physical activities she participated in the volleyball team and took archery as a special activity. She was on the social arrangements committee for school affairs.

D. In her *pre-high school vocational career choices* the student expressed an interest in finding an occupation that enabled her to work with children, in homemaking activities, or in either art or music. She was undecided as to her specific areas of concern in her high school program.

Senior High School.   In her senior high school program, the student took the general basic studies block. She enrolled in general science, humanities and foreign language courses. She took all the home economics that the school had to offer. She entered the home nursing course, the vocational child-care cluster, and continued with her studies in music and art. She continued an interest in volleyball and participated in the school glee club. She was a member of the Future Homemakers of America.

Upon graduation she planned to enter a community college in the child care program. In her second year in a child care services program at a community college, she was faced with the need to decide between a position as an aide in a Head Start program or attending the state university to major in elementary education or child development.

Discussion.   This case is not atypical of the girl who has a range of artistic interests and abilities and centers into a career which is culturally legitimated for her sex and congruent with the value system in which she was reared. With her abilities and obvious drive, it is not unlikely that regardless of her decision, she will eventually find her way into a program where she will acquire more advanced professional training. Her school program, however, has helped her explore possibilities, given her opportunities for preparation consistent with her aspirations, and has enabled her to make a choice which seems to be compatible with her values, even if it doesn't as yet appear to be the maximum possibility for utilizing her full potential. In this instance, as well as in the others, the school has helped her develop her human capital in ways in which both she and society profit. Her interest in art and music, certainly within the realm of career possibilities, will become an avocational interest from which she should be able to derive a great deal of satisfaction.

CASE 7: A FEMALE STUDENT WITH HIGH ACADEMIC POTENTIAL

Data Derived From Elementary School Records.   The student's father, an attorney working for the federal government, earned a modest income. Her mother had been a secretary, but had not continued with her employment after her first child was born. The girl was the younger of two children. The home provided a rich and stimulating environment for academic interests. The family was traditionally middle-class in its values and aspirations.

The girl learned reading and the other basic skills very rapidly. She was highly motivated to seek out new learning experiences and she brought references to her discussions about her subjects of study at home into the classroom. She read extensively beyond the requirements on all assignments, and she displayed a considerable leadership potential in her homeroom activities. She liked to read, wanted to be accepted by her peers, and desired to gain the recognition secured from being elected to offices.

Because of the rapidity with which she was able to complete assignments, she assisted the teachers with low level achievers in her class, and she seemed to derive satisfaction from this experience. She had acquired several pen-pals in foreign countries and shared her letters with the class. In units on community workers she wanted to explore teachers, social workers and secretaries.

She was a high achiever in all subjects and displayed more interest in social studies and literature than in math and science. While she was still in elementary school, through participation with her parents she had developed hobbies in sewing, gardening, and reading.

Junior High School.

A. *Vocational career explorations.*

7th Grade
a.   Careers in health occupations.
b.   Careers in the computer world.
c.   Careers in science.

8th Grade
a.   Opportunities in agriculture.
b.   Opportunities in journalism and writing.
c.   Opportunities in consumer homemaking.

9th Grade
a.   Office occupations.
b.   Careers in utilizing foreign languages.
c.   Opportunities in the educational professions.

B. *General Exploratory Areas.* The student took a program emphasizing social studies, foreign language, humanities, homemaking and speech.

C. *Avocational, Physical, Aesthetic and Expressive Areas.* The student elected swimming, school service club, journalism and dramatics. She was chairman of a committee that initiated the school grounds beautification project.

D. *Pre-High School Vocational Career Choices.* The student indicated she was interested in a career in the United Nations. As a second career, she considered teaching foreign languages.

Senior High School.   The student enrolled in the academic basic studies program. She took two foreign languages, social studies, humanities, and secretarial science. She was active in student government and the French club and was editor of the high school paper in her senior year. Upon graduation the student entered the state university, majored in French, took her teaching credential, and upon graduation secured a position as a simultaneous translator in the State Department.

Discussion.   This is the girl in whom the traditional school would delight. She doesn't present much of a problem for any type of school, save to keep her sufficiently challenged. In her career choices, she has the possibilities of expanding career opportunities, which may be realized in later life. She also has some potential in further development of her leadership capacity. She has some salable skills through her secretarial science program. In all probability, few people have the straight line path to fulfillment of their careers she seems to have.

Conclusions

It would be deluding to think of the careers curriculum as a panacea for all our educational ills in this century. It would also be deluding simply to reject the concept without carefully assessing its potential. If fully developed into an operating conceptualization of the curriculum, it has the potential for providing the flexible curriculum, adaptable to the needs of each youngster, and directed toward realistic goals, which conditions in our society require. It turns the emphasis of the curriculum away from purely academic goals, and it re-directs the knowledge mission of the school away from the purely integrative and more toward the applicative dimensions. Knowledge is not an end in itself but a means to ends, a tool used by human beings and human society to achieve definite ends. The schools will still fail to meet all the needs of every child at times, but hopefully it will meet a much larger range of needs of more children than is presently the case.

A great deal of research and development is needed before this model can be fully implemented. Some of the tasks that need to be accomplished include:

1. Materials need to be produced which explore all fields of human endeavor, particularly for students in the middle grades. These materials should provide the vast amount of information which help students adequately explore the field in which they may have potential for involvement. *The World of Construction* and *The World of Manufacturing* are two good beginnings toward this end.

2. Projection of sequences of occupational exploratory activities need to be carefully made. Conceptualization of the structure of occupations, including functions, fields, clusters, and specific occupations must be developed and made useful in terms of the vocational options available to youth.

3. Implications of this curriculum design for teacher education must be explored. Obviously, changes must be made not only in the preparation of vocational teachers but in the preparation of all teachers at all levels and in all fields. Not only must the task of pre-service teacher education be delineated, but a greater job remains to be done in the proper conceptualization of the problems of in-service education.

4. In connection with the above, materials for teacher education must also be developed. A vast range of materials will be necessary to acquaint teachers with the range of problems they will confront in implementing this type of program and in developing the knowledge and skills they will need to assist students use knowledge effectively in making careers decisions.

5. Specific curricular patterns on all grade levels need to be explored.

6. Patterns of instructional strategies indicating anticipated consequences need to be simulated.

7. This curriculum places high emphasis upon team effort by teachers occupying differential roles in the instructional areas. Models of such team efforts need to be developed and given careful analysis so role descriptions of different assignments can be made. Protocols for assisting the training of teachers in team patterns need to be developed.

8. The school envisaged here is built upon a new clinical model of the school. This model needs to be explored through careful systems analysis.

9. The program of this school is high individualized. Systems procedures for determining optimum means for individualization still need to be explored.

10. We still do not know enough about the life styles and personality characteristics associated with various careers. Until we gain more knowledge in these areas, we will be lacking a much needed knowledge base upon which to refine this curriculum.

11. The school devoted to helping children become effective in their life roles cannot exist as an entity apart from the community, selfishly guarding its operations in seclusion from the community. The school must become a part of the community, and the community must become a part of the school. School resources and community agencies must be employed in coordinated fashion to maximize the development of the potentialities of our children and youth. New forms of mutual employment of resources and coordinating and governing structures must be developed. The perspective of a school organization integrated with the total community has been emerging, although slowly, for many years and has been particularly stimu-

lated in periods of crisis. Such a period exists today and provides the opportunity for its accomplishment.

I am sure there are a host of other things that also need to be accomplished. In the long run, the model is suggested in the hope that it will stimulate discussion which helps to establish the concrete patterns through which the educational resources of this country can realistically and relevantly capacitate human potentialities and stimulate human self-fulfillment.

FOOTNOTES

[1] Nels Anderson, *The Dimensions of Work.* New York: David McKay Co., Inc., 1964, p. 33.

[2] Plato, *Laws.* I.644.

[3] Dennis Gabor, "Education for a Future World of Leisure." In Werner Z. Hirsch (ed.), *Inventing Education for the Future.* San Francisco: Chandler Publishing Co., 1967, pp. 46-47.

[4] Conrad M. Arensberg, "Work and the Changing American Scene," in Sigmund Nosow and William H. Form (eds.), *Man, Work and Society.* New York: Basic Books, 1962, pp. 24-28.

[5] E. A. Friedmann and R. J. Havinghurst, "Work and Retirement." in Nosow and Form, *op. cit.,* pp. 41-52.

[6] Nels Anderson, *op. cit.,* p. 80.

[7] Robert Dubin, *The World of Work.* Englewood Cliffs, New Jersey: Prentice-Hall, Inc. 1958, p. 252.

Frank C. Pratzner here discusses the research and theoretical considerations undergirding an approach to career education. In Pratzner's view, the dual functions of education in the American system have been those of social maintenance and individual self-fulfillment. Pratzner concludes that education has concentrated upon its social maintenance functions and neglected its individual concerns. As a consequence, it has failed in both.

Pratzner analyzes the distinctions between college preparatory, general education, and vocational educational programs. In his estimation, each is insufficient in itself, and a combination of at least two of the elements is essential for the school's performance of its two major functions.

In discussing the outcomes of the career education program, he suggests that the program results in increasing the options for students, encouraging greater emphasis upon individualized instruction, and greater opportunities for utilization of the affective domain in the improvement of learning.

Dr. Pratzner is Chairman for the Instructional Systems Design Program at The Center for Vocational and Technical Education at The Ohio State University.

Frank C. Pratzner

CAREER EDUCATION

Roles of Education

Most sociologists agree that the individual has a number of different social institutions available which provide the contexts for his interactions with society (e.g., the familial, educational, political, etc.). He assumes different role identities within each context and attempts to achieve a level of individual self-fulfillment. One of the goals or functions of the educational system is to provide for individual self-fulfillment in socially acceptable ways. At the same time, the educational system is charged with a social maintenance role which, in general, provides for the knowledges and skills required to understand and improve the society (e.g., through satisfactory citizenship, values and beliefs, and through other culture-carrying activities). These two essential roles of education are depicted in Figure 1.

We have set up a highly sophisticated and elaborate system of education in this country in order to meet the social maintenance role of

This paper was written for use in staff seminars at The Center for Vocational and Technical Education at The Ohio State University. The views expressed herein are those of the author and do not necessarily reflect Center views or policy.

FIGURE 1

A MODEL OF A CAREER EDUCATION SYSTEM

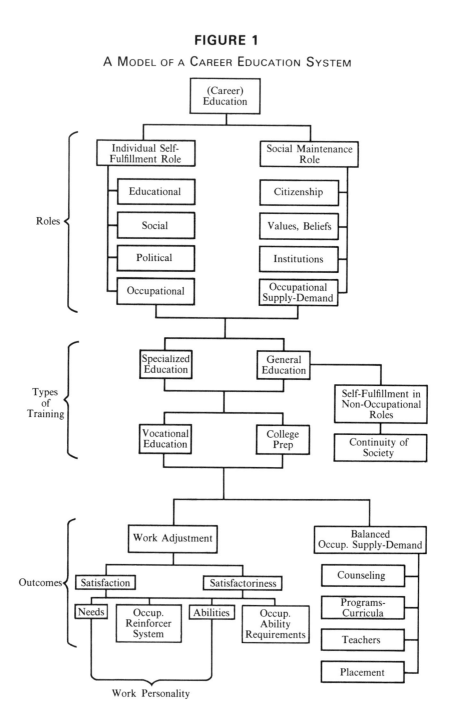

education, but have failed in the past to give equal or adequate attention to the individual self-actualization function of education. The result is a system which does not perform either of its roles optimally. For example, (a) many students drop out of school before completion; (b) half of the students who prepare for and enter college never complete the full four years; (c) those who do not complete college, and even some of those who do, are not adequately prepared for successful and satisfying employment; and (d) even if one argues that there is not a high level of unemployment, under-employment and mis-employment are prevalent in spite of manpower shortages in some occupational areas.

Thus, at some point recently, all levels of the educational system and types of educational programs, from elementary through post-secondary, have been decried as irrelevant. The thesis presented here is that the conditions above are not so much the result of a failure of the educational system to meet its social maintenance function (although performance of this function is certainly curtailed) or the result of inadequate or inappropriate program characteristics, as much as it is the result of the failure of the system to provide adequately for the individual self-actualization role of education.

Several explanations can be suggested for the current imbalance in the way the system has provided for its two major roles. One plausible explanation seems to be that we have relied almost exclusively upon the individual differences conceptual model from psychology for achieving the social maintenance function of education and have virtually ignored the sociological base for achieving the individual self-fulfillment function.

We have, of necessity, done the things we were best able to do relying almost exclusively upon information and techniques derived from the field of psychology because this was the easiest, most opportunistic thing to do. We have not appropriately drawn upon the fields of philosophy or sociology.

Philosophy has always been an obscure discipline for most educators, and in American society in general, the discipline itself has not been a dominant force. Americans are often characterized as action-oriented, and as a society, seldom described as a self-reflective people, characterized by critical and prolonged analysis and thought prior to our actions.

On the other hand, we have not appropriately drawn upon the field of sociology because its development as a discipline has closely paralleled that of education. It is a relatively recent field of inquiry and therefore has not developed its domain or its methods of inquiry to the level of sophistication that psychology has.

As a result, we have often used a psychological base for deriving content and developing instructional methods. A more appropriate strategy would give more consideration to sociologically-derived information and

FIGURE 2

<small>Types of Specialized
Education</small>

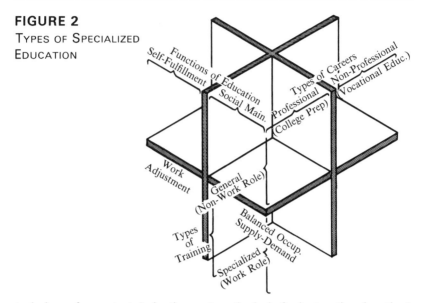

techniques for content derivation and particularly for instructional methodology. For example, we have taken for granted that the one-to-one
relationship between a teacher and student, using the Socratic method of
instruction, was the ideal instructional situation for *all* types of content and
in *all* learning environments if only we could achieve it. We are beginning
to realize, probably since the advent of programmed instruction and computer-assisted instruction, that this piece of educational folklore has often
lead us astray. Thus, we rarely make good instructional use (as opposed to
school organizational use) of the fact that most of modern education takes
place in a classroom or group context and that this context can often
determine, to a large extent, instructional approaches and learning outcomes. Moreover, we continue, for the most part, to inappropriately use
notions derived from psychology to legitimate the relative ranking and
grading of student achievement (e.g., for motivational, negative reinforcement and disciplinary purposes), rather than emphasizing learning and
achievement as a function of, and relative to, the social context in which
it occurs. Several suggestions in the latter discussion of career education
should serve to further clarify these points and to illustrate potential approaches based upon a sociological view of education.

Types of Training

PROFESSIONAL AND NON-PROFESSIONAL TRAINING

The vocational program and the college prep program represent two
types of specialized education. Other types of specialized programs (outside

of the public educational system) include on-the-job training programs, privately operated occupational training programs, and occupational correspondence programs.

Reference to Figure 2 will indicate that the only real difference between college and college prep programs, and vocational programs, is in the types of careers for which they provide training.

Vocational education programs provide training for less-than professional level careers, while college prep programs provide training for professional level careers. Both are forms of specialized education and both are components of career development.

GENERAL AND SPECIALIZED TRAINING

Like all of education, specialized education has both individual self-fulfillment and social maintenance roles. Unlike the rest of education, it focuses upon the occupational-work aspects of the interaction between the individual and society.[1] On the one hand, specialized education is primarily concerned with the economic institution of society and with the individual's work role within this institution. It is primarily designed to help individuals achieve self-fulfillment or self-actualization[2] through their specialized work roles. On the other hand, specialized education's primary social maintenance responsibility is to contribute to a balanced occupational supply and demand.

These unique responsibilities of specialized education are balanced by the responsibilities of general education. Specialized education should have a concomitant positive impact upon the general (non-occupational) satisfaction of individuals and upon his contributions to society. General education has a similar impact upon specialized education. General education (a) increases the potential for productivity in *all* occupations (professional as well as non-professional), (b) is prerequisite to specialized occupational training, or (c) is needed for the continuity of society and individual self-actualization in non-occupational roles. It is, therefore, not substitutable for or interchangeable with specialized education.

One of the important and unique characteristics of the emerging concept of career education is the requirement for a more appropriate mix and timing of general and specialized education. Since the influence of the work and non-work roles cannot be completely separated from each other within the individual, the potential outcomes and program characteristics of both general and specialized education must be considered together. Thus, the hard programmatic and course distinctions between general and specialized education are confusing and unnecessary because the two are not separate identities which can be substituted for each other. Rather they represent arbitrary and convenient referents to knowledges and skills required along the occupational/non-occupational continuum.

Career Education

The discussion thus far has attempted to describe career education as an emerging construct and mechanism for achieving (a) a better balance between the two essential roles performed by the educational system, (b) a better synthesis of general and specialized education, and (c) a more appropriate distinction between vocational and college programs. Based upon the discussion, career education can be further defined as education:

(1)   consisting of general and specialized training
(2)   to help individuals achieve self-fulfillment through their work roles, and
(3)   to help society achieve a balanced supply and demand for professional and non-professional manpower.

In the broadest sense, career education is an attempt to *humanize* education and in particular vocational education. The point was made earlier, that while the social maintenance role of education has been elaborately provided for, the individual self-actualization function of education has not. There is still a long way to go. But this is not to say that nothing has been done. In fact, we have even passed federal legislation in an attempt to better provide for the individual aspects of an education.

Consider, for a moment, some of the changes in vocational education which have resulted from the emphasis and tone of the Vocational Education Act of 1963 and the Vocational Amendments of 1968 represented by the following quote. ". . . Never before has attention to the individual as a person been so imperative." The statement implies that while the importance of the individual as a person was always an important belief in our society, changes in the society (e.g., scientific, social, and technological) now require greater emphasis and attention to this belief. For example, ours has become a service-oriented society with the bulk of the labor force more and more involved in rendering services rather than in producing goods. This is of extraordinary importance for specialized education,

> . . . some of the most interesting jobs will increasingly be jobs that depend ultimately for their effectiveness on the relationship among individuals . . . How do we educate people to be non-exploitive and non-manipulative in their relations with other people? How do we educate for rapport and empathy?[3]

Changes in policy and emphasis, new thrusts, programs and activities have resulted not only from the legislation but from a belief system, a set of basic assumptions underlying the system, and a variety of important and supportive research findings.

Harman has succinctly summarized a large amount of information and research data into four well-established sets of findings with important implications for career education (Figure 3).

> All of this data would appear to support the conclusion that, . . . if self-expectations and self-image are as important as seem indicated, the deliberate development of a high self-image would seem to command almost central attention in curriculum and program planning.[4]

FIGURE 3

SOME WELL-ESTABLISHED FINDINGS
WITH IMPORTANT EDUCATIONAL IMPLICATIONS[5]

---

1. The breadth and magnitude of human capacities and resources far exceed present levels of actualization within persons or societies.
   a. The ratio of latent to manifest capacity indicates that only a small fraction of human potentialities is currently being actualized.
   b. Latent-manifest discrepencies (underdevelopment) is particularly apparent regarding perceptual and emotional sensitivity/awareness, empathic communication, altruistic love (toward persons, materials, objects), imagination, and creative life styles.
2. World- and self-perceptions are strongly conditioned by familial and social learning as well as personal needs and motives.
   a. The nature and scope of self-expectations constitute a major determinant of actualized potential.
   b. The expectations of others strongly influence self-expectations and may impair or enhance actualization of potentialities.
   c. Self-expectations are generally lower and narrower than optimal (or maximal) and as a result severely limit full actualization of one's capacities.
3. Unconscious processes comprise a major portion of significant human experience (perceiving, learning, thinking).
   a. Access to unconscious processes is facilitated by attention to feelings and emotions.
   b. Access to unconscious processes is facilitated by imaginal thought (visual imagery) in contrast to verbal-associative thought.
4. Basic attitudes and beliefs (self-and world-views), conscious and unconscious, tend to be self-fulfilling.

Thus, career education can be viewed as an attempt to balance and synthesize the several components of the educational system in order that the system might be more responsive to the individual reasons and requirements for an education: as an attempt to *humanize* education. The process will likely require three major and interrelated thrusts directed at three levels within the system: (a) increased program and curriculum options (at the program level), (b) greater emphasis and development of individualized instruction (at the instructional level), and (c) a major effort to understand the affective domain and to utilize this understanding to improve learning (at the individual level).

INCREASED PROGRAM OPTIONS

The following list (Figure 4) identifies some of the more apparent developments at the program and curriculum levels which might reasonably be attributed, at least in part, to the emerging educational policy—renewed emphasis on the individual as a person. While the list is not exhaustive, it does point out the greatly increasing number of program options. But more importantly, it also suggests that the methods for pursuing the options are becoming more varied as well.

FIGURE 4

SELECTED EXAMPLES OF ATTEMPTS
TO INDIVIDUALIZE THE EDUCATIONAL SYSTEM

Selected Program Developments	Selected Curriculum Developments
•Remedial and enrichment programs (e.g., Job Corps, COPS)	•Individualized instruction
•Emphasis on programs for the disadvantaged	•CAI and PI development and expansion
•Renewed emphasis on the concept of "leisure"	•Emphasis on updating and revision (e.g., Urban/Rural Development Program)
•Recommendation for "residential schools"	•Modular scheduling
•Emphasis on curriculum for service occupations	•Non-graded classes
•Emphasis on integration of work, education, and leisure	•Small-group techniques (e.g., brainstorming, discovery methods, encounter groups, etc.)
•Emphasis on pre-vocational programs (e.g., world of work exemplary program)	•Move toward emphasis on affective domain

INDIVIDUALIZED INSTRUCTION

The work on individualized instruction is only beginning and much of this work will continue to be directed toward the development of associated hardware and to the development of appropriate techniques and strategies. But consider, for example, the variety of options and choices available to the school and to the learner as reflected in the following continuum or types of individualized instruction (Figure 5).

FIGURE 5

OPTIONS FOR PURSUING INSTRUCTIONAL OBJECTIVES AND STRATEGIES[6]

TYPES OF INDIVIDUALIZED INSTRUCTION	INSTRUCTIONAL OBJECTIVES		INSTRUCTIONAL STRATEGIES	
	School	Student	School	Student
Individually diagnosed and Prescribed Instruction	X		X	
Personalized Instruction		X	X	
Self-Directed Instruction (Learner-Centered Instruction)	X			X
Independent Study		X		X

More of an effort will be aimed at the development of new applications of types of individualized instruction. Within the context of career education, and a greatly increased number of available programs, additional approaches need to be devised for putting together individual learning programs because they represent one of the best approaches to date for personalizing the educational system and making it more relevant to student career needs and more responsive to the individual role or function of the system.

However, increased program options and more individualized instruction will not, by themselves, bring about career education as described herein. They are not likely, by themselves, to cause a better balance between the two essential functions of an education or a better synthesis of general and specialized training required by a system for career education. What is likely to bring this about is a greater attention to the affective components and outcomes of specialized education.

AFFECTIVE OUTCOMES: KEY TO CAREER EDUCATION

Figure 1 indicates that the outcomes or goals of a career education system are (a) individual work adjustment (i.e., a stable work personality), and (b) a balanced supply and demand for skilled manpower. Work adjustment is the concurrent degree of correspondence between the individual's abilities and the ability requirements of his work (satisfactoriness) and between individual needs and interests and the reinforcer system of the work environment (satisfaction).[7]

The ultimate goals of career education are individuals with stable work personalities who are (a) adjusted to and satisfied with their occupational role and with their other roles in society; (b) satisfactory to both their employers and to the society of which they are a part; and (c) employed in an occupation contributing to a balance in the supply and demand for professional and non-professional manpower.

> As he grows and develops, the individual's sets of abilities and needs undergo change, some abilities and needs are strengthened. Others disappear. New abilities and needs are added. The strengths of abilities and needs become more stable as the individual develops an increasingly fixed style of life. Eventually they crystallize, at which point successive measurements of ability and need strength will show no significant change. The individual can then be said to have a stable work personality . . . work adjustment is premised on a stable work personality.[8]

Because we know so little about the formation and change of abilities, needs and values, career education cannot be confined to the school years K through 12. Rather, it must be viewed as a continuous process occurring throughout the school years, and beyond, during which the influence of prior training and experiences diminish somewhat in importance as new learning and experiences are acquired until a point is reached where successive measurements of ability and need strengths show no significant changes.

Specialized education for professional level occupations, by-and-large, does not appear to have done as well in providing for either work adjustment or a balanced supply and demand for skilled professional manpower. Probably much of this is due to the fact that college prep and college training are rarely viewed as preparation for professional-level careers. (Except, perhaps, in colleges of engineering, and in other colleges, at the Ph.D. level).

In specialized education for non-professional level occupations, the satisfactoriness correspondence appears to have received more attention, and is better provided for by vocational education, than is the satisfaction correspondence. For example, in terms of abilities, of the available psychological tests and measures, ability tests are better developed, more reliable, valid and useful than many other types. In terms of ability requirements of occupations, there are a number of methods and techniques currently available which provide information for assessing the ability requirements of occupations or clusters of occupations (e.g., trade and job analysis, task analysis, and job inventory analysis).

A concerted effort by the profession on the satisfaction correspondence of work adjustment to develop comparable knowledge, instruments, and techniques for assessing the needs, values, and attitudes of individuals and the reinforcement patterns provided by different occupational environments, and a similar effort to better understand the work personality (i.e., the combination of the individual's needs/values system and his skill/ability set) may well be the "missing links" required for a career education system.

Some Immediate Steps Toward the Development of Career Education

In the meantime and concurrent with the research and development work suggested above, several things, in addition to those already suggested, can be done in a programmatic or curricular sense and in an attempt to individualize instruction through the application of sound psychological as well as sociological research findings.[9]

For example, the contemporary view of the self-concept holds that it is more the product of the social development of the individual than an innate attribute of personality. G. H. Mead's description of the awareness of the self has been discussed as a process through which,

> . . . the attitudes others communicate to him, and the evaluations which they make, gradually become assimilated into the person's own perception of himself. The self is thus considered to be a purely social product arising out of communication between individuals. From this point of view the self could only arise in a social setting, and without social communication there could be no awareness of self.[10]

Dewey, Goffman, and others consider the self-concept to be developed or actualized through, ". . . the reciprocal influence of individuals upon one another's actions when in one another's immediate physical presence."[11] Cartwright has further suggested that a strong, cohesive classroom group can control those aspects of the members' behavior traditionally thought to be expressive of enduring personality traits. "Recognition of this fact rephases the problem of how to change such behavior. It directs us to a study of the sources of the influence of the group on its members."[12]

A variety of courses might be devised at the elementary, junior high, and senior high school levels the purpose of which would be to create an interest in occupations. The emphasis within such courses should be on a broadened awareness and a more accurate concept of the structure of an industrialized society, on the relationships among the individuals who compose it, and on their opportunities and responsibilities within it.

For example, expanded and improved work-study programs at the senior high school level are needed consisting not only of on-the-job training but including school activities centering around in-depth occupational studies for the purpose of narrowing occupational preferences. These might be supplemented by organized individual or small group classroom activities (a) to evaluate work experiences in relation to the individual's self-concept, needs, and attitudes toward different occupational opportunities; (b) to develop work habits and attitudes; and (c) for the measurement and student-teacher analyses of personality, attitude, ability, and interest test scores and their relation to the development of a "mature vocational plan."

All of these approaches should provide the opportunity and emphasize activities designed to permit guided exploration of the individual's self-concept, as well as exploration of the individual's needs and interests relative to work and leisure. It requires that instruction be sequenced and timed and that learning opportunities be arranged to maximize the relevance of the content for the learners' self-concept by providing opportunities for exploratory communication among learners around two overriding themes based upon the two essential functions of career education:

(1) the individual self-fulfillment function—the role expectations, requirements, and interrelationships among individuals in various occupations. The theme here is what Samler has described as "The Psychological Man,"

> . . . the worker's role, his ability to work at a task that is congruent with his identity, the exercise of his values and attitudes, consideration of status, ways of meeting anxiety, patterns of interaction with others, out-of-work style of life, and totally, the way in which his personality needs will be met.[13]

(2) the social maintenance function—the nature, economic requirements and societal needs for occupations: what Samler calls "The Economic Man" and centering on,

> . . . economic considerations, wages, competitive conditions of training and education, duties performed in payment for wages received, lines of advancement, certification and union membership conditions, and so on.[14]

Most of the above are steps which can be taken NOW toward the development of career education.

Summary

The discussion began with a description of the individual self-fulfillment and social maintenance roles of education. Inadequate provision for the individual self-fulfillment function of education was proposed as one of the main concerns behind the development of career education. A distinction was made between general and specialized education. Two types of specialized education were described as primarily concerned with individual self-fulfillment through specialized work roles, either in professional-level careers (through college prep and college) or in non-professional careers (through vocational education), and with the social maintenance responsibility of contributing to a balanced supply and demand for skilled manpower.

Evidence and examples were cited to demonstrate the need for emphasizing the individual role of the educational system and to describe career education as an attempt to meet this role by humanizing and personalizing the system, thus correcting the imbalance of the current system.

Career education was defined as: (a) consisting of general and specialized training, (b) increased program and curriculum options, (c) broader development and use of individualized instructional strategies, (d) a major emphasis on the affective domain in both the content and methods of education, and (e) a continuous process of adjustment going beyond the K–12 school years.

The goals of career education are, first, to help individuals achieve work adjustment within their occupational roles and a stable work personality over time: individuals adjusted to and satisfied with their occupational role and with their other roles in society, and satisfactory to both their employers and to society; and second, to help society achieve a balanced supply and demand for professional and non-professional manpower.

It was further suggested that the successful development of career education was probably largely dependent upon our ability to better understand the components of the work personality, and particularly, the satisfaction correspondence between the needs, values and attitudes of individuals and the reinforcer patterns of different occupational environments.

Several approaches were proposed as immediate steps toward the development of career education which were consistent with the description of career education and the roles of the educational system.

Conclusion

Career education is essential to the continued improvement of life in this country both from an individual and a social perspective. It can become a viable educational system if we do two things sequentially:

(a)   if we re-examine the desired goals and outcomes of the system and improve the specificity and clarity of the model, paradigm or conceptual framework of the system, and

(b)   if, using this framework, we pursue the development of the system with the attitude and required stamina to MAKE IT WORK.

But the sequence of (a) then (b) is extremely important and requires a note of caution. The dilemma is that to do (a) without later doing (b) is a waste of time. To do (b) without first doing (a) is a disaster, yet historically it is far more likely. As Daniel Bell has aptly noted,

> Although action is typical of the American style, thought and planning are not; it is considered heresy to state that some problems are not immediately or easily solvable, that it might take . . . perhaps a generation for real improvement to occur. A sense of historical time is absent from American thought, and a desire for "instant" reform or "instant" solutions is deeply ingrained in the American temper. . . .[15]

FOOTNOTES

[1]Moss, J. *et al.* "Project Improve," *American Vocational Journal.* 45:49-52, February 1970.

[2]Self-actualization is considered to be "the directional trend which is evident in all organic and human life—the urge to expand, extend, develop, mature—the tendency to express and activate all the capacities of the organism, or the self." (Rogers, C. R., *On Becoming a Person.* Boston: Houghton Mifflin Company, 1961.)

[3]Michael, D. M. "The Plausible Future: Some Trends, Some Questions, and Some Answers." Mimeographed paper delivered at a Vocational Guidance Association Conference at Airlie House, Warranton, Virginia, December 12–15, 1965, 12 pp.

[4]Harman, W. W. *Belief Systems, Scientific Findings, and Educational Policy.* Menlo Park, Calif.: Stanford Research Center, EPRC 6747-4, November 1967, p. 9.

[5]*Ibid.* p. 5.

[6]The table was constructed from information in: Edling, J. V. *Individualized Instruction: A Manual for Administrators.* Corvallis, Oregon: Teaching Research Division, Oregon State System of Higher Education, N.D., 137 pp.

[7]Betz, E. *et al. Seven Years of Research on Work Adjustment.* Minneapolis, Minn.: Industrial Relations Center, University of Minnesota, 1966, p. 5.

[8]*Idem.*

[9]Much of the following is based upon the discussion in: Pratzner, F. C. "Development of the Self-Concept: A Theoretical Framework and Suggestions for Classroom Action Research," *Journal of Industrial Teacher Education,* 7:31-37; Fall, 1969.

[10]Blocher, D. H. *A Study of the Relationship Between Self Descriptions and Stereotypes of Occupations With High and Low Claimed Interests.* Unpublished doctoral dissertation. Minneapolis, Minn.: University of Minnesota, 1959.

[11]Goffman, E. *The Presentation of Self in Everyday Life.* New York: Doubleday-Anchor, 1959.

[12]Cartwright, D. "Achieving Change in People: Some Applications of Group Dynamics Theory," *Human Relations,* 4:381-93, 1951.

[13]Samler, J. "Psycho-Social Aspects of Work: A Critique of Occupational Information," *Personnel and Guidance Journal,* 34:458-65, February, 1961.

[14]*Idem.*

[15]Bell, D. "Toward the Year 2000: Work in Progress—The Trajectory of an Idea," *Daedalus,* Vol. 29, Summer 1967.

If a satisfactory career education curriculum is to be developed, it must provide for a cumulative experience in career decision-making and related understandings and skills. Dr. Louise J. Keller, who is Chairman of the Department of Vocational Education at the University of Northern Colorado, Greeley, presents a rationale for such a program based upon the integration of the customary three domains of the school—academic, vocational, and general. She emphasizes that the integrating elements of the curriculum is the career development theme. This theme is of particular importance in that it provides students with a conceptual map of the world of work, to which they can relate their own interests and aspirations.

Dr. Keller briefly presents the four phases of career development as they are related to the various levels of the school. Her plan includes an outline of the six principal components which should be included in a career development curriculum.

Louise J. Keller

CAREER DEVELOPMENT— AN INTEGRATED CURRICULUM APPROACH, K-12

Introduction

There is a new and exciting adventure in education. The need for the adventure is well documented in the professional literature and research. Few educators or school districts, however, have designed directional maps for us to follow. Such an adventure is profound because we must seek new ways to integrate into our existing curriculum those knowledges, skills, and attitudes which are vital to build a society in which all people can function with optimum mutual satisfaction.

The Problem

We have always contended that educational goals'and objectives are affected by the society for which these exist and by the social and economic factors prevailing in that society. I contend that

Revised from a keynote speech delivered June 8, 1970, at the University of Northern Colorado, Greeley, Colorado, for a workshop on career development.

education does not reflect the realities of our society. One such reality is that men and women spend most of their adult life in an activity we call *work.*

The history of education reflects that we have yet to accept this fact. The early high schools were developed to prepare youth for college. This purpose or mission naturally affected the entire curriculum. The classical tradition of a liberal arts education continued to be the standard of education with its subject-centered curriculum aimed at normal college or university matriculation. High schools gradually established a Carnegie unit of organization which allowed colleges and universities to identify those individuals who had successfully completed those courses which best prepared them for collegiate-level education.

Through the years various sets of goals were delineated to give new directions to curriculum designers—these included the "seven cardinal principles of education," the "ten imperative needs of youth," etc. Yet, the curriculum of yesterday and today essentially remains a subject-centered, college preparatory type of curriculum.

As new courses and programs were developed, we tended to separate these into three domains—academic, vocational, and general. Secondary schools, especially after World War II, were organized as comprehensive schools and still reflect separate educational spheres or domains which seldom interact and relate.

Knowledge through the years has been identified, classified, and compartmentalized. This phenomenon has permeated the entire system of education. The education of teachers for this type of curriculum organization is also compartmentalized. The interrelationships of learnings with those realities of life such as work are often not perceived by individual teachers. Teachers find it difficult to integrate and relate categorical knowledge from a specific discipline to situations different from those in which they were taught.

The academic domain, composed of the ancient seven liberal arts, has long dominated the educational scene and the impregnability of this domain by other educational objectives gave the rationale for the creation of other educational domains such as vocational education and general education.

Writers through the centuries have differentiated between education and training. Plato described training as illiberal and preparation for work as training—not education. This concept was perpetuated through the centuries, and in order for vocational education to emerge within the framework of public school education it was given legislative incentives to be conceived, nurtured, and protected.

The demands for academic, general, and vocational education through the years have created, therefore, the three domains which exist in varying degrees in most comprehensive schools. There have been many attempts to overcome this type of compartmentalization through the establishment of a variety of curriculum principles such as correlation and integration. But these attempts have been thwarted for many reasons. For one reason, there is a social status habitually associated with an academic education and college degrees. Subsequently, there is an inherent bias of many teachers, elementary through university. This bias reflects the attitude that success is achieved by the acquisition of academic content which is not occupationally relevant. These two factors do exist—the first in the home and community and the second in the classroom. These attitudes tend to stigmatize both individuals and programs having goals related to the world of work with the exception of those occupations classified as the professions.

If "work" is a reality of our society, then should it not be an integral part of our total education system? This rationale has brought to the forefront of educational thought the concept that career development is a responsibility of the total school and cannot be limited to a single discipline, department, or grade level. Career development is perceived as a continuous process from early childhood throughout life—developmental in nature. All teachers, the elementary teacher, the secondary school counselor, the college professor, therefore, are accountable for career development.

Perhaps much of the floundering of young men and women in our society is due to the fact that they lack a conceptual map of the world of work for use in interpreting information about occupations and in understanding the probable consequences for career decisions.

Teachers who have worked with the elementary and junior-high-age student know that boys and girls often choose each day a new occupation, but this is relatively unimportant during the early years of development. The significant thing is that they do choose occupations—they do identify with work models. We so often forget that the work one does and the environment in which one does that work constitute one of the few elements of our culture that affect mankind from the cradle to the grave.

Regardless of how long individuals stay in a college-sheltered environment, they too are headed for the realities of the world of work. It is conceivable that career development can be the theme which integrates vocational, general, and academic learnings. Career development can be the principal vehicle for the inculcation of many of the basic intellectual skills.

One way of rendering school experiences more relevant to the needs of all students is to organize the school around a career development theme. This, therefore, is the major thesis of this paper.

Career Development

Career development seems to be a process which is not only developmental but cyclical in nature. An empirical examination of the cyclical nature of career development may well serve as the basic educational components of a career development education model. The following components are suggested as a possible model for designers of curriculum—elementary through adult education. The six proposed components are: Career Awareness, Career Exploration, Career Identification and Orientation, Career Preparation, Career Entrance, and Career Assessment and Recycling.

These components would suggest that a realistic approach to career development would be to consider these components in relationship to the existing educational structure. For example, career awareness would begin in the elementary schools with a realistic picture of the world of work. The fundamental purpose of this component would be to (1) familiarize the student with occupations related to his developmental level and environment, (2) integrate work knowledges and skills into the existing curriculum, and (3) foster proper work habits and attitudes.

Career explorations at the middle school and junior high level would attempt to (1) provide the student with the intellectual tools for assessing career options, (2) provide an economic orientation to the world of work, (3) allow for discretionary and prescriptive career cluster explorations, and (4) assist each student to prepare a career blueprint with educational alternatives.

Career identification and orientation is that phase of the individual's development which requires the individual to identify with a given occupation or cluster of occupations and to become aware of the requirements for career entry and career mobility through planned orientation experiences.

This phase should come at the beginning of a critical entry point within the educational structure; for example, the first year in high school, or community college, or four-year institution. Career identification and orientation represent synoptic experiences. These are experiences which interface self-identity with occupational information. It is here that a student should revise his career blueprint and state in writing his long-range career goal as well as his short-term (immediate) career path objectives.

Career preparation is that component better known as Vocational Education which has as its major goal the preparation of individuals for job entrance, job success, and job mobility. Career development education does not supplant Vocational Education but enhances its role within the total developmental process. Vocational Education has struggled through the years for recognition as an integral part of the total education process. The concept of career development education recognizes Vocational Education as a major component.

Career entrance is a reality for most people and often a difficult transition. The "cooperative" education method is an ideal method for "bridging" the two worlds—school and work.

Career assessment and recycling is a component appearing more frequently within individual career patterns. A satisfactory career pattern may call for frequent re-assessment and educational experiences which recycle the individual through the career components but at a different rate and different degree of emphasis. Career development is a continuous process. Through education we help plan a career by interspersing at appropriate times blocks of education to supplement the working/learning components of life. Jobs and education should be integrated to build a satisfactory career. For many individuals this means re-education for upward mobility. Cooperative Vocational Education will someday be tried in reverse. Students will leave work for coordinated educational experience.

Career development in the past has been the responsibility of a few individuals. *Some* teachers advise *some* students with respect to educational plans and decisions. School counselors, of course, are involved to some extent in occupational guidance, but their efforts tend to be concentrated on a few students, usually those who already have well-developed occupational interests.

In other words, career development education begins when youngsters become *aware* of roles in our society. "Thinking" about occupational roles begins very early in our society, perhaps even prior to kindergarten in some cases. Thus, occupational decision-making is a more or less continuous process which in our society begins as a tentative, groping search for self awareness, which interfaces with occupational awareness. Thus process referred to as "career development" can be roughly divided into the six components which prescribe themselves to levels of education. These components, of necessity, do and should overlap to accommodate individual needs at a given time. Thus, career development is a "complete program" needed by an individual to understand, identify with, make a choice in, prepare for, enter into, achieve success in, and even change occupational goals. All educators play an important role in this scheme.

An Integrated Career Development Education Curriculum

The title of this paper is "Career Development —An Integrated Curriculum Approach, K through 12." Webster defines *integrated* as a unity composed of separate parts, a total. Curriculum is usually defined as the total learning activities of a school. Thus, an integrated career development curriculum is the sum of the learning activities regarding the world of work.

To the best of my knowledge, no highly integrated career development curriculum currently exists. Many ideas have appeared in the literature. One of the early writers was James W. Altman of the Institute for Performance Technology, American Institutes for Research (1966). Bottoms and Matheny (1969) prepared "A Guide for the Development, Implementation, and Administration of Exemplary Programs and Projects in Vocational Education," and the subsequent position papers delivered at the National Conference on Exemplary Programs and Projects at Atlanta, Georgia, in March, 1969, contributed to the present day career development education rationale.

In Colorado, Governor Love appointed a Juvenile Delinquency Planning Project Committee, and one of the appointed ad hoc committees (1970) developed a position statement on the role of occupational education for the elementary school. This same committee wrote a paper titled "An Integrated Occupational Program for Public Schools in Colorado." Another early thrust taken to identify the work habits and attitudes which needed to be integrated into elementary curriculum was undertaken by the Rocky Mountain Educational Laboratory in Greeley, Colorado (1968). Much of the work in Career Development Education at the University of Northern Colorado, Greeley, is a continuation of these early thrusts.

FIGURE 1

MODEL FOR CURRICULUM DEVELOPMENT

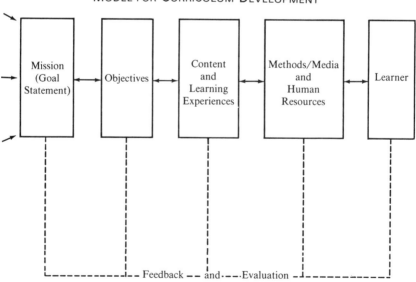

To begin the dialogue in a school district, a frame of reference often helps individuals organize their thinking. The initiatory model for curriculum development (Figure 1) implies that the curriculum designer must consider the forces which affect the school's mission—one such force is the world of work—and the model also indicates there are significant curriculum development components.

The above model also may be used to analyze the entire educational continuum or as a tool for dissecting elements at a given level of education.

Any school system accepting the challenge of career development education will struggle initially with the problems of focus, analysis, synthesis, and implementation. The purpose of the six components earlier described was a means of providing some direction as to the "focus" of career development within the present educational framework. The model for curriculum development suggests the matrix for analyzing the career development components in terms of curriculum development.

A further examination of the above model shows the learner as an important component. We mortals often forget the most obvious component when curriculum is being considered—the learner. In short, we forget a rather simple question—What do we want our children to become? The answers to that question should help schools focus on their mission and select the kinds of experiences we want our children to experience so they can become what we think they ought to become.

For example, a group of elementary teachers in a workshop at UNC in Greeley, Colorado (Summer, 1970) on restructuring curriculum K through 12 decided to begin with the Career Awareness component dealing with work habits and work attitudes. The group developed a mission statement which declared that the elementary school in their community would integrate into their existing curriculum the habits and work attitudes which could be measured.

From this focus the group moved to the next block within the model for curriculum development. The task to be delineated was the identification of attitudes characteristic of successful employment that should be considered as part of the developmental process. The following attitudinal concepts were considered as highly important to this group: Desire to Work, Responsibility-Dependability, Loyalty, Life Aspirations, Appreciation for Quality, Value of Cooperation, Personal Satisfaction, Dignity of Work Well Done, Pride in Accomplishment, and Adaptability. As the teachers considered content, learning experiences, methods, media, a decision was made to design an instrument which would assist the teacher to integrate specific attitudes into their daily lessons. A lesson plan sheet was designed which required certain identifications: Unit, Lesson Title, Duration, Content Objectives, Attitudes to be Stressed, Lesson Features, Teacher Activities, Student Tasks, Teaching Resources, Evaluation of Students, and Teacher's Evaluation of the Attitudinal Elements of the Lesson.

When a school begins to translate the question—What do we want our children to become?—into somewhat more operational smaller questions, curriculum development is transformed and transplanted into a meaningful level.

An integrated career development program requires a systematic approach to curriculum development. The initial steps are still obscure, but those who have worked on a curriculum restructuring, K through 12, would probably agree with the following statements:

1. The school board and school administrators must be committed and be willing to be involved personally in the inservice education program.

2. Inservice education will require time, support, encouragement, and facilities.

3. Teachers will need freedom to experiment and innovate—this means freedom to innovate on the spot without continuous reference to committees and higher authorities.

4. A total school system commitment—not an isolated group of teachers and counselors working on a specific task—should be marshalled for curriculum articulation.

5. Curriculum restructuring does not mean overthrowing the present structure but does mean a systematic procedure for working within the present framework.

6. The inservice education begins with extensive orientation sessions followed by individual schools identifying and discussing the philosophical ramifications of career development education.

7. An outside consultant should be hired to give direction. It is imperative that teachers, counselors, and administrators work together but it is equally important that administrators not assume the role of group leaders.

8. A simple position paper should be written which elucidates the group's commitment and mission.

9. Interfacing committees should be established. Though the initiatory meetings involve all the educators, work groups will need to be established.

10. An organizational scheme which has proved to be successful begins with the entire faculty of a school system meeting and as dialogue focuses on tasks to be completed, the following management pattern originates.

1.0 Entire faculty and staff
   1.1 Elementary

        1.11 Grade levels K–3

        1.12 Grade levels 4–6

     1.2 Secondary

        1.21 Vertical Articulation by Disciplines—7 through 12.

        1.22 Horizontal articulation by grade levels (This often is not feasible until after specific disciplines are able to identify how each discipline can relate its curriculum to the world of work. At this point commonalities can be identified which become a means for correlating and integrating content and learning experiences.)

  11. Throughout the inservice education process certain concepts need to be reinforced by the consultant(s):

     a. The first task is to develop in teachers a commitment to the equal worth of each individual and hence of each child's development and growth, whatever his so-called native capacities.

     b. Curriculum is based on goals, not hurdles.

     c. Motivated learners can reach most goals if the school provides directional alternatives.

     d. Teaching and learning processes also occur outside the classroom and school.

     e. Curriculum development does not mean each teacher must become a producer of new materials. Teachers do need to be exposed to the vast array of world-of-work materials that already exist and be given the tools for selecting and organizing these instructional materials.

Two major problems often appear when school systems attempt to integrate the curriculum around the career development theme. First, many of the arguments about how to organize the curriculum stem from different conceptions regarding the role of the school. The traditional role has not considered the realities of work as a legitimate academic pursuit. A second factor must be recognized—an integrated approach is most difficult because educators often lack knowledge for conceptualizing and attacking the problems and issues under study.

Because of the awesomeness of the task, I am fearful that the following alternatives will be implemented. The responsibility for designing and implementing a career education program will be placed in the hands of a few counselors who are already burdened with too many students and too many unrelated activities. World-of work media will be purchased and placed in a center but not integrated into on-going program activities. In an attempt to provide for some career orientation and explorations, a course will be designed to impart career information.

Should an integrated approach not be possible, the greatest tragedy that could befall education would be for educators to confuse career development education with Vocational Education and a dual track system be developed—academic education and career education.

Career Development Education in the Elementary

Let's begin by stating a goal for career development education at the elementary level. For the time being, we shall say our goal is to develop a system whereby the existing elementary curriculum can be related to the realities of the world and reinforce positive work attitudes.

Kindergarten is an "entry point" into the schools for many children. The kindergarten is an essential time for development of foundations for learning and includes readiness activities and essential developmental concepts. Reading skills are necessary for children, but before children are ready to read they must be able to see, hear, discriminate, remember, and associate. They must have meaningful experiences upon which to build. Before children can make personally realistic choices, accept responsibility, and achieve satisfaction, they must have experiences, knowledge of alternatives, consequences, and success. They must have experienced responsibility.

The kindergarten is concerned with oral language. A child cannot learn to read until he has adequate understanding of oral language. Attention, therefore, at the kindergarten level is directed to the development of oral language. In this context the child can identify with a worker—his father, mother, and other significant persons. The concept of working can become an essential part of his thinking, speaking, and his playing.

The elementary school curriculum deals with those things which are considered to be the common need of all. The curriculum is concerned with those things that tend to unify or integrate people. Work that was formerly carried on in the home is now performed by factories. Children no longer observe and share the work of the family. Boys and girls today know almost nothing about the production of the clothing they wear or about any product they use. This appalling ignorance of products, occupations, and industries is the outcome of an educational program that does not accurately reflect our society.

Industry has come to occupy an ever increasing place of importance in the social, economic, and political aspects of life today. There are abundant reasons why this element should be added to the humanistic and scientific elements already in the elementary program in order to help children adjust to the important and large industrial element which surrounds them.

Students in the elementary should acquire simple manual and mental skills in the performance of a number of work tasks. Instruction in the use of common tools and materials is needed. Such a study should develop an understanding of the tools, materials, processes, products, occupations, and problems of industry. As a culminating experience, students in the upper elementary or middle school should plan an integrated unit of study, perhaps a study of a major industry, and then perform certain constructional activities that demonstrate their understanding of both the subject matter and the method. Such an exploratory unit can incorporate what I like to call the "survival skills"—speech, mathematics, reading, and English usage. Projects related to the world of work should be an early part of the learning process. Such experiences permit creativity, expression of self-image, development of concepts and skills, and success.

Schools may wish to experiment with mini types of work experience programs for some youngsters at the elementary. These experiences should be highly people oriented. The occupational cluster which would lend itself well to this activity would be the so-called "helping" careers within the personal services occupational cluster.

One educational area which lends itself well to career development is social studies in the elementary. Here is an example of an integrated career development curriculum through the social studies program—a proposed curriculum by the Governor's Juvenile Delinquency Planning Project Committee, 1970:

Kindergarten   living in the immediate environment; child learns about work in his home; mother, father, and other members of his household.

Grade 1   living in the home and school; child learns about work in his immediate environment; home, school, church, neighborhood.

Grade 2   living in the community; child learns about community helpers who protect and serve him, as well as familiar stores and businesses in the community.

Grade 3   living in the community or expanding community life; child studies transportation, communication, and other major industries.

Grade 4   life in other communities and/or life in our state; child studies world of work at state level, main industries of the state, etc.

Grade 5   living in the United States or living in the Americas; studies broaden to cover the industrial life of the nation. Major industries of the various sections of the U.S. are selected for study.

Grade 6 our American neighbors or life on other continents; studies expand to include Canada, South and Central America as contrasted to life in the U.S.

But not only facts or knowledge must be taught; we must also foster proper work habits and attitudes. Some children have to be taught behavior patterns that are acceptable in our society. They cannot learn these by watching; they have to be taught. Along this line we must not forget that appreciation of the culture of minority groups is another area of concern. The elementary teacher has the responsibility of helping youngsters understand and appreciate the contributions minority groups have made to our society.

The role of the elementary teacher is very important. It is in the elementary school that we detect particular styles of learning. Some children learn better through listening, others through looking, and still others need both listening and looking. A few may need to manipulate, feel, and trace, as well as hear and see. To begin our adventure into the world of work at the elementary level, the teacher must identify:

1. What can be taught about the world of work (I call these the "knowing" objectives). This is an elementary concept of career dynamics and alternatives. An understanding of the relationships of education and learning to a satisfying career, the study of occupations that youngsters can identify from their environment.

2. What skills must be developed through specific learning activities. (These are the "doing" activities which give meaning to those knowing objectives.)

3. What world of work attitudes and habits should be integrated into the daily lessons.

Career Development Education in the Junior High

The junior high school has traditionally been known as the "exploratory" phase of education. Little has been done to explore the world of work except in those courses designed for the low achiever—occupational units often appear in general math courses and social-living type courses.

The attitude of teachers and administrators toward the world of work at this level is critical. Too many junior high school programs have structured dual track systems. For example, there are educators who look upon the industrial arts program for boys only and for boys who are not going to college. If all our youngsters—even the girls—will be working most of their adult lives, then should not all of them have the opportunity to explore various aspects of the world of work?

The goal for the junior high should be to develop a system whereby the curricula can be utilized to disseminate occupational information, to provide *all* students an opportunity to explore various work categories, and to assist students in developing coherent, flexible, tentative career blueprints.

The following career development activities are proposed as a means of implementing a truly career explorations program. The curriculum would be built around (a) Occupational Clusters, (b) Career Supports, and (c) Career Guidance. The process of learning would be a combination of prescriptive and discretionary learning experiences.

An *occupational cluster* represents a group of occupations which have been arranged for related exploratory purposes. These experiences range from self-directed learning activities to teacher-directed activities. Each occupational cluster is subdivided into sub-clusters. An occupational cluster can be pictorially presented to students in the form of a wheel. The wheel, which is divided into the different sub-clusters, is further partitioned into exploratory functions. The size of each of the latter partitions or segments denotes the "time" established in the master schedule for those teacher-directed instructional activities. These latter segments can also be explored through self-directed activities designed around learning activity packets which are housed in the school's Center for Career Development. Each segment could also be coded to indicate time required for teacher-directed learning and self-directed learning and could also indicate the learning level or degree of difficulty.

Career Supports represent those areas of the curriculum which have been restructured to enhance career development education, namely, mathematics, English, social studies, science, physical education, etc. The career supports would also be clustered as to required sub-clusters and discretionary sub-clusters for students who desire more indepth study.

Career Guidance and Counseling become the means by which both occupational clusters and career-support experiences are coordinated for personalizing the learning experiences. The aid of computer terminals with print-out capabilities, career explorations, resource centers, simulation occupational laboratories, etc., become the new educational centralities for assisting learners, teachers, and other supportive personnel.

Each student entering the junior high would be required to explore at least one sub-cluster from each of the cluster wheels—both occupational and career-support clusters. The student conceivably could, through random choice or through directed prescriptions, explore as many clusters as time, energy, and capabilities permit. Through guidance and counseling, career exploration program plans and schedules would be established for each student. Some students may be able to plan their complete program while other students may need a more prescribed plan.

Career development activities at the junior high level must be held responsible for (a) helping students acquire the necessary cognitive tools for assessing one's internal and external environment—this includes a conceptual map for analyzing and synthesizing occupational information in order to establish goals, career plans, and career alternatives; (b) providing exploratory opportunities which are occupational and career supportive in nature—these experiences need to be both prescriptive and discretionary; (c) acquainting students with role models for future identification purposes; and (d) assisting individual students design career blueprints for reaching both short-term objectives as well as long-range career goal(s).

A *career blueprint* is not some absolute declaration. The fact that so many young people today lack goals and directions would seem to indicate that educators have the responsibility for helping young people focus attention on those aspects of life which will affect future activities. Teachers, regardless of their subject specialization, need some tangible source of information to help them better understand students and relate their instructional program to individual objectives and goals. Yes, the junior high school becomes the centrality for decision making.

Perhaps this is the best place to present a notion developed by the Institute for Performance Technology, American Institutes for Research, Pittsburgh, Pennsylvania, and introduced by Dr. James W. Altman at the 1965 AVA convention in Miami Beach, Florida. The research, funded under a grant from the Ford Foundation, was titled: "Research on General Vocational Capabilities (Skills and Knowledges)." Six principal components for an integrated career development curriculum were identified. Excerpts from the 1965 American Vocational Association speech and the 1966 final report are elucidated below in hopes that some individual will become intrigued with the relevancy and the curriculum feasibility it could engender.

**Six Principal Components for an
Integrated Career Development Curriculum**

Society and Work

This area of the curriculum would be concerned with importing basic knowledge about the institutions and dynamics of our society which generate, define, and lend meaning to occupations. It must interface with social studies throughout the school system.

This component can be sub-divided into four major sub-headings: (1) components of a working society, (2) the economics of work, (3) how work roles and values are defined, and (4) change in the working world. Further delineation of these sub-headings is possible.

1.   Components of a Working Society

Financial institutions	Trade unions
The public	Workers
Government as a third party	Managers
Government as an employer	Owners
Technical and professional societies	Commerce and business
Labor unions	Industry
	Agriculture

2.   The Economics of Work

Cost of Living	Risk
Prices	Investment
Wages	Increasing wealth
Costs	Wealth and its changing meaning
Profit and loss	

3.   How Work Roles and Values are Defined

The relationship of social status to occupations
The impact of labor policies
Labor negotiations and disputes
Relationship of jobs to functions performed
Relationship of jobs to products produced
Education and occupational opportunity
Work and leisure

4.   Change in the Working World

The interpretation of occupational trend data
Sources of occupational change information
Methods of measuring and predicting occupational change
The impact of industrialization, automation, and technological change on
    occupations
The nature of technological change

Occupational Information

This area would present information concerning broad occupational groups, families of related jobs, and individual jobs. It must be coordinated with occupational counseling activities of the school system and should draw heavily upon the results of job and task analysis for its content. May I suggest that if you are interested in the first component you take a look at the teacher's manual for *Manpower and Economic Education—Opportunities in American Economic Life,* published and distributed by the Joint Council on Economic Education, 1212 Avenue of the Americas, New York, 10036. For information on how one state is developing a "system" for career development, I suggest you look at the Wyoming system for career development publication.

Occupational information also has some major sub-headings. These are (1) job areas —opportunities and requirements, (2) job opportunities and hierarchies within different industrial areas, and (3) information concerning specific jobs (available selectively to students).

1. Job Areas (opportunities and requirements)

    Professional workers (physicians, lawyers, teachers, engineers, scientists, etc.)

    Officials and managers (corporation executives, public officials, plant supervisors, store managers, etc.)

    Technicians (electronic technician, X-ray technologist, computer programmer, laboratory technician, etc.)

    Craftsmen (carpenters, auto mechanics, electricians, air conditioning mechanics, plumbers, welders, etc.)

    Clerical workers (stenographers, typists, file clerks, secretaries, bookkeepers, etc.)

    Distributive occupations (salesmen, buyers, stock clerks, wrappers, etc.)

    Operatives (assemblers, inspectors, machine operators, drivers, deliverymen, etc.)

    Service workers (policemen, firemen, waiters or waitresses, barbers, beauty operators, etc.)

    Laborers

2. Job Opportunities and Hierarchies within Different Industrial Areas

    Apparel
    Agriculture
    Communication
    Construction
    Education

Electric light and power
Entertainment and sports
Equipment manufacturing
Finance, insurance, real estate
Food and lodging
Government
Health and welfare
Maintenance and repair
Materials manufacturing
Merchandising and retail trade
Metal production
Personal and protective services
Research and engineering
Transportation

3. Information Concerning Specific Jobs (available selectively to students)

Specially prepared job descriptions
The nature of social contribution
Nature of tasks performed
Success and failure criteria
Causes for demotion or termination
Skill and knowledge requirements
Advancement prospects
Training opportunities
Employment opportunities
Remuneration
Work schedule
Work environment
Personal, family and social demands
Travel required
Status connected with the occupation
Education, training, and other entry requirements
Relationship to other occupations
Probable change due to technological or social change

Self-Knowledge

This area of the curriculum provides the student with the information needed to make accurate and relevant self-assessments in relation to career choices and related education plans. It must be an integral part of the total testing, grading, and evaluation program of the school system. It may draw heavily upon the techniques and findings of the behavioral sciences for its content. When developing curriculum around this component, teachers need to consider the student's capacities and motivational factors.

1. Capacities

Assessing one's bargaining position with respect to a job
Evaluation of demonstrated proficiency with reference to occupational
    requirements
Evaluation of age, sex, physical characteristics, and handicaps in relation
    to occupational requirements
Financial status and training costs
Scholastic aptitudes and educational achievement as indications of proba-
    ble future educational success
The aptitude profile and occupational requirements
The sources of useful self-evaluation information

2. Motivational factors

Assessing one's values with respect to job demands
Assessing one's economic, social status, and individual dominance needs
    with respect to occupational opportunities
Evaluation of interests and aspirations as these related to occupational
    choice
Sensitivity to the following as sources of satisfaction, motivation, and
    dissatisfaction
    Opportunity for creative effort
    Responsibility
    Recognition
    Accomplishment
    Amount and type of interaction with others
    Repetitiveness of tasks
    Status
    Wages
    The physical environment
    Working hours
    Failure and criticism
Full use of capabilities as a source of satisfaction
The development of capabilities as a source of satisfaction

Career Planning

This area of the curriculum involves the student's using information about the world
of work and self-knowledge and making effective (we hope) career choices and
training plans. Career planning must be phased with the student's level of maturity,
with the occupational and self-knowledge available to him, and with the educational
choices available to him.

Career Planning has three sub-divisions—(1) a plan for combining occupational and
self-knowledge, (2) an educational plan, and (3) actual work experience.

1. Combining Occupational and Self-Knowledge

    Allowing for occupational change
    Avoiding under- and over-employment
    Choosing among employment opportunities
    Evaluating a potential position
    Matching individual characteristics to occupational profiles

2. Educational Planning

    Post-employment training as a route to advancement
    Part-time and cooperative school-industry employment opportunities
    Sources of financial aid for education and training
    Costs of training and time required
    The relationship of education to occupational achievement
    Alternative routes to career objectives
    How to develop a reasonable career plan
    The sequence of career-relevant choices
    Strategies of learning for flexible occupational proficiency
    Matching educational and training programs to occupations
    Sources for post-high school training

3. Securing a Job

    Making the initial impressions on the job
    The employment interview: behavior and appearance
    Resumes and application forms
    Placement services and sources of job availability information
    Common employment and personnel practices

Basic Technology

I am not sure our schools are ready for this component because it requires a reorganization of the entire curriculum. At this point the school is asked to examine the world of work and restructure the curriculum around the basic knowledge and skills useful in a wide variety of occupations. This component draws heavily upon findings in the fine arts, engineering, sciences, and humanities for its content. In this area there are *eight major sub-headings.*

1. General work habits
2. Machines and mechanical principles
3. Electrical principles
4. Structures
5. Chemical and biological principles
6. Numerical operations

7. Verbal communications
8. Human relations

Specific Occupational Training

If we have a truly career development curriculum we will provide all students with entry skills/knowledges, attitudes. However, some students will want more specific training. This component of our curriculum will be initiated only when the student has made a relatively firm occupational choice, or is approaching sufficiently close to his planned education terminal point that further delay in specific training will be likely to preclude an opportunity to obtain employment which will fully use his capabilities. Specific occupational course content must be based on the results of job and task analysis.

To you, the junior high teachers, your responsibilities as I view them are to make sure that:

1. Each student can make a sensible tentative choice between career support clusters and occupational cluster explorations
2. Each student has a coherent and flexible education plan (career blueprint) in writing.

Keep in mind that a small percent of the students that make it through high school will never receive a college degree. Don't allow them to develop a high school program without building into it marketable skills/knowledges, attitudes. Your task, therefore, is to decide what kind of curriculum will accomplish these objectives.

Career Development Education in the Senior High

The senior high school in many schools has three well-established tracks—the academic track for those going to college, the vocational track for those not going to college, and the general track for the drop-in and drop-out type of student.

Again, our philosophy has not accepted the premise that all students will eventually work and that all students should be able to enter a series of job-entry positions regardless of future work objectives. A tentative goal for the senior high school is the development of a system which integrates the three tracks and provides all students entry-level occupational training. Such a goal will require the small community to develop a viable mechanism through which the school system can mobilize available resources to provide occupationally relevant learning experiences and services for all students. One of these services is job placement of all students who reach the occupational standards established—at least the first level or rung of a career cluster lattice. As educators we must be held responsible for placement and followup of students who leave our high schools or drop out of college. You may not see this as an educational role, but is this not the real test of a school's curriculum—what happens to your products—the student-customer/consumer?

It is necessary that high school drop-outs, graduates, business and vocational school students, community college graduates, and college graduates be prepared to begin a job. Those of us at the university level who prepare teachers are very much aware of the need for even college graduates to be able to do more than teach.

You must begin preparing people for more than one job. The choice of occupations is seen as a continuing and refining process. It is expected that automation will continue and that changes will require people with basic skills and the ability to think to continually adapt and re-train. Therefore, problem solving with its essential analysis of facts and selection of alternatives plus positive attitudes toward adaptation and learning need to be emphasized in our high schools. Because occupational choice requires a selection, some alternatives are eliminated. Women in the future can be expected to fill a very different role. Traditional role expectations will not be appropriate. It is anticipated that women will have greater opportunities for occupations outside the home. There will be shifts in patterns of interaction on the job, in the home, and in the community as the role is modified. Both men and women will need broader understanding and a number of alternatives for the future.

1. I believe the high school has the responsibility to help students develop and/or refine realistic career plans (note I said plans—these may be both career supportive and occupational in nature).
2. Each student should develop basic vocational capabilities. (If you study the six principal components, you will get a better idea of these vocational or occupational capabilities.)
3. Some students should enter specific career training programs. Even the small community can provide an effective occupational training program, especially if it is based on a career lattice approach.

A career lattice is a way of looking at occupations at a given level. As educators we ask ourselves what skills, knowledges and attitudes can we teach which will permit students to be able to enter one or more of these occupations, thus providing for horizontal mobility.

Students, as well as teachers, need to understand better the occupational hierarchy which exists. Lattices will not all look alike—some are simple, some are much more complex. But we need to be able to show youth as well as adults that this is the point where you begin. You can move horizontally, or with additional education and experience, career mobility of a vertical nature is possible.

When I work with senior high school teachers regarding career development education, I ask them to do three things:

1. Give a brief statement (in writing) about the course(s) taught—their mission, so to speak.
2. Take one sheet of paper, if the course is one semester in length or two sheets if the course is a full year. Block off (calendar) the major topics or units to indicate *what is taught,* how much *time* is devoted to the topic.

    This activity forces teachers to take a good look at what they teach. It helps them discover where career information and learning experiences can be integrated by the teacher. It may help them defend budget requests. It will help them better plan, refine, update curriculum. This activity also helps communicate to others what teachers are doing.

    This all may seem trite, but the best place to start restructuring curriculum is with the present structure—its content and learning experiences.
3. The third question would be to ask teachers about their employment of strategies to facilitate the teacher/learning processes.

Of critical importance to the successful implementation of a career development education curriculum at the high school level is the collaborative role of the elementary, junior, and senior high schools.

The senior high school program must not ignore the efforts of the elementary, middle, and junior high schools. A suggested mode for development would be for each discipline/department within the senior high school to consider the writer's six components of career development, especially components three through five—career identification and orientation, career preparation, and career entrance—in relationship to the proposed curriculum structure for the junior high school: occupational clusters, career supports, and career guidance.

Students entering the senior high school, having experienced career explorations at the junior high, should be able to identify with one or two clusters for more indepth career orientation. Some individuals may view career identification and orientation as the same as career explorations. The difference lies in career focus and depth of experiences. For example, students wishing to pursue a program which would prepare them for some occupation related to the field of office work should have an opportunity to reorient themselves to the skills, knowledges, and personal characteristics related to the business and office occupations cluster as well as relate this information to the various possibilities within the community and/or area for more indepth "vocational" preparation.

Just as each teacher in the lower grades is an integral part of the career development program so should this be true at the senior high school level. Through the years there has been a proliferation of courses by departments, often unrelated to each other, but seemingly essential for the implementation of departmental goals and objectives. An interesting and exciting approach to curriculum restructuring around the career development theme would be one that considers the following initiatory strategies:

a. Each discipline or department represented in the high school would analyze its curriculum for common elements for all students.

b. These elements or units would be assigned to the career support core. A teacher from each of the disciplines/departments would also be assigned to the career support area as a member of the instructional team. This assemblage of general, academic, and vocational educators would design a new correlated curriculum. Each team member would also be the liaison person between the correlated career support curriculum and the career development curriculum—the last being composed of all the disciplines/departments within the existing high school.

c. The career support area would represent those common learnings essential for citizenry in the twenty-first century. Examples of the career support units are: communication, courts and correction systems, fine arts, humanities, financial systems, transportation, social psychology, social assistance and rehabilitation, development and control of physical man-made environment, health delivery systems, biological science and technology, etc. The core is "now" and "future" oriented.

d. The major portion of the high school curriculum would be integrated and correlated career cluster preparation. The same disciplines/departments which support the common core experiences would also interface with each other. Block-of-time approaches would be established in order to permit team teaching, integration and correlation of subject-matter.

Educators are beginning to realize that the most insidious and subtle barrier to our future is not our goals and objectives but the process we have used to invoke or implement these goals and objectives. The so-called innovative programs which have emerged over the past decade indicate that if we are to reach people we cannot fragment the learning situation. Youth do not learn in an atmosphere of subject matter hermetically sealed off from the rest of life or from other factors which influence their perceptions.

The exciting exemplary programs today are those that found new ways to combine content, methods, strategies, and instructional media to bring our isolated general, academic, and vocational objectives into a continual interplay. There is no earthly reason why a student enrolled in a science career cluster program could not be involved with a method of instruction heretofore viewed strictly as vocational—the "cooperative" method which coordinates actual on-the-job experiences with classroom instruction.

Restructuring the high school program around the theme of career development education with its career supports, occupational clusters, and career guidance and counseling would indeed make for a more relevant approach to meeting the needs of all students.

Some Concluding Remarks

There will be those who read this empirical promulgation on "Career Development—An Integrated Curriculum Approach, K through 12," as a nefarious treatise. Still others will accept and/or refute some of the notions. All would be justified, whatever their declamation. At the beginning of this discourse, I mentioned that the profoundness of such an adventure is not yet understood. What is understood is that the educational system of the 1970's must find ways to develop students into productive, independent, rational persons who are productively employed and use their leisure time not only for fun but also for public service and self-actualization. The mode by which the transition from an educational system subdivided into three domains toward a more realistic, humane approach would be the sincere consideration of restructuring the curriculum around the concepts of career development education. I believe this approach will emerge toward the latter part of this decade as a viable structure for preparing citizens for the twenty-first century.

Did I hear you say that people will not be working in the twenty-first century? Perhaps a new definition of work will also emerge—work being the expenditure of one's time and energy for the benefit of self and society.

Part III EMERGING CAREER EDUCATION PROGRAMS IN THE PUBLIC SCHOOLS

In this section, four examples of materials developed in emerging career education programs in public schools are presented. Each example was selected because it represents an approach which can be used in any school district which allocates the proper resources for the development of career education programs of various depths. Each example represents the work of public school personnel with or without the assistance of personnel from state departments of education and universities. These do not necessarily represent fully developed career education projects. But they do represent programs in operation and which appear to be having some success in providing a sound basis for career development for children and youth.

These materials were selected from a large number of examples which were reviewed. Any number of other examples could also have been included if space permitted. A review of these materials leads one to conclude that there is a great deal being done in career education in the United States, with or without the assistance of Federal funds. What appears now to be most needed is a comprehensive, integrated model which can be generally diffused throughout the school systems of the country.

CAREER EDUCATION: CAREER AWARENESS (K–6)

Introduction

"By demanding educational reform now, we can gain the understanding we need to help every student reach new levels of achievement; only by challenging conventional wisdom we need to educate our young in the decade of the 70s."

President Richard M. Nixon
Education Message
March 3, 1970

The public schools in Oregon are responsible for providing every young person with educational opportunities that will enable him to develop to his full potential. The Oregon Board of Education has interpreted this to mean that schools have a three-fold objective: to help young people (a) discover their individual interests and abilities, (b) explore the many avenues of

This material was developed by the Intermediate Education District, Marion, Polk, and Yamhill Counties, Oregon, under Regional Coordinator, Jack Tilton. It was originally issued by the District in booklet form.

productive activity that might challenge and enlarge their individual talents and (c) learn the wise exercise of freedom of choice, self-direction, self-discipline and responsibility. Hence, a concern has developed with the new increasing perplexities of living which students must cope with not only in school but even later as they become productive citizens of society.

With the foregoing concern considered to be of paramount importance, there has been almost unanimous cooperation by many elementary teachers toward contributing written indications of actual recognized career awareness-type situations which were and are being shared with the students, grades K–6. It is our intent to share with all interested persons a composite of all contributed career awareness type situations, for it is their belief that the individual teacher approach to career development is most effective when the teacher utilizes resources available in the community and the expertise of teachers from other disciplines.

Special recognition should be given to John Fessant, Claude Morgan, and Tom Williams, Specialists with Oregon Board of Education, and to C. B. "Pat" Daly, Consultant, Oregon State University, for their efforts and contributions which they have made to this publication.

Jack Tilton
Regional Coordinator
Career Education

PHILOSOPHY OF EDUCATION

1. Education is for all people.
2. Education should perpetuate the cultural heritage.
3. Education should afford the student with experiences and knowledge for self-realization.
4. Education should afford the student with experiences and knowledge to establish a positive self-image.
5. Education should afford the student with experiences and knowledge for understanding of self, community, and self within the community.
6. Education should afford the student with experiences and knowledge to allow him to establish constructive life goals.

PHILOSOPHY OF CAREER EDUCATION

1. Career Education is for all people.
2. Career Education should prepare a student for a successful life in which employment plays a major role.
3. Career Education should lower the barriers between education and work.
4. Career Education should emphasize the student's natural ability.

5. Career Education should equip the student to compete successfully in a changing society.
6. Career Education should prepare the student with job entry skills and provide continuing education opportunities.
7. Career Education should allow the student options and alternatives in his future employment.
8. Career Education should offer the student cultural and avocational experiences and opportunities.

DEFINITIONS

1. *Vocational Education* is that area of education that pertains to instruction and skill development directly related to employment.
2. *Career Education* is the attitudes, skills, and knowledge that pertain to a full and productive life in which employment plays a major role. It may be all of education.

STATEMENT OF THE PROBLEM

1. Education has not met the needs of all the students.
2. Education has created artificial barriers between man's preparation for "the good life" and life itself.
3. Education has created norms to which each person must conform.
4. Education has prepared students to compete academically rather than economically.
5. Education has been geared to preparation for higher education rather than a useful and productive life in which employment plays a major role.
6. Education has not equipped the student to enter the labor market.
7. Education has not provided opportunities for retraining and upgrading on a continuing basis.
8. Vocational education has often provided skilled training in dead-end jobs.
9. Vocational education has not provided broad-based education to allow the student options and alternatives in his future employment.
10. Education has not provided the student with decision-making skills.
11. Education has not provided the student with the background to establish life goals.
12. Education has not encouraged the development of a positive self-image within each student.
13. Education has not developed within each student a concept of himself in relation to his society.

CAREER AWARENESS—WHY?

A. Students will learn to know themselves in their immediate environment and begin to relate to the broader environment beyond the family and school.

B. Students will develop identification with workers, fathers, mothers, or other significant persons.

C. Students will acquire simple manual and mental skills in the performance of a number of work tasks.

D. Students will at the upper elementary level become aware of factors that may have an impact upon their future.

E. Students will acquire satisfaction in the task of learning itself.

F. Students learn to get along and work with peers.

Career Awareness—Why?

The essence of a recent publication from the Office of Education indicated that for large numbers of American youth the public school system represents a maze of meaningless activity leading nowhere. They fail to see any relationship between their current school experiences and some identifiable *next step* beyond school. Such a view is especially common to the large percent who do not go on to higher education. Education at any level should be evaluated in terms of the extent to which students are prepared for, and are assisted in taking, *the next step.*

The prolonged period of dependency required to today's youth by certification requirements and union regulations intensifies the feeling of uselessness and alienation which many youth experience as a result of their school experiences. Many youth have limited contacts with work role models from which they might pattern their behavior and aspirations. With the passing of the guilds, farm work, and small businesses within the home, the sight of formal work has become farther and farther removed from the lives of modern youth. Perhaps the school is the single most appropriate agency for systematically preparing youth to enter the World of Work. Such a systematic effort should help to bridge what many youth see as a "credibility gap" between the announced purposes and the actual outcomes of public education.

Since work is the next step for over 60 percent of the nation's high school youth, transition from school to work is too important to be left to chance. Work-bound youth need at least as much assistance as college-bound youth; indeed, the immediate alternatives available to them are in some respects broader and more complex.

The school must do more than match student and employer. The school must assume responsibility for assisting a student in the clarification of his goals; providing him with knowledge about the labor market; helping him in evaluating his qualifications and abilities in terms of job opportunities; assisting him in developing the flexibility needed for adjusting to a fluctuating society; providing him with appropriate preparation for entering a job; and providing special assistance to many students to help them maintain employment and move up from dead-end entry level jobs.

The goals of career development are sufficiently broad and expansive to preclude their accomplishment by any single worker however well trained. Such goals frequently include: (a) helping the student to view himself as a worthwhile person; (b) assisting the student to experience success in his own eyes; (c) assisting the school in providing *meaningful* experiences for all students; (d) helping the student to consider, understand, and assess the values of a work-oriented society; (e) assisting the student to develop an appreciation of his own talents and interests; (f) helping the student to make appropriate choices from the widest possible range of alternatives available; (g) helping the student to formulate plans for implementing decisions which he has made; (h) helping the student to accept personal responsibility for such decisions; and (i) providing the student with the kind of education that will prepare him to implement the decision he has made. The Herculean nature of this task is compounded by the sagging self-concepts of slum children; the limited range of experiences, work and otherwise, available to minority group and rural students; and the increasingly crowded conditions within the urban schools. The attainment of these ambitious goals will require the active support of personnel both inside and outside the school.

The more promising programs and practices of vocational education must be fused with the broader curriculum and with the guidance program of the school to facilitate the student's career development and acquisition of other skills and understanding. Exemplary programs and projects should be designed to influence and involve the total school in the creation of an environment wherein all students do in fact acquire skills, knowledge, understandings, and attitudes necessary for career development. The entire education process, including vocational education, is currently failing to provide an appropriate educational experience for nearly one-half of the school population.

There are other concerns such as the proper use of leisure time and the establishment of sound interpersonal relationships which also should be stressed throughout the school experience. The effort to infuse the curriculum and the guidance program with career development interests is not intended to preclude concern for these other important aspects of life.

If the college choice can be seen as something other than an end in itself, as an intermediate step in career development, then it is safe to say that all students need help with career development. Not only do students need such help, they want it! Studies which examine the elementary and secondary student's concern for his career development repeatedly conclude that he is strongly interested. Efforts to demonstrate the relationship between courses of study and the World of Work are likely to render the teaching of such subjects more relevant to student interests. Six assumptions underlie this effort to develop the school around a career development theme:

   I. Vocational education is the right of everyone who can profit from it, and it is the responsibility of the school to provide it;
  II. Vocational education, like general education, is a responsibility of the total school and cannot be limited to a single discipline or department;
 III. Vocational education programs can be developed which serve as nonblocking career ladders, and they can be planned to be consistent with the goals of both general and vocational education;
  IV. Vocational education should be a continuous process from early childhood throughout life;
   V. Vocational education provided more opportunities than other aspects of education for youth to perform adult work roles which are essential to promoting the career development of youth;
  VI. Vocational education experiences can serve as a vehicle for teaching basic academic skills to those youth whose learning activities are less appropriate for highly abstract learning experiences.

Concern for career development cannot be a one-shot approach that takes place at the junior or senior high level. It is too late when the student reaches the point of making the transition from school to work. Career development should be conceived of as a pyramid offering a broad base of exploratory experiences at the elementary and junior high school levels and gradually narrowing to a decision point as the student acquires appropriate preparation for his next step beyond school.

Occupational preparation should begin in the elementary schools with a realistic picture of the World of Work. Its fundamental purposes should be to familiarize the student with his world and to provide him with the intellectual tools and rational habits of thought to play a satisfying role in it.

The career development program at the elementary level should be informational and orientational in nature. The effort should be directed toward expanding the student's awareness of self and of the occupational structure. More specific objectives toward which career exploration programs should be directed are given as follows:

First, students learn to know themselves in their immediate environment and begin to relate to the broader environment beyond the family and school.

Second, students develop identifications with workers, fathers, mothers, or other significant persons.

Third, students acquire simple manual and mental skills in the performance of a number of work tasks.

Fourth, students at the upper elementary level become aware of factors that may have an impact upon their future.

Fifth, students acquire satisfactions in the task of learning itself.

Sixth, students learn to get along and work with peers.

There is little question that a career development program at this early level can be effective if it is geared to the readiness of elementary children. A recent study demonstrated in two socio-economically different elementary schools that measurable improvement in vocational knowledge, level of occupational aspiration and realistic occupational choice can be attained through a planned vocational guidance program. Another study found that eight-year-olds could be taught, through an organized guidance program, respect for other people and the work they do, the advantages and disadvantages which occupations have for the worker, and some of the interdependent relationships of workers.

It has been suggested that the younger the child the greater the interest in the actual job performance itself. Most children are natural-born actors; they want to act out in order to understand what it feels like to be a carpenter or a ball-player. Observations suggest the appropriateness of dramatizations, role-playing, and simulation games at this level. These action-oriented activities appeal to the concrete nature of the conceptualization of elementary children and furnish them a thoroughly enjoyable means of gaining vocational information. Other appropriate activities include films, displays, field trips, and visits to the classroom by occupational role models representing a wide variety of occupational areas and levels. Special care should be exercised to acquaint children with jobs representative of the entire occupational array since past efforts have seriously slighted lower level occupations, the very level at which many children will later work.

Other Suggested Career Awareness Experiences for Grades K–6:

1. Bring into the class people from the community who will be willing to talk to the children about the jobs they hold.

2. Ask students to interview their parents, then report what they do in their jobs. In this way, students are taught interviewing techniques

and the skills of oral communication. The students can develop a questionnaire reflecting the kinds of questions they have and the things that interest them. (Appropriate from kindergarten through sixth grade).

3. As a follow-up, invite the parents to come to the class, bring in some of the tools of their trade, talk to the children for a short time, and have the children ask questions.

4. The school is a great resource for occupational information. Invite the different workers around the school to come in and talk about their jobs. (Suggestions: custodian, secretary, cafeteria worker, nurse)

5. Encourage students to dream about what they would like to do as an adult. Have them pantomime a job and let other students guess who they are or what they are doing. Encourage them to do research—even as early as first grade. Suggest that they observe somebody working and then act out the job in the class. Children interested in the same profession can work together. Those interested in medicine, for example, could act out surgeon, nurse, anesthetist.

6. Ask students in the upper grades who have interesting hobbies to explain them to your children. Perhaps go a step further and relate different occupations to those hobbies. Lower grade children often have hobbies, such as collecting coins, that could be used in the discussion.

7. Upper grade children who have part-time jobs (paper routes, babysitting, yard work) can explain the satisfactions they get from their jobs; what they don't like; how they are going to spend their money. All speakers that come into the classroom should be encouraged to talk about the satisfaction they gain and the skills they need for their job.

8. Have students write a resume of their own skills (weeding, babysitting, cutting grass, ironing). Encourage them to sell their skills around the neighborhood. This could begin a discussion on what kinds of skills different grade level children have that could be used to make money. Center another discussion on how the children should present themselves for a job.

9. Have discussions in the classroom about the importance of all kinds of jobs and how they relate to society.

10. Have workmen such as auto mechanics or TV repairmen work on small jobs in the back of the classroom. No lecture involved; merely have the person stay there several days doing his job in the back of the room. Let the children ask questions when they want to know something. This has been tried in several schools and proved very successful.

11. Have students draw something about occupations they are familiar with. When they are finished, have them describe the meaning of their drawing. Project the students' drawings and read their explanations for the whole class. Discuss the families the occupations belong to and explore methods of obtaining occupational goals. Ask students to volunteer to gather photographs and other information about the occupations representative of different families and present them in class at a later time.

12. Have the students work on a newspaper. Give each person in the class the opportunity to write something. They can advertise things they want to sell, they can write a story about anything. Have them go through the whole process of collecting the data, writing about it, setting the type if you have a small printing press; follow up with a trip to a real newspaper plant.

13. Take field trips. Prior to the field trip, contact the person in charge and tell him the kinds of questions your grade level children are likely to ask and the things they might be interested in.

Career Awareness—How?

The great temptation in all curriculum planning is to leap immediately to the questions: "What content shall we teach?" "What topics must we cover?" "Will it take extra time?" Consideration of the last question especially prompts me to say that the basic concept of Career Development Education is to employ all disciplines already included in the curriculum; this is extremely important to remember for as you already know, education is geared to the readiness of the student.

When a student comes to school, he is usually open to new experiences. If the instructor is sensitive to the student's needs and maintains maximum flexibility with minimum restrictions, the young person's drive to learn about his environment can be productive and satisfying. I can see no greater opportunity for accomplishing the opportunity for this learning than through a meaningful series of career awareness situations. The sensitive teacher does help the student keep his basic motivation of "wanting to know" by offering, as many of you already have done, situations of real live interaction with persons who can readily relate often far better than you the answers to the student's interests which are derived from his trying to make sense out of a confusing world. It is from this honest educational endeavorment that, hopefully, his open and questioning attitude will continue after completion of his formal education.

Each of you already have your instructional objectives, no matter at what level, but an instructional objective describes an intended outcome rather than a summary of content. You, the teacher, must decide what changes you want to see in the student's ability to perform as a result of his learning unit or course. These changes in behavior are based upon the student's development of concepts, understandings, and skills as well as new attitudes. Each of you already have received a broad array of prepared changes which were written by me, and possibly they will be helpful; but I do believe that the individual teacher must take an active role in determining his or her own expected student changes according to his or her philosophy of education. You, the teacher, must take the initiative and design or implement meaningful situations of career awareness while maintaining a constant effort to permit full exploration and flexibility in your teaching effort.

Figure 1 is a sample sheet which indicates a possible method of creating orderliness in your career awareness planning. It is only a sample and created simply to indicate a logically planned sequence of expected student outcomes and activities which will facilitate their reality. It is hoped that each of you will adopt a similar method not only for your own use (one of which may be to periodically evaluate the success of your activity) but also for the possibility of sharing with your fellow instructors.

Contributed Career Awareness Experiences Grades K–6

Note: Similar duplicated situations are usually indicated in this listing only once for the purpose of clarity except where there is indicated additional valued experience. Sincere appreciation is extended to all contributors.

1. A trapper visited the class with a dead badger relating expertise of trapping to the class.
2. Visit a bakery. Make a cake in class and emphasize the units of weights and measures.
3. Missionaries visit the class and show film of their travels and experiences.
4. Carpenter working on a project in class offering the students an opportunity to relate to his work and tools.
5. Show films about the construction trades which indicate the many different types of workmen.
6. Scuba diver appeared in diving gear and related to the students the role of a professional scuba diver.

FIGURE 1

CAREER AWARENESS, INFORMATIONAL AND ORIENTATIONAL,
GRADES K–6

Carpenter Appears at School and Actually Constructs Project
WITH STUDENT HELP. . . . . GRADE K

EXPECTED OUTCOMES

Students gain concept of cost and money . . .
Students develop identification with lumber yard workers . . .
Students relate to broader environment . . .
Students acquire simple manual and mental skills . . .
Students develop reading habits . . . .
Students learn to get along and work together . . . .
Students acquire satisfaction in the task of learning . . . .
Students develop decision-making . . . .
Students begin to understand responsibility . . . .
Students begin to know themselves . . . .
Students begin to appreciate citizenship . . .

DOING ACTIVITIES

Class visits lumber yard and purchases materials . . .
Class views films related to wood and wood products . . .
Class reads books on construction . . .
Class views building under construction . . .
Class paints project and possibly sells project . . .
Class shares learning with another class . . . .

221

7. Use of vocabulary lists—words often related to different types of careers.
8. Discussion of postal workers culminating with the students building a post office with each student taking a turn at selling stamps to be posted on valentines to be mailed. Two students worked as mail sorters. Play money was used, and students were required to make change.
9. Use of films, magazines, and books leading to discussion of careers.
10. Police officer and firemen visit classroom.
11. Farmers visit classroom and relate the importance of raising crops.
12. Each student related to other class members the nature of their parent's occupation.
13. Field trip to Foster Dam, tree farm, and fire department.
14. Students gather articles from newspapers, magazines, etc., about astronauts and had a lively, meaningful discussion in the classroom.
15. Veterinarian visits classroom and relates to care of animals.
16. Dentist discussed care and repair of teeth to class.
17. Observation of regular important school employees, custodians, cooks, secretaries, teachers, and the principal.
18. Dioramas made depicting logging and sawmill operations after discussion in social studies.
19. Sheep rancher visited the school with a bummer lamb and explained sheep ranching culminating with the son of the rancher bringing in many items of necessary equipment used in sheep ranching such as ear markers and tags.
20. Postal employee, the father of a student, visited the school and discussed the postal system.
21. Field trip to Foster Dam—students observed various jobs being done. They saw the machine shop operation complete with machinist working. They also saw a fish biologist who was involved in helping the fish get over the dam.
22. Filling out employment applications. Students found difficulty in reading, understanding, and completing the forms. They gained the realization of the importance of reading. A mock employment interview culminated the activity.
23. Chicken rancher visited the classroom and related to the students the various tasks, responsibilities, and requirements necessary for the raising and marketing of chickens.
24. Former logger, now an instructor, discussed logging and the characteristics of a logger's living habits.
25. Visit to Foster Dam where students gained an awareness of natural resource conservation, electricians, and engineers. The gained concepts were further developed through discussion, report writing, and art work.

26. Commercial fisherman visited class and discussed commercial fishing to the class. Films pertaining to fishing were later shown.

27. Different inventions discussed in class during a social studies period. Airplanes, cars, telephone, telegraph, electricity, steel making, and railroads were discussed.

28. A unit was done on advertising techniques. Different methods of advertising were learned and students were given the opportunity to write their own ads.

29. School newspaper began; each student had specific duties to perform in order to get the paper ready for distribution.

30. Flannel boards, puppets, plays, and coloring books used with discussion of various careers.

31. Clown visits classroom, circus films shown and later puppets were made.

32. Doctor visits school, gives shots to students, shows and explains many of his tools.

33. Garbage collection discussed, students watch men pick up school garbage. High school students are permitted to visit the classroom and relate on ecology.

34. Class visits city library and check out books.

35. Make butter and ice cream in class using measuring devices.

36. Use teletrainer kit—later construct tin can telephones.

37. Visit state capitol for gaining concept of public officials.

38. A student's father constructed an incubator and actual eggs were hatched in class. Constant observation was made and a record kept of development. This was culminated by a hatchery worker appearing before the class and a visit to a hatchery was planned.

39. A trip to the coast where students see an actual diver working at the Underseas Garden.

40. A trip to a fish cannery enabled the students to observe the preparation of fish by many different workers. Many students did not relate the necessity of mechanics required for canning fish.

41. Students enter into track competition and are given an awareness of athletes who make athletics a career.

42. A comparison was made of job opportunities today as contrasted to 100 years ago.

43. A trip to Oregon State Marine Science Laboratory where students were introduced to an oceanographer who eagerly related aspects of his profession.

44. A student related to the class the occupation of his father, an excavator. Other students related the occupations of their fathers later.

45. Students are directed to pretend they are employed on a job and are instructed to research the occupation, describe it, and report it both orally and written.

46. Discussion concerning the advantages and disadvantages of skilled and unskilled jobs.

47. Discussion on different types of homes, trailers, apartments, etc., with an in-depth discussion of the different kinds of people who inhabit them. An example used is the construction worker who often lives in a trailer house.

48. Class visited a bank where students were given a complete tour of facilities and were shown how the many complicated machines operated.

49. Class visited bakery where students were given an actual demonstration on commercial baking.

50. Class visited an optometrist and were shown the process of fitting glasses and of the machines used to check eyes.

51. Class visited warehouse where persons employed related where articles were to go and how they would be sent.

52. Class visited local florist where they saw how plants were cared for and how floral arrangements were made.

53. Class visited zoo by bus. The bus driver's occupation is thoroughly discussed along with the persons who work at the zoo.

54. At the beginning of the school year all students are taken on a tour of the school. They meet the principal, secretaries, cooks, custodians, and librarians. The occupation and duties of each are discussed.

55. Class participation in activity entitled "classroom duties." Students rotate weekly, becoming room helpers. Children relate to the custodian's duties by picking up, putting things away, arranging desks, etc. Students take weekly turns at being lunchroom helpers, going to the lunchroom for straws, napkins, silverware, etc. They relate this to waiters and waitresses. The students get acquainted with the cooks and bakers.

56. Classroom is arranged with interest centers which permits the students to learn the workings of different machines such as tape recorders, record players, viewmasters.

57. Model store set up in classroom after visit to grocery store. Students assumed different role playing in the store situation.

58. Viewed a comprehensive film distributed by the Goodwill agency which does indicate many people with handicaps doing many different kinds of jobs.

59. A trip to a cheese factory where the students have an opportunity to learn cheese-making process and the roles of the workers involved.

60. A high school student came to class and took a lawn mower apart. He discussed the role of a mechanic and further related to gas station attendant tune-up men.

61. An O.C.E. professor presented material on Northwest Indians. The students not only learned about Indians, but also about college professors.

62. A comprehensive unit in the optical field by a knowledgeable person included studying parts of eye, eye safety, diseases of the eye, and the role of the optometrist and opthalmologist, and the making of glasses, which included how glass is made and then ground. This was culminated by actual dissection of several cow's eyes where certain parts were identified.

63. Classroom officers are elected and a discussion is held as to what attributes are necessary for becoming public officials. Not only officials on local and state level are discussed but also on the federal level.

64. The role of the weatherman is discussed with the aid of actual weather reports, newspapers, etc.

65. Mathematics is related to building construction in a unit and measure class period.

66. A real estate person has come to the classroom during social studies and related the real estate business in Mexico while the students were studying that particular country.

67. A dentist visited the classroom and related experiences of dentistry he encountered while visiting some primitive Indian tribes.

68. Reading in class the magazine "Jack and Jill" which has regular articles entitled "My Father Works at. . . ."

69. Students are directed to interview their parents concerning their occupations and then make a report to the class.

70. At the beginning of the school year an occupational goal inventory is taken of each student. Relationship to the students' chosen occupational goal is then related to their studies in the classroom. Along with relating the academic studies to an occupation, the integrity, and honesty holding value in preference to the get-rich-quick schemes is discussed.

71. A student's father who works in a plywood mill brought some plywood to school and related how the plywood was made; this culminated with a trip to a plywood mill.

72. A student's parent taking a correspondence course in art came to class and related the basics of art and the role of an artist.

73. A piano tuner came to class and tuned the piano.

74. Hobbies are stressed. In stamp collecting the students discuss different people from different countries, their occupation, etc.

75. Class took a train trip to Portland. The students were introduced to persons working on the train.

76. When class discusses social studies and questions come up that cannot

be answered, the student is asked to talk to his parents and bring back an answer.

77. Show film to the class entitled "Why Fathers Work?" and follow with students writing what would happen if everyone stopped working.

78. Have students paint a picture of themselves in the role of an occupation they would like. (One student painted himself in the White House.)

79. Class forms a committee which will plan a community indicating what businessmen will be there, etc. This includes dozens of careers.

80. Class visits a pheasant farm and students become knowledgeable of the persons who work there.

81. A trapper visited the class and brought several beavers to school. He explained to the students the art of trapping, processing, and selling furs.

82. Class visited television studio where they became acquainted with the persons who worked there.

83. Drug abuse officer visited the class and related the hazard of drugs and further described his occupational role.

84. Class plans a trip to a commercial airport where students will have an opportunity to become acquainted with the many different kinds of workmen there.

CAREERS EDUCATION CENTERED GROUP GUIDANCE FOR SECONDARY SCHOOLS (7-12)

I. Statement of the Problem

INTRODUCTION

The staff, students, and patrons of Springfield School District #19 are, no less than others in our society, extremely concerned about the nature and quality of its educational offerings. Of particular concern has been the realization that only a minority of its students are prepared upon graduation to assume a meaningful, productive, and self-fulfilling role in the occupational world, or at least to be embarked upon a well-defined path toward such a role. There has been some fear that for many the schools are those of which Commissioner Marland spoke that, "... only result in additional millions of young men and women leaving our high schools, with or without benefit of diploma, unfitted for employment, unable or unwilling to go on to college, and carrying away little more than an enduring distaste for education in any form, unskilled and unschooled."

This material was developed cooperatively by Project C.O.R.E. (Careers Oriented Relevant Education) of Oregon State University, Cas F. Heilman, Director, and by the Springfield School District #19, Springfield, Oregon, Bobie Newman and Carl E. Marking, Coordinators.

ROLE OF THE SCHOOL

The Oregon Board of Education has declared that public schools in Oregon are responsible for providing every young person with educational opportunities that will enable him to develop to his full potential. The Board has defined this to mean that schools have a three-fold objective to help young people: (a) discover their individual interests and abilities, (b) explore the many avenues of productive activity which might challenge their individual talents, and (c) learn the wise exercise of freedom of choice, self-direction, self-discipline, and responsibility.

II. The Rationale for Career Education

BACKGROUND

The rationale for Career Education has many dimensions. Over the past 50 years various names have been given to similar programs—vocational education, manual training, occupational education, etc. These programs have all had at least one purpose in common—to prepare students for work. Various degrees of success have been achieved through these programs. Our society, which has tended to use the college degree as a measuring stick for success, has prevented enrollment in vocational programs from increasing and vocational curriculum emphasis from occurring. Recently, many educators, businessmen, and industrial leaders have seen a need for a change in attitude. Further commitment by society and education needs to occur before needed career education opportunities will be made available to all students.

There are many values for students participating in an educational program aimed at preparing students for the world of work: (1) All students should have some skill and knowledge for the work world. (2) The economic values of having people prepared for work are obvious. (3) It is certainly desirable to prepare high school graduates with the ability to be self-supporting. (4) College bound students will benefit from some knowledge of occupational opportunities and they will also benefit from some exposure to practical educational experiences.

GOAL CENTERED EXPERIENCES

Since most students are goal-centered, students' goals should be the prime consideration in establishing curricula. The task of education should be to assist students in setting and attaining goals. Experiences based on students' future careers should be available on a continuous basis throughout elementary and junior high schools. Students should then be able to make a realistic choice of programs at the tenth or eleventh year level. When, *after adequate counseling,* a student changes his goals, every effort should be made to assist him in proceeding in a new direction.

CAREER CLUSTER PROGRAMS

In the past "Vocational Education" has been offering programs which trained students for specific jobs. In our changing technology many of today's jobs require additional training, in many cases even before the student begins work. Most eleventh and twelfth year students are not ready to choose a *specific* occupation. Therefore, Oregon and the Springfield School District proposes a career cluster program wherein juniors and seniors select a *family* of occupations (cluster) upon which they desire to concentrate for two or three hours per day. For example, students enrolled in a construction cluster would be exposed not only to carpentry, but also concrete work, masonry, plumbing, electrical wiring, framing, roofing, etc. This student would then be well aware of the construction occupations and should have attained many job entry level skills and knowledges. There are 18 career clusters which have been identified by the Oregon Board of Education together with state advisory committees from business and industry. This cluster approach to occupational education at the senior high level seems appropriate for high school students who need a background to be able to select an occupation after graduation. It also enables students to *readily* make career changes which he desires to make and to adapt to changes occurring in industry.

INTERDISCIPLINARY APPROACH

The basic courses in math, science, communications, etc., are very essential to the student's achievement in a career cluster program. Efforts must be made by all teachers to interrelate other academic skills with each student's career interest. Examples from the world of work should be integrated into the classrooms.

III. The Objectives

1. To provide sufficient experiences and information at all grade levels so that students will be aware of their abilities and therefore make wise selections of career goals.
2. To prepare students at the secondary level with skills and knowledge necessary for entry into *future* employment in an occupation or group of closely related occupations (clusters).

3. To provide education that is socially and economically relevant to the needs of the individual and to the manpower requirements of the nation, state, and community.
4. To provide adequate and continuous guidance of students to assure proper placement in career education programs.
5. To provide curriculums in career education which link general education (3 R's) to the world of work.
6. To utilize all personnel—administrative, supervisory, teacher education, state department, teachers, and counselors in the achievement of career education objectives.
7. To provide systematic evaluation of programs by administrators, teachers, and advisory committees *to assure its relevance* to a dynamic and changing world of work.

IV. The Principles

During all of the changes which have occurred over the past in vocational education, certain sound principles have remained through these changes. The degree by which these principles have been adhered to has varied according to economic and social conditions but they remain the important challenge in maintaining quality programs. The following should be some of the principles of the Career Education Program:

1. Programs should be relevant to the world of work.
2. Advisory committees composed of members who have current and substantial knowledge of their field should be effectively used.
3. Programs of instruction should be based upon and designed to meet individual and community needs.
4. Vocational guidance should be adequate for *all* students.
5. Follow-up should be made of all students completing and dropping out of career cluster programs.
6. Placement assistance for students into all types of post graduate programs should be made available (military, occupational, apprenticeship, community college, 4-year college, entry level jobs, etc.)
7. All students who need, want, and can profit by instruction should be allowed to enter programs. After adequate counseling, if a student wishes to change to a different program, this change should be made as smooth as possible.

8. Education for work is a continuous process and should not be limited to high schools.
9. Facilities and equipment used in instruction should be comparable to those found in the occupation for which training is offered.
10. To be most effective the training should be offered as close to actual job entry as possible.
11. The cluster training programs offered should be based on projected employment needs at the local, state, and national level.
12. All programs K–14 should be articulated and coordinated so that students can move freely from one level of instruction to another without excessive repetition or serious gaps.
13. Cooperative work experience programs should only be offered to as many students as can be placed and supervised *adequately.*
14. The conditions under which instruction is given should duplicate, as nearly as possible, desirable conditions in the occupation itself and, at the same time, should provide effective learning situations.
15. Teachers should be competent in the occupation for which they are giving instruction and possess adequate professional qualifications for teaching. All cluster teachers should return to their occupation periodically.
16. Youth groups which provide leadership and social development opportunities should be a planned part of the career education program.
17. Flexibility should allow the programs to change with our changing technology.
18. Periodic evaluation by staff and students and citizens should be made to determine if programs are meeting objectives and goals.
19. Inservice training should be available for career cluster teachers due to the changing nature of the subject matter which should be taught.

V. The Challenge for Career Education

The preceding rationale, objectives, and principles will serve as guidelines for program development. Efforts will need to be made to continuously examine programs in relationship to them. Presently, certain gaps exist between these guidelines and the present operating programs. The following is an attempt to identify and analyze this gap.

Gap #1 There needs to be complete acceptance of career education by educators, parents, and the community so that students participating in these programs are not degraded, discouraged or insulted by their career choice.

Gap #2 Correlation between skill training in the business, homemaking and industrial classes and the exploratory (SUTOE) classes is necessary so that more realistic goals can be established by students.

Gap #3 Thorough staff understanding and commitment to true cluster programs is needed to achieve our goals.

Gap #4 Guidance and counseling departments need to re-evaluate their goals and priorities.

Gap #5 New and innovative approaches to adding relevancy to our general academic education programs need to be explored.

Gap #6 Occupational awareness approaches to elementary level career education programs need study.

Gap #7 Program evaluation on a regular and planned basis is necessary.

VI. What We Know About the Learner

A. *1969 Graduate Follow-Up Study*

The following factors from a follow-up study of 256 students from the graduating classes of 1969 Springfield High School and Thurston High School seem significant to long range career education planning. (Conducted within 6-9 months after graduation, returns were about equally received from males and females.)

1. Approximately 7% were married

2. 68% indicated they had seldom, and 9% indicated they had never, seen a counselor in High School
63% indicated they needed more counseling in High School
27% indicated they needed more *educational* counseling in High School
38% indicated they needed more *vocational* counseling in High School

3. 37% of the students "knew what they wanted to do" when they were in the 12th grade; 18% in the 11th; and 12% in the 10th grade (total: 67%)

4. Of the 64 students indicating that they had participated in a work experience program (Distributive or Business Education or work release):

> 50% indicated—very valuable
> 25% indicated—take it or leave it
> 2% indicated—rather taken another elective
> 23% did not respond

5. Graduates indicated the "most help in planning for your education, career, or life's work" from the following sources in rank order (number in parentheses indicates responses):

1. Parents—(130)
2. Teachers—(104)
3. Friends—same age (88)
4. Reading material—(87)
5. Adult friends—(76)
6. Relatives—(48)
7. Counselors—(35)
8. Coaches—(24)

6. Graduates indicated that the following sources assisted them in finding their first job after graduation:

1. Friends and relatives (111)
2. Newspaper ads (18)
3. Teachers (13)
4. Public employment offices (8)
5. Private employment offices (7)
6. School counselors (3)

7. At time of survey (6-9 months after graduation):*

> 68% (174) had continued their education
> 18% 4-year colleges
> 41% community colleges
> 3% private colleges
> 3% business colleges, trade or military school, correspondents, etc.
> 3% other
> 8% entered armed forces
> 13% were working full time
> 22% were working part time
> 6% housewives
> 18% unemployed looking for work
> 7% unemployed not looking for work
> *Totals over 100% due to duplicate answers.

8. Most graduates indicated a lack of help in choosing a vocation and in securing a job.

Survey of 1970 Cluster Program Graduates (October, 1970)

In a survey of 1970 graduates of who participated in cluster programs, the following statistics were obtained:

31% continued their education; ½ of these in a field closely related to their cluster program in which they participated in high school

28% employed in the field in which they were trained

13% employed in job *not* related to training

2% entered the armed forces

13% were unemployed

4% were housewives

9% no response

B. *We know these things about the learning process which tend to indicate that small group work, individual understanding and varied learning media might make the vocational counseling process more successful than it has been in the past.*

1. By nature, humans prefer active involvement as opposed to passive learning acts. This is particularly true of young people, the younger the more applicable.
2. Facts memorized, unless continually used and reinforced, are quickly forgotten.
3. Learning rates differ markedly.
4. All students are not ready to profit from the same learning experiences at the same time.
5. Concepts acquired from a given learning situation are greatly influenced by the background of experience which the learner brings to the new situation and how he perceives this situation.
6. A single media will not communicate the same thing to all students at the same time.

C. *When thinking about vocational counseling and career choices we become aware of some of the students needs.*

1. A student needs to feel that someone is concerned about him as an individual.
2. The student needs to see the relevance of what he is doing in the classroom and the school situation to what is actually occurring in the world about him.
3. A student needs to be understood according to how he views reality.
4. A student needs to understand himself.
5. A student needs an opportunity to learn to better understand his motivations, abilities and opportunities.

6. A student needs to have a positive attitude about himself and his abilities before he can develop a positive attitude about the world about him.
7. Some students need a "home" at school, a place or a person where there is no pressure or threat.
8. A student needs to have an opportunity to develop a positive attitude about himself.
9. A student needs to experience success.
10. A student needs to know where he is before he can plan where it is that he is going.
11. A student needs to know where there is to go.
12. Students need experiences and educational counseling which make him aware of his abilities, values, and aptitudes at any level of his educational program.
13. Students need to develop an understanding of the inter-relatedness of occupations in order to make intelligent choices.
14. Students need a knowledge and understanding of significant data about self and the kinds of data needed for self-appraisal.
15. Students need a knowledge of the educational and vocational resources available to him in order to utilize these to maximize self potential.
16. Students need to understand that decision-making is a chain process rather than an event.
17. Students need to develop the ability to deal selectively with the environment by modifying it, as circumstances require.
18. Students need to know the additional educational opportunities available after termination of the high school experience.

D.   *We are also aware of these things about Vocational Choice and the student should also be aware of them.*

1. Vocational choice is a process rather than an event.
2. Vocational development consists of a series of stages.
3. The different stages can be identified.
4. Different personalities are attracted or repelled by certain occupational environments.
5. Needs both consciously and unconsciously affect vocational choice.
6. Accident plays a large role in vocational choice and development.
7. There is multipotentiality in both jobs and careers.
8. To some extent vocational choice is irreversible.
9. The self concept is influenced by contact with people and changes throughout life.

10. Success can have a decided effect on vocational choice and development.
11. An occupation has an effect on life style.
12. Vocational decision making consists of many compromises between both the individual and the occupation.

VII. Present Accomplishments in Vocational Awareness

A. *S.U.T.O.E.*

A number of devices have been tested in Springfield District in an effort to develop a viable career education program for the school and community. During the fall of 1969 Springfield junior highs initiated a new approach to career-decision-making called S.U.T.O.E. (Self-Understanding Through Occupational Exploration). The purpose of the S.U.T.O.E. program is to instill ideas concerning one broad aspect of the decision-making process, the investigation and evaluation of information about career opportunities and societal needs.

B. *C.O.R.E.*

A project begun in January of 1969 titled Careers Oriented Relevant Education (C.O.R.E.) has as its primary objective the development of a basis for a total program of curriculum decisions based upon a careers centered approach. One of its features is the concept of guidance services which replaces the traditional counselor-student relationship with a procedure whereby groups of personnel work with the student as a participant in decision-making. They mutually determine the sequence and career content of the student's educational program. Current career information is a vital part of three major steps in the sequence of learning experience as outlined in the C.O.R.E. concept. They are: (1) Discovery—discovering the world of careers, the requirements for engaging in them, etc. (2) Selection and Repetition—making choices which help an individual identify on an increasingly mature basis the direction which his life will take. (3) Refinement—gaining more knowledge of requirements, expectations, life styles, and occupational specialization in order to narrow choices to a specific field of endeavor.

In an effort to implement the above and broaden the offerings of the school district, the following programs were initiated.

C. *House: Student-Faculty Discussion Groups*

Initiated at the junior high level, the house program attempted to provide students with an opportunity to learn more about themselves, other students, the school, the community, and the world at large. This began in the form of a special time set aside in the schedule for student-student, and student-advisor interaction. House guide books were developed to assist teachers in working with students in the above setting and "clinics" scheduled to provide additional information and direction for the program. Surveys conducted in June, 1971 indicated that approximately one half the students and faculty felt that "house" was a success and wanted to continue the program. For the remaining one half, "house" appeared to lack sufficient structure and direction.

D. *Curricula Revision*

Increased utilization was made of team teaching, independent study, education "teacher aides," shorter length courses, and broader course offerings, particularly in previously established cluster areas.

E. *Work Experience Program*

A more meaningful work experience program was provided students enrolled in clusters. Students had an opportunity to: experience real life interviews, obtain valuable training, work and interact on a semi-equal basis with adults, and to develop job responsibilities, and the possibility of consequent full-time employment in their occupational area.

F. *Expanded Counseling Facilities*

The following expansions of existing counseling facilities and program occurred:

1. A work experience coordinator and a vocational counselor were hired to work with students in career education in the district.
2. VERIFY was implemented as a followup report to be plugged in to the student's career cluster and work experience and will be followed up through his Social Security number to determine subsequent job placement.

A common element present in each of the above was a focus on career education, community involvement, and increased awareness and understanding by and of the student. However, by and large, the school has continued to operate essentially in the same manner in which it has always operated with few basic concessions to the realities of the problems faced in a complex society.

VIII. For Improved Vocational Counseling

The Staffs of Thurston High School and Springfield High School are aware of the problem, the rationale, learning processes, student needs and the Oregon Board's emphasis of Career Education. With this awareness they have already implemented some programs which have been mentioned. Further they are recommending some approaches to improving career awareness, vocational counseling and the students self understanding.

The Thurston High group recommended a group guidance program that would promote faculty and student involvement in a common exploration of the four life roles: career, avocation, family life and citizenship. The base would be a common interest of a faculty member and a student in a subject or special interest area.

The Springfield High group has proposed an exploration of the four life roles in which a seminar type of format would be utilized.

It is possible to establish a base for exploration that would accomplish the same outcomes and would be a composite of both school proposals and with the addition of the Oregon State Board's clusters that would greatly expand the possibilities of achieving the stated outcomes in depth.

IX. A Model for a Career Education Centered Group Guidance

A. *A career education centered group guidance program could be established in which a student would:*

1. Be oriented to all of the clusters and C.O.R.E. four life roles.
2. Begin to build a personal profile sheet.
3. Select interest area under a heading established from the O.B.E. established Cluster Areas.
4. Be assigned to a staff member who has also indicated an interest or expertise in that cluster area. Interest would be sufficient or there could be a common search supported by very active research personnel.

B. *Staff would be involved in at least these things before receiving students:*

1. Oriented to career clusters

2. Oriented to C.O.R.E. and the four life roles
3. Orientation to the type of evaluative instruments being used in building the student personal profiles.
4. Possibly some orientation to some theories of individuality.

C. *Occupational interests or commitment would then be the base for exploration into the three remaining life roles:*

1. Avocational
2. Family
3. Citizenship

Particular consideration should be given as to how the student would relate himself to them in terms of potential occupational choices. That is, what sort of training is required and available; what are employment opportunities locally, regionally, nationally; What sort of family life do people in that occupation have? (Policemen have largest divorce rate in the nation.); What do these types of people do during their leisure time?; What sort of citizenship activities do people in this occupation become involved in? This will give the student some idea of the type of life style and interest that would help lead to optimum development and fulfillment in that area.

X. Operational Schematic of Career Education Centered Group Guidance

Steps for Student's Cluster Selection	Steps for Staff Cluster Selection
1. Career Cluster Awareness	1. Career Cluster Awareness
2. C.O.R.E.—four life roles exposure	2. C.O.R.E.—four life roles exposure
3. Personal profile sheet begun	3. Inservice on testing (profile sheet)
4. Student selection of cluster	4. Theories on individuality
	5. Selection of cluster

CLUSTERS

Metals
Construction
Electronics
Clerical
Bookkeeping Accounting
Secretarial
Marketing

Health
Food Service
Forestry
Agriculture
Industrial Mechanics
Graphic Arts
Child Care
Architecture and Engineering
Life Science and Medicine
Business Management
General Studies
Social Science and Law

Note: Activities will be planned to take students and staff through steps listed above prior to establishing guidance groups based on career clusters.

The student and the staff member would then explore the four life roles using the cluster and the profile sheet as base. Support for this common enterprise would be:

1. School staff
2. District Staff
3. Community people, Advisory people, etc.
4. Lane I.E.D. personnel
5. Lane Community College personnel
6. U. of O.–O.S.U. and other four year college people
7. State Board of Education people
8. Personnel from other school districts

XI. Implementation

Career Cluster, C.O.R.E., Orientation

There are many people who can be of invaluable aid in the implementation of the Career Education Model. They are people within our own school, our own district, Lane I.E.D., Oregon Board of Education, O.S.U., U. of O., other districts and the community. These people can and should be used for very valuable insight and input.

Some suggestions for the manner in which this orientation to Career Clusters, C.O.R.E., the four life roles, understanding evaluative instruments, individuality and vocational choice could be:

1. Over all presentation by various and appropriate resource people of necessary information to staff and students in large group settings, i.e., faculty meetings, student assemblies.
2. Development of "strike groups," a small core of people to include a faculty group, a student group, and a student-faculty group. These groups would be orientated in the several areas by the resource people. Once this is done the groups would move out to small group information sessions. These could be during prep periods, before school or after school, classrooms, lunch periods or whatever.
3. A combination of the two would be possible, overall presentation, and then the development of "strike groups" with the subsequent activity.

Once the orientation has been accomplished with the student and staff member and they feel well enough informed to make a sensible selection, they can make a selection and move into the Guidance groups. At this time any sort of scheduling arrangement that fits into the school system could be implemented to accomplish the objectives.

XII. Rationale for Career Education Centered Group Guidance

1. Career Education is the Oregon way.
2. Career Clusters have been established, after much research by the State Department of Labor and the Oregon Board of Education, as being relevant to the world of work.
3. Our school district has committed itself to career education and the Cluster Concept.
4. Thurston High School is a comprehensive high school that is committing itself to career education and the Cluster Concept and will be adding at least six more clusters to the six we already have by school years 1957–1976, four years from now.
5. Springfield High School is a comprehensive high school that is committing itself to Career Education and the Cluster Concept and will be adding six new clusters to the eight now offered.
6. The traditional curriculum could suggest for a group guidance base lacks some relevance as is pointed out by the very fact that we have C.O.R.E. and are searching for ways of making what we are doing more meaningful.
7. The State Board of Education has supportive services in each cluster area which would be a tremendous resource aid.

8. Lane I.E.D. is organizing its supportive services on the Careers Education Cluster Base.
9. The community colleges within Oregon are organized and organizing new programs on the Careers Education Cluster Base which will make the students articulation between high school and community college much more facile.
10. Articulation is now being established along these lines. There are cluster guides available which offer much information as to the future opportunities, skills, and talents required, etc.
11. The Northwest Regional Laboratory has compiled a huge listing of vocational and career relevant material that will be available this fall. It is listed under occupational classifications similar to clusters, not subject headings.
12. School life has been historically separated from life, work, and the community (i.e., relevant) and to base Group Guidance on subject matter heading would continue the process rather than initiate needed change.
13. Testing and Counseling- Administer Armed Forces Tests, Interests Tests, O.V.I.S., Edwards, Strong, and GATBY are established on an occupational basis rather than a subject base.

XIII. Student Objectives

1. Each student will be able to define realistic career goals based on interests and aptitudes.
2. Each student will demonstrate the ability to locate and apply information relative to career opportunities and requirements.
3. The student will understand and demonstrate an ability to go through a career decision-making process.
4. Each student will be able to list the entrance requirements or procedures for the following post-high school programs:
   a. Community College
   b. Junior College or University
   c. Training School
   d. Apprenticeship Programs and Requirements
   e. Armed Service Careers
   f. Post-high school job areas
5. Each student will be able to provide feedback concerning local career oriented programs and institutions, including:
   a. Lane Community College
   b. University or College

    c. Local Business Schools

    d. Other post-high school programs

6. Each student will demonstrate an awareness of the life style associated with the career(s) in which he is interested.

7. The student will be able to complete in writing an outline of the courses necessary and/or desirable to help fulfill his career goals.

8. Each student will be able to identify the career clusters available to him within school district #19.

9. Each student will be able to indicate through discussion with his teachers and classmates the relationship of the family life role, the avocational life role, and the citizenship life role to his tentative career choice.

10. The student will understand the overall picture of career education in Oregon.

K–6	7–9	10–12	13–16
Awareness	Exploration	Emphasis	Specialized

XIV. Staff Objective

1. Schools are a microcosm of the community. Students upon completion of high school enter the community for employment or post high school training. Therefore, schools need to develop an effective articulation with all segments of the community related to the educational program of the student.

2. The curriculum is, in many cases, too general and too often irrelevant to the needs of the student and society. One of the goals of Springfield School District is to provide a training ground for the student as an independent economic being. Therefore, the school will provide a comprehensive career education program utilizing the occupational area to explore the remaining life roles (avocational, citizen, family). Each teacher will, therefore, need to reevaluate course content and objectives in light of the four life roles.

3. In order to develop a student's maximal potential and to meet student and community needs, each school will provide placement services for the student's next life phase be it education or employment. Consequently the teacher will need to be aware of placement opportunities.

4. Staff and students will begin to see school in terms of career education.

5. The teacher will understand the overall goals and objectives of career education in Oregon.

6. The teacher will understand the four life roles as being a vehicle for evaluating relevance of present and planned curriculum.

7. The teacher will demonstrate a degree of competency in defining career cluster areas and/or in locating source materials dealing with career clusters.
8. The teacher will utilize resource and evaluative personnel in guidance sessions to widen the scope of his program, as he sees the need.
9. The teacher will be capable of assisting the students in determining realistic goals, in inventorying abilities and skills, and in establishing criteria for the selection of goals. (Interest tests, personal interviews, informal discussions, occupational research, etc.)
10. The teacher will gain in professional and personal growth through added knowledge of student needs, and the student as an individual, as well as an evaluation of his own responses and self-concept in the student-student and student-teacher interaction process.

XV. Resource People

Here is a partial listing of resource people who may be helpful in implementation.

C.O.R.E.	CAREER CLUSTERS	THEORIES OF INDIVIDUALITY	
District No. 19	District No. 19	Jerry Patterson	ORI
Chuck Crone	Cluster Instructors	Dick Withycomb	John Adams HS
Bob Myers	Carl Marking CWE	Marv Harmon	HRVHS
Stewart Pfeifle	Frank Alexander	Chuck Bowe	HRVHS
Conrad Roemer	Hartley Troftgruben	Dick Littman	U of O
Don Kalstad	OSU		
Bob Tormey		Contact Carl Marking for more information on these people.	
Jerry Bishop	Dr. Henry Tempest		
Sue Powell	Dr. Richard Spansiani		
OSU	OBE		
Dr. Cas Heilman	Dr. Rich Schmidt		
Dr. Keith Goldhammer	John Pheasant		
Dr. Dick Gardner	Monty Multanan		
OBE	Lane IED		
Dr. Dan Dunham	Bill Manley		

A wealth of people are available from the "ESCAPE" Program at the University of Oregon. Tutors, Counselor Aids, Teacher Aids. These people can be great time savers as well as beneficial to the program.

Note: Resource contacts with O.S.U. and the Oregon Board of Education should be made through Mr. Frank Alexander or Hartley Troftgruben in the Career Education Supervisors Office.

Note: The profile sheet that has been mentioned has not been developed. This should be done soon, because it will form the basis for initial interaction. The Profile Sheet would contain such information as:

Aptitude test scores (not IQ)
Achievement Test Scores
Interest test Scores
Classes taken . . . grades
Special interests
Achievements

FACULTY TALENTS AND INTERESTS SURVEY

NAME_____

I. The purpose of this survey is to identify cluster areas, or interest areas staff have which may have application as resources to be used in the establishment of Guidance Groups.

II. Among the interest areas from which the students will choose, make a first, second, and third choice on the basis of your own talents.

____Mechanical and Repair	____Social Services
____General Clerical	____Graphic Arts
____Basic Marketing	____Health
____Agriculture Occupations	____Metals Work
____Food Service	____Bookkeeping
____Construction	____Woods
____Secretarial	Professional
____Electronics	____Architecture and Engineering
____Social Science and Law	____Life Science and Medicine
____General Studies	____Business Management

STUDENT INTEREST AREA SURVEY

(to be used in forming cluster advising groups)

NAME_____ CLASS   10 11 12
    (last) (first) (middle initial)   (circle one)

M   F
SEX   (circle one)

From the fifteen areas below, select the one which interests you most:

____Mechanical and Repair	____Social Services
____General Clerical	____Graphic Arts

____Basic Marketing

____Agriculture Occupations

____Food Service

____Construction

____Secretarial

____Electronics

____Social Science and Law

____General Studies

____Health

____Metals Work

____Bookkeeping

____Woods

Professional

____Architecture and Engineering

____Life Science and Medicine

____Business Management

CAREER- CENTERED CURRICULUM FOR VOCATIONAL COMPLEXES IN MISSISSIPPI: AN EXEMPLARY PROGRAM

Introduction

The career-centered concept views the total school experiences of students as preparation for life, with earning a living a prime focus. The concept views people as needing three types of skills to be successful in life, namely: (1) sociological skills in order to adjust to and participate in changes in the local community, state, nation, and world; (2) psychological skills to enable the individual to achieve self-awareness and develop desirable personal characteristics; and (3) occupational skills which afford the individual an opportunity to earn a living and which serve as a base for continuous growth and advancement in a career.

The career-centered curriculum in Mississippi is designed to provide these minimal skills for the students. Components of the entire school system are focused upon the career development concept in order to increase the awareness of career choices among students.

This exemplary program was developed in the Jones County School System, Mississippi, pursuant to a grant from the U.S. Office of Education and the Division of Vocational-Technical Education, Department of Education, State of Mississippi, under the supervision of J. Harold McMinn, State Exemplary Program Director.

The career-centered concept begins in the elementary school with students being introduced to a realistic picture of the world of work. It then progresses to occupational exploratory experiences for the student in the junior high school. As the student progresses, the exploratory experiences narrow toward the point where students make decisions concerning educational preparations and/or occupational choices. As students' decisions are reached in high school, additional occupational training becomes available to them through the area vocational complex. Occupational education of a more specialized nature is also available to interest students in a post-secondary vocational-technical program in the area.

Location

The exemplary project, a *Career-Centered Curriculum for Vocational Complexes in Mississippi,* is located in the Jones County School System. The system is located in the Coastal Plains area of the southeastern part of the state. The county is classified as being depressed and has a high rate of unemployment.

The school system is made up of ten elementary schools which feed into three combination junior-senior high schools. The three high schools serve as feeder units for a centrally located vocational complex. In addition, a community college which includes a post-secondary vocational-technical program is located within the county.

The Jones County School System has an enrollment of approximately 8,000 students, with a professional staff of some 380 teachers and administrators. It serves a school district with a population of approximately 61,000, of whom 25 percent are described as being "disadvantaged."

Purpose

The goal of this exemplary program is to provide guidelines and give impetus to the development of career-centered curriculums for vocational complexes in Mississippi. It is designed to develop and demonstrate to teachers, administrators, and the public a coordinated and integrated program of career development from the first grade through post-secondary vocational-technical education.

Emphasis is being placed upon demonstrating that exploratory occupational experiences are essential ingredients in the educational experience of all students if they are to arrive at sound career decisions. This is being accomplished through relating the exemplary program to existing educational opportunities at the elementary, junior high, secondary, and adult levels.

Objectives

- To relate occupational instruction and counseling to elementary students and faculty members.
- To establish an intensive program of occupational guidance and counseling in the junior high and secondary schools.
- To implement the Occupational Orientation Program for all students in the junior high schools.
- To provide cooperative education (work-experience) through local businesses and industries.
- To provide a wide variety of occupational training programs through the vocational complex and post-secondary vocational-technical center (community college).
- To provide intensive occupational training programs during the day or evening for those about to leave school without salable skills.
- To establish the career-centered curriculum as an integral part of the school system's curriculum.
- To provide adequate placement and post-training work counseling for students.
- To develop curriculum guides and instructional material which might be utilized by other career-centered programs.
- To stimulate career-centered curriculum development in other school systems.

Procedure

The procedure designed to implement the career-centered concept spans all levels of the educational ladder. It places heavy emphasis upon reorientation of the traditional school concept about occupational education. During the process, students are exposed to occupational education as they enter the elementary school and continue learning about, and preparing for, the world of work as they progress through elementary, junior high, secondary, and post-secondary schools in the area.

The procedure views the levels of occupational education as being a pyramid, with students making decisions about careers and needed training based upon broad exploratory experience and counseling obtained through the program. As students narrow their choices about occupational selections, individual occupational experiences become more sophisticated and intensified.

The process begins with the elementary schools providing students with sufficient occupational information and counseling to meet the needs of all children according to their interests and abilities. To accomplish this basic goal, local exemplary program personnel are providing basic services to the elementary faculties. These services include obtaining occupational information, providing counseling, and providing resource persons to be utilized by the elementary faculties. In addition, workshops, seminars, and field trips are held to assist the elementary faculties to incorporate career development into the regular instructional program.

In the junior high school, students expand and intensify their exploratory experiences in the world of work through a specially designed course, Occupational Orientation. In Occupational Orientation, the students' self-awareness of the world of work is increased by capitalizing upon the introduction to occupational information received at the elementary level. The course is designed to provide exploratory experiences in a broad range of occupational categories and levels, with opportunities for students to make comprehensive educational and occupational decisions rather than being forced into limited choices. In the course, the students are brought to grip with self and society, self and occupation, and self and personality development. Throughout the course, the students see career development in logical sequenced steps traversing the entire occupational choice process.

The career-centered curriculum at the senior high school level is a continuation of exploratory experiences received by students in the elementary and junior high levels, with additional emphasis being placed on occupational preparation activities. Students receive assistance in planning for and attaining vocational goals and preferences, either in the form of additional vocational training or work experience. These experiences are obtained by the students through the vocational programs of agriculture, auto mechanics, building trades, cooperative education, consumer home economics, general metal trades, industrial drafting, industrial electricity, or office occupations, which are offered either in the three high school attendance centers or the area vocational complex.

A concerted remedial program is operated for students who are identified as potential dropouts in conjunction with the exemplary program. This remedial program is equipping potential dropouts with competence and skills necessary for pursuing further vocational training in keeping with their occupational objectives.

The career-centered concept is enhanced by the availability of extensive vocational-technical training available through an area post-secondary school (Jones County Junior College). The vocational programs at the junior college are open-ended and accept students at any level who can make progress in the occupational training programs. Offerings available in the post-secondary facilities include: forestry, horticulture, livestock technology, distribution and marketing, supermarket training, practical nursing, data processing, secretarial science, building construction technology, drafting and design, electronics technology, mechanical technology, air conditioning and refrigeration, auto mechanics, horology, machine shop, radio and television repair, and welding.

Evaluation

One of the major components of the exemplary program from its implementation has been evaluation. The gathering of evaluative data has been a constant process which has aided in: (1) redirection of programmatic efforts; (2) annual and long-range program planning; and (3) meeting accountability requirements.

The very nature of the exemplary program prevented the use of established arbitrary evaluation standards. However, meaningful evaluation information of another nature is being utilized in assessing the effectiveness of the program.

The evaluation system consists of a thorough study of the process through which the program was inaugurated and is being conducted. It is focused upon the impact it has upon the career development of students in the Jones County School System. The evaluation system may be summarized into four major stages of evaluation:

1. Environmental Analysis—Involving an analysis of factors affecting the program and the students.

2. Resource Analysis—Involving an analysis of financial resources, facilities, equipment, personnel, etc., which are utilized in the operation of the program.

3. Process Analysis—Involving an analysis of the actual procedures being employed to meet the stated goals and objectives of the exemplary program. (Methods and techniques utilized, policies, training experiences, etc.)

4. Product Analysis—Involving an analysis of the extent to which the program has brought about changes in the educational system's product—the student.

Evaluation activities are being conducted by three specific groups, namely: (1) local exemplary program personnel; (2) State Division of Vocational Education personnel; and (3) independent evaluation specialists. Evaluative information from all three sources is being utilized by local program personnel and administrators, and the State Exemplary Program Director to improve the operation and effectiveness of the program during its operation.

A UNIVERSE MODEL OF OCCUPATIONAL EDUCATION FOR PIKEVILLE, KENTUCKY

Introduction

Pikeville is a mountain community of approximately 6,000 people and located in the largest and eastern most county of Kentucky. The city is the smallest community to have a Model Cities program. While Pikeville is a major service center for the county of about 60,000 people and a geographic area which includes nearly 200,000 people, the primary economic activities are coal mining and education.

There are two school systems in Pike County. The larger is the Pike County School District which includes all of the County except the city of Pikeville. The career education program is in progress in the Pikeville Independent School District, which serves only the city of Pikeville. There are nearly 1,300 students enrolled in one elementary school, one junior high school, and one high school.

Under Project Director, John D. Jenkins, this material was prepared for the Conference on Career Education, Lexington, Kentucky, October 14-15, 1971. In conjunction with the Pikeville Model Cities Program, the project is a cooperative effort between the Pikeville Independent School District, Pikeville, Kentucky, Charles Spears, Superintendent, and Eastern Kentucky University, Richmond, Kentucky.

253

The Model Cities program has assumed the challenge of improving the physical, social, economic, and educational conditions in Pikeville. As a portion of the total effort, a Part D, Exemplary Educational Project was funded for the Pikeville Independent School District. The project was prepared, submitted, and funded through Eastern Kentucky University. Certainly there were multiple motivations for seeking funds for a career development program. Some of the major reasons for selecting career education as a mechanism for educational change in Pikeville were:

1. Career education provides the opportunity to re-orient the focus of schools to be directed more toward life applications of education than before. Until the project was funded, the primary emphasis was on academic education which led a high number of students to select a college education as their career objective.
2. It is expected that the changes in the educational program in Pikeville will make the community more attractive to families who might want to move into Pikeville.
3. If the economic base in Pikeville is to be adequately diffused, new business and industry must have an ample supply of competent employees. The career education program in Pikeville should provide a system to develop a labor force to fulfill the employment demand.
4. For years the young people in eastern Kentucky have been migrating out of the area to the larger cities where they can secure employment. In many instances the young people have been unable to effectively compete for the jobs in the cities. While one of the overall objectives of the Model Cities program is to reduce the out-migration, it is doubtful that the objective will ever be completely fulfilled. The career education program will offer those students who leave, the opportunity to attain skills which will permit them to function on an equal basis with others.

Several other educational programs are either planned or are in operation in places other than in the schools. The nurse training program and a mining technology program (Pikeville College) are examples of programs which are currently functioning. The focus of each of the programs will be career education. When all of the programs are implemented, Pikeville will have a "birth-to-death" educational program with career education as the primary focus.

SCOPE
Over the three year period, from July 1, 1970 to June 30, 1973, career education programs will be introduced for students in grades 1–12. Initial efforts have been devoted to the elementary school (1–6) program. The

major focus of this year's activities will be devoted to the development of the junior high (7–8) programs and improving and increasing career offerings in the high school (7–12). During the final year of the project, attention will be placed on total program refinement and increasing the quantity and quality of high school programs for career education.

PERCENT OF STUDENTS INVOLVED

When the program is complete, 100 percent of the students in grades 1–12 will be involved in career education programs. Currently 100 percent of the students in grades 1–8 are directly and actively involved in career education activities. Approximately 50 percent of the students in grades 9–12 are participating in career development programs. The 50 percent figure will expand to 100 percent because all programs in the school will be directed toward helping students achieve life oriented goals.

GOALS AND OBJECTIVES

Below is a list of overall goals followed by several more specific objectives for each segment of the career education program in Pikeville.

A. To establish curricula in the elementary school on two levels, 1–3 and 4–6, which will employ occupational orientation as the principal vehicle for the teaching of basic education.

If this goal is realized, the following will be characteristic of the students completing the first six years of formal education:

1. Students will have developed an appreciation for work as a means of self-satisfaction in a full and fruitful life.
2. Students will have developed an understanding of the social and economic importance of a number of easily identifiable occupations and occupational families.
3. Students will attain basic education skills to a degree that is equal to, if not greater than, that which is now possible.
4. Students will have developed a degree of self-realization and awareness that will lead them to seek careers commensurate with their abilities and aptitudes.
5. Students will have developed an understanding of the impact of technology on the world of work and the necessity of developing a career strategy which will enable them to cope with a changing labor market.

B. To establish in the junior high school a curriculum which has as its core a study and exploration of specific occupational families, the career opportunities in these families, the skills needed for job entry into a specific cluster of related occupations, and the paths available for obtaining job entry skills or upgrading skills in chosen careers.

If this objective is realized, the following outcomes will be characteristic of students completing grade eight:

1. Students will be aware of the occupational opportunities within all the major occupational families, e.g., agriculture, health, technical, service, distribution, business and office, homemaking, and professional.
2. They will be able to plan a strategy for attaining a specific career choice within one of the major occupational families.
3. They will have developed an awareness of self-realization that leads to the selection of an appropriate career with realistic aspiration levels.
4. They will have developed habits and attitudes which are needed for successful and continued employment.

C. To provide guidance and educational opportunities for students in grades 1–12 to establish positive relationships between school and the world of work.

More specifically, this goal may be expressed in terms of the following:

1. To explore occupations whereby elementary school children, 1–6, can see positive relationships between school and the world of work. To begin particularly with grade four and be concerned with concepts of self, work, interest, and skills.

    If these objectives are realized the following will be characteristic of students at the completion of the first six years of formal education:

    a) Students will have developed positive concepts of self.
    b) Students will have attained varied and wide interest in the world of work.
    c) Students will have developed the ability to make wise decisions and choices regarding occupational goals.
    d) Students will have realized opportunities to express and develop goals and aspirations in the world of work.
    e) Students will have been exposed to some of the skills basic to some selected occupations.
    f) Students will have been exposed to the fact that skills must be developed commensurate with abilities and interests.

g) Students will have been exposed to occupational information not only in the community but on an international and national basis.

h) Students will have learned some of the skills and the extent of education and preparation required for entry into certain job areas.

i) Students will have had many opportunities to express interests, exercise talents, and explore areas in which interests and talents might be developed.

j) Students will have learned the value and dignity of all types of work and skills.

k) Students will have learned that all workers contribute to the positive over-all welfare of our society.

l) Students will have developed a positive attitude toward work and preparation for work.

2. In grades 7–9 an attempt will be made to instill realistic objectives toward occupational considerations. Counselors and teachers will cooperate to build a more realistic understanding of occupational requirements.

If the goals of this objective are accomplished, the following factors can be observed in students completing grades 7–9.

a) Students will have gained knowledge about occupational and educational opportunities on a variety of levels.

b) Students not finishing high school will be provided information and opportunities to seek other training and/or employment.

c) Students will have gained knowledge of broad fields of work which will assist the individual in making long-range vocational plans.

d) Students, especially potential drop-outs, will be provided opportunities to study intensively a few selected occupations of their choice.

e) Students will have been provided opportunities to explore their abilities, interests, and aptitudes.

f) Students will follow curricula that best satisfy individual needs.

g) Students will be provided, if possible, opportunities to match what they have discovered about themselves with facts discovered about the worker in the occupational areas studied.

3. To establish in vocational guidance, in grades 10–12, opportunity for students to learn more about themselves, ways of working with

others, and psychological aspects of jobs as they relate to their own temperaments, personalities, and values.

If these objectives are accomplished, students will exhibit the following characteristics:

a) Students will have become aware of continued change in the world of work.
b) Students have acquired broad knowledge in major occupational fields.
c) Students will have developed an understanding of the need for continuing education and training in the various career areas.
d) Students will have become acquainted with information concerning schools, colleges, and other training programs.
e) Students will have developed realistic attitudes toward the dignity of all work and workers.
f) Students will have developed a realistic understanding of themselves regarding career decision-making.
g) Students will have acquired information regarding present and future employment trends and opportunities.

D. To provide within the high school, grades 9–12, an expanded and improved program of vocational preparation for those youth who plan to terminate their formal schooling at grade 12, to include (1) improvement of the present program to reflect preparation for a cluster of related occupations rather than for specific occupations, (2) the expansion of offerings through incorporation of work-study and cooperative vocational programs, and (3) the development of a program geared specifically to meet the needs of the handicapped.

If these objectives are realized, the following will be characteristic of those students completing grade 12:

1. Students will have the background necessary to further their career preparation by attending technical schools, colleges, and other post secondary technical programs, or they will have saleable skills necessary for job entry.
2. Students planning to terminate their education upon graduation from high school will possess the types of skills, attitudes, and work habits necessary for employment in a cluster of closely related occupations.
3. Handicapped students will have attained the basic education and vocational skills that are within their individual capabilities.

E. To establish a short term intensified program of vocational preparation for the students who have not previously been enrolled in vocational programs and who have chosen to terminate their formal education before the completion of grade twelve.

If this objective is realized, the following will be characteristic of the high school drop-out:

1. School drop-outs will have attained, to a degree, attitudes and habits which are necessary for successful job performance and successful living.
2. To the extent that time will permit, school drop-outs will have acquired a degree of specific skills which could qualify them for entrance into a cluster of occupations requiring a relatively low degree of skill.

INSTALLATION STRATEGIES

Different strategies for program installation are being used with the various program elements. This is due to the scope of the activities at the different segments, existing local program structure, teacher attitudes, and constraints which are perceived to exist after the funding period has terminated. The fundamental concept underlying all strategies is to be sure that the local people will be able to assume the responsibility for continuation and growth of the program.

Elementary (1–6)   The original approach was to ask that 20 minutes daily be devoted to career education. While it was generally considered that the activities could occur as part of the social studies section of the grade levels, an attempt has been made to encourage the teachers to integrate the career education aspects with the most appropriate subject matter areas. Through the use of a regular weekly in-service program, the teachers prepared lesson plans for their respective grade levels. The teachers were provided with broad content outlines which were prepared by the project staff and revised on the basis of teacher suggestions. The lesson plans, which are about two-thirds complete at this time, will serve as a coordinating device and will be a means of record keeping for subsequent revisions.

Ultimately, it is expected that the career education elements of the elementary curriculum will be integrated with the other subject matter areas. In fact, some of the teachers have already recognized the need for such revisions in their plans.

Junior High (7–8)   Like most other junior high schools, the school in Pikeville is organized as a departmentalized system as opposed to the self-contained classroom in the elementary school. Until this year the only junior high school program that could be considered career education was the industrial arts program in Pikeville and approximately 25 seventh grade students and 25 eighth grade students were enrolled in the program. Several additional practical arts areas are being offered to all junior high school children during this school year. In addition there will be an in-service program to help regular classroom teachers introduce career education in their classroom. The cluster approach is being considered as a means of providing wide coverage of occupational opportunities. Several of the clusters are already in operation in the school and others will be introduced this year and in the future years.

High School (9–12)   At this point in the development of the programs, the high school has received the least attention. Business education and home economics education were the only two vocational programs offered at the beginning of the project. If one wants to consider industrial arts as having "vocational education" value, approximately 75 high school students were enrolled in that program last year. Certainly industrial arts has career education value. Supplementing the above high school programs, an agriculture program was identified this year with the main focus being horticulture. Planning is in progress to begin a cooperative education program as soon as acceptable personnel can be secured.

Pikeville Independent School District participates in the "area vocational extension center" and has secured space for approximately twenty students. This program requires that the students leave the home school each afternoon and enrollment has been less than encouraging in the past two years. Last year only one student was enrolled and this year only seven students are attending.

Program development in subsequent years will include improvement of existing programs, developing the in-school educational offerings to provide the base for effective cooperative education in a wide variety of local occupations.

A new physical facility is in the planning stages which will support the necessary in-school entry level type course. The facilities have been designed to facilitate a dynamic program. It is expected that there will be few enduring programs and that the facility will be used by multiple local agencies.

Functionally the entire high school program will emphasize career planning and decision making. That is, optimally each course will be directed at preparing the students to assume a career role or assist the students to obtain additional education which will lead to the attainment of a career goal.

The teachers of the "academic" course will be the key to the success of the career education program in Pikeville. It is vital that the teachers help students understand that the knowledge, skills, and attitudes are learned because they are tools which help people function in society and are not merely abstract obstacles which must be overcome to get out of school. Certainly, considerable work must be done to assist the academic teachers change their courses to focus on applications of the course content. It would, however, be misleading to let the reader assume that the magnitude of change in the academic offerings will be as great as the change expected of the courses leading to entry level skill attainment.

SUPPORTIVE SERVICES

Two kinds of supportive services are available either directly or indirectly to the students. The first service deals with staff which is supported by project funds to assist with the extra load required during the initial stages of the project. Examples of the services are clerical staff, curriculum coordinator, and resources specialists.

The second, and most directly related to the students, is the group of staff people who make up the "guidance team." They include an elementary counselor, junior high school counselor, high school counselor, placement coordinator, pupil personnel coordinator, and nurse. In addition, the services of several local agencies are available to the students. Examples of out-of-school resources are the Mountain Mental Health Service, Employment Security, and the State Department of Rehabilitation. Among the services which will be provided by the guidance team are placement, guidance, counseling, follow-up, home visitation, and assessment. Where feasible, an attempt has been made to utilize teachers as an extension of the guidance service.

First Grade: Basic Content Outline

FAMILY ENVIRONMENT
I. Structures of families
    A. Families have members and the members are related to each other.
        1. Names of members (Mother, father, sisters, brothers, uncles, aunts, etc.)
        2. Members' relationships to each other
        3. The structure of a family differs from family to family
        4. Immediate family usually lives in a single structure or house
        5. Related family often live in other places
        6. Sometimes people become good enough friends to be considered as part of the family.

   B. Members of a family interact with other members of the family.
1. Communicate
2. Work
3. Play
4. Eat
5. Sleep
6. Argue
7. Learn
8. Protect
9. Help
10. Share

   C. The structure of families changes.
1. Number of members
2. Age of members
3. Responsibilities of members

   D. Families are mobile (rural to urban; urban to rural; within geographic area; and country to country).
1. Families move to secure different housing.
   a. better housing
   b. more economical housing
   c. different environment
2. Families move to secure different jobs.
3. Families move to be closer to jobs or schools.

   E. Families make decisions.
1. Some decisions are made by older members of the family.
2. The entire family makes some decisions.
3. As members of a family become more mature (have experience) they participate in making more of the decisions.
4. Family decisions are affected by the size of a family.
5. The educational background of a family often determines family decisions.
6. Occupations of the parents often affect family decisions.
7. Some decisions are made only because of family's tastes.

II. Families are consumers and producers.
   A. All families are consumers of food, clothing, and shelter.
1. Define consumer and producer.
2. Food, clothing, and shelter are essential to life.
3. Food, clothing, and shelter can be consumed without buying the items.
4. Kinds and quantities of food, clothing, and shelter consumed vary among families.

B. Families are consumers of things other than food, clothing, and shelter.
  1. Families consume material goods.
  2. Families consume services.
C. People have a conflict between unlimited wants and limited resources.
  1. People want to have many goods and services.
  2. Most people do not have the resources to obtain everything they want.
  3. People must get need things first.
  4. If any resources remain after needs are obtained, wants can be obtained.
  5. Priorities are established for the wanted items.
  6. Sometimes the resources which remain are not enough to buy the most wanted items.
  7. People can spend resources on less important wants or save for more expensive items.
D. Not all families consume the same things or services.
  1. Economic structure of a family determines how much they can consume.
  2. Some items are not available to certain people.
  3. Different families consume things because they like or dislike the items.
E. Before things or services can be consumed, they must be produced.
  1. Products and services are produced by the family.
  2. Products and services are produced by the people outside the family.
F. Some members of a family are producers, some are preparing to become producers and some cannot produce.
  1. Family producers are members who provide for goods and services that would otherwise have to be purchased.
  2. Members who obtain resources to obtain goods and services are producers.
  3. Members who are going to school or learning to do something are preparing to be producers.
  4. Very young, old, sick, handicapped members often are not producers.
G. When possible everyone should be a producer.
  1. It is the economic and social responsibility of people to be producers.
  2. It is a family responsibility to be a producer.

       3. It creates a feeling of satisfaction and well-being to be a producer.

III. Families divide labor and develop specialities.

    A. Each person usually does only certain jobs in a home.
        1. Some jobs are done by women and some by men and some by both.
        2. Some jobs are too difficult for certain family members.
        3. Specific jobs are usually given to individuals in the home.
        4. As people grow, they are usually given additional jobs and more responsible or difficult jobs.

    B. Dividing labor is more efficient.
        1. Quantity of work takes a given amount of time and effort.
        2. When several people do a specific amount of the total task, the task takes less time to complete, than if only one person does the total task.
        3. When one or more does not do his task, everyone else will have to do more.
        4. Family members become interdependent.

    C. Learning and practice help people become more efficient and accurate when doing a job.
        1. People learn how to do jobs.
        2. People become more proficient in doing a job because of the practice.

IV. Families have free time.

    A. Families produce goods and services in the home.
        1. Members of families make material goods in the home.
        2. Families do things in the home that could be done by people outside the home.

    B. Families play or pursue hobbies in the home.
        1. Members play as individuals and as groups.
        2. Hobbies or interests occupy family members' time.
        3. Hobbies can develop into occupations.

    C. Families sometime can save money by producing goods and services in the home.
        1. When people have sufficient time and ability they can produce items that would have to be purchased.
        2. When material goods are produced in the home, the family saves labor cost.
        3. Many services done in the home would be too expensive if they were done by people outside the home.

    D. It sometimes is more expensive to produce goods and services in the home than to have someone else do the work.
        1. Tasks requiring specialized equipment.

        2. Tasks requiring skilled people.

        3. When task requires time that would be devoted to securing income.

   E. Families make decisions about what work they will do in the home.

        1. Conflict between using free time for work or using free time for play.

        2. Some families can afford to have more work done by people outside the family.

        3. Some families want to see that all work is done in the home and others do not care if certain work is not done.

        4. There is often too much to complete and families decide what work is most important.

V. Implements aid people in their work.

   A. Tools and machines are available to make jobs efficient and accurate.

        1. Many different kinds of tools in a home.

        2. Tools usually built for specific purpose.

        3. Man has developed tools throughout the years.

        4. Tools and machines can be used to reduce time required to do a job.

        5. Proper tools and machines can help people do a better job.

   B. Tools and machines must be used by people.

        1. People must learn to use tools and machines.

        2. Tools and machines will not work—people have to make them do work.

        3. Tools and machines can be dangerous if man does not use them safely.

   C. Tools and machines are expensive, they must be maintained, and they must be repaired.

        1. Tools and machines must be purchased or made.

        2. The more specialized or complicated a tool or machine is, the more expensive it is.

        3. Tools will wear out faster or will not do the job as efficiently if they are not maintained.

        4. Tools often break or wear out and must be repaired.

   D. Transportation increases mobility of people and things.

        1. Transportation is a means of moving people or things from one place to another.

        2. The larger the item, the more expensive it is to move.

        3. The farther the item must go, the more it costs.

        4. The faster the item goes, the more expensive it is.

        5. Man has developed transportation devices too.

E.   Devices make communication more efficient.
  1. Improved communication lets people do work in places without going to the places.
  2. Improved communication lets people know what is happening all over the world shortly after it happens.
  3. The more rapid the communication, the more expensive.
  4. The more people involved in communication, the more expensive it is.
  5. Man has developed devices to make communication more efficient.
F.   Devices have evolved because man wanted to make his work more efficient.
VI. Some workers come to school to work.
A.   Some school workers must have special training.
  1. Superintendent
  2. Principals
  3. Teachers
  4. Nurse
  5. Counselor
  6. Librarian
  7. Cook
B.   Other workers are semi-skilled or unskilled and receive on-the-job training.
  1. Cafeteria workers
  2. Custodians
  3. Delivery man
  4. Teacher aide
  5. Bus drivers
C.   School workers divide the labor like members of the family.
  1. School workers depend on each other.
    a. Each person is expected to do a specific job.
    b. All jobs are important and contribute to the total job.
    c. When one person doesn't do his job others have to work harder.
  2. Some jobs are more difficult or require more responsibility.
    a. Physical difficulty
    b. Intellectual difficulty
    c. Risk because of responsibility
  3. Work is divided on the basis of worker qualification.
    a. Special education
    b. Special training
    c. Unique experience

D. School workers are producers of services.
     1. Provide services to people
        a. Help students learn
        b. Protect children
        c. Transport children
        d. Feed children
     2. Provide services to things
        a. Cleaning
        b. Repairing
        c. Installing
        d. Altering
        e. Moving
     3. Provide services to data
        a. Record
        b. Collect
        c. Distribute
E. Some jobs require workers to wear special clothing.
     1. Appearance
     2. Protection
     3. Sanitation
F. Some school workers need special tools and machines.
     1. Janitor
     2. Cafeteria workers
     3. Teachers
     4. Nurse
     5. Secretary

Lesson Plan

Major Unit: *Structure of Families*   Grade Level   <u>First</u>
Lesson No. 1: 2 or 3 days
Title: Families have members and members are related to each other.

Definition: A family is a group of people who are related to one another.
               The family members may be: Father, mother, brother, sister,
               grandfather, grandmother. These members share work and
               play. They share feelings of love, joy, happiness, sadness and
               sorrow.
Objectives: As a result of this lesson the child will be able to:
               1. Orally state the name of his mother and father.
               2. Orally state what members comprise a family.

3. Tally number of brothers and sisters in his family on chalk board.
4. Orally make the sound of Ff.
5. Follow dotted lines to make the letter Ff.
6. Suggest sentences for experience chart.
7. Identify pictures of objects that are big and little.
8. Cut pictures from magazines to represent his or her family and paste in family album.
9. Draw the face of their family members on paper plates.

Activities:
1. The children will cut pictures from magazines to represent their family and paste on construction paper to make family album.
2. The children will draw faces of their family members on paper plates (These may be strung together in family groups.)
3. The children will listen to the poem "Celebrating Dad."
4. The children will observe filmstrip, "Our Family."
5. The children will make chart story about one family member.
6. The children will follow lines to make the letter Ff.
7. The children will select pictures that are big and little.
8. The children will discuss the topic about family membership.
9. The children will orally make the sound of Ff.

Teaching Procedure:
1. Show pictures of family groupings.
2. Ask the following questions:
   a. Which family is most like yours?
   b. Do the families look alike?
   c. Do you see a country family?
   d. Do you see a family who lives in the city?
   e. Are these families the same size?
   f. Who cooks your dinner?
   g. Who reads to you?
   h. Who buys your clothes?
   i. Who takes you for walks?
   j. Who can't walk in your family?
   k. Who helps you get ready for school?
   l. Do all children in your family go to school?
   m. Who drives the car in your family?

Relationships:

Reading readiness: Make experience chart.
Writing: Write the letter F f.

Phonics: Sound of letter F f.

Language Arts: Read poem, "Celebrating Dad."

Math: Use chart family picture to distinguish big and little. Who has the biggest family in our class?

Tools, Materials, Equipment, and Teaching Aids:

Magazines, scissors, paste, construction paper, newsprint, chart paper, writing paper, poem, pencils, paper plates, crayons and string.

Bibliography: Ginn Co., manual for *Little White House,* p. 10.

Silver Burdett, Primary Social Studies

Families and Their Needs, pp. 6, 7

Filmstrip: *Our Family,* Home & Community series (Encyclopedia Britannica)

You Are Here, Benefic Press, Chicago, pp. 8–10.

Evaluation: Were the children able to complete their family album?

Could each child name his father and mother?

Did most children participate in discussions and answering questions?

Was handwork done with efficiency and ease?

Lesson Plan

Major Unit: *Structure of Families*   Grade Level <u>First</u>

Lesson Number 2: Two days

Definition: Close family members live in a single space. All people need structures for protection and for maintenance of a way of life. People do things in the home and the home is arranged to meet the needs of the family.

Objectives: As a result of this lesson the children will be able to:

1. Orally state the purposes of structures
2. Orally describe the place where they live and distinguish features about other homes that are different from their home
3. Name the rooms in their home
4. Name and describe three kinds of structures used by families—Single family home, multiple family home, and mobile home.
5. Name, by sight of a picture, and describe the use of the living room, bedroom, kitchen, and bathroom.

Activities:

1. The children will observe the filmstrip, "Why We Need Houses" Encyclopedia Britannica (Library #366) and discuss among the children.

    2. Children will describe orally and the class will discuss features about the following kinds of pictures—(1) single family house, (2) multiple family house, (3) apartment and/or townhouse, (4) mobile home (possibly several), (5) home with brick outside, (6) home with wood outside, (7) home with stone outside, (8) home with flat roof, (9) home with angle roof, (10) kitchen, (11) bedroom, (12) living room, (13) bathroom.

    3. Have children cut paper (see next page) and fold into shape of house, open folds, and draw in different rooms in his home.

    4. Have children make a chart story about the topic of homes.

Teaching Procedure:

    1. Show filmstrip, "Why We Need Houses." Ask questions to stimulate discussion.

    2. Show pictures of items listed above and encourage discussion.

    3. Pass out paper, have children cut, fold, and draw the pictures of rooms in their homes.

    4. Encourage children to contribute to chart story.

Relationships:

Reading readiness
Science: All living things have family and homes
Writing: Chart story

Tools, Materials, Equipment, and Teaching Aids:

    1. Pictures
    2. Paper for making house
    3. Chart paper
    4. Crayons
    5. Pencils
    6. Dry Mark
    7. "Why We Need Houses" Encyclopedia Britannica, #336 in the library
    8. Filmstrip projector

Bibliography: *The True Book of Houses,* Childrens Press, Chicago "Why We Need Houses" Encyclopedia Britannica (#366 in library)

Evaluation: 1. Informal questions relating to the activities.

    2. Were the children able to draw the rooms of their home (do not evaluate the quality of the drawing—only whether they could identify the rooms).

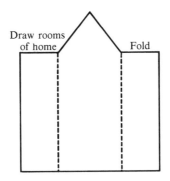

Lesson Plan

Major Unit: *Structure of Families* Grade Level <u>First</u>
Lesson No. 3
Title: The structure of families differs from family to family.
Definition: The structure of families differs in size, composition, and relationships.
Objectives: At the end of the lesson students should understand differences in family structures by being able to:
  1. Count members of their family compared with others.
  2. Tell names of members of family.
  3. Tell relationships of these members.
Activities: 1. Draw members of their immediate families.
  2. Draw picture of another family that differs in structure.
  3. Show and tell differences and relationships of people in pictures.
  4. Bar graph showing size and relationship of family.

Teaching Procedure: Show children pictures of Dick's family and list names of members on board. Note as many likenesses and differences as possible. Show pictures of Tom's family (Do the same as above) Let children draw conclusion about the families. Number of children, size, sex, color, etc. Relate how these families are like their own.

Relationships: Math, tally number of boys in class families.
  Tally number of girls in class families.
  Writing: Our family has _____ members. Total number in all. Count fathers, mothers.

Tools, Materials, Equipment, and Teaching Aids: Fun With Our Friends, On Cherry Street, newsprint, crayons, chalk board, chalk, pencils, duplicated worksheet, writing paper.

Bibliography: Scott Foresman Co., *Fun With Our Friends*
    Ginn Co., *On Cherry Street*

Evaluation: Mark X male members of family. Circle female members of family. Mark smallest member of family with blue crayon. Mark tallest member of family with red crayon.

Part IV CAREER EDUCATION: PROMISE

Introduction

One of the more obvious reactions to the preceding papers might be that most of what is proposed is not new. Greater emphasis upon occupational preparation as a fundamental function of public education has been proposed at various times since Benjamin Franklin's proposal of his Academy. It was a fundamental factor in the establishment of the Land-Grant College Act. It was a central concern of the Cardinal Principles of Education, along with the de-emphasis of the purely academic and a call for the development of educational programs to help students become prepared to fulfill their life careers or roles effectively. About thirty years ago, following Havighurst's identification of the developmental needs of youth, both the Educational Policies Commission (of the National Education Association and the American Association of School Administrators) and the National Association of Secondary School Principals took the bold stand that every high school graduate should receive training for some "salable skills" before leaving high school. The statement of *Purposes of Education for American Democracy,* prepared for the Educational Policies Commission by the historian Charles Beard, included a broad statement of educational functions related to the total life needs of children and youth.

How, then, did it happen that these statements were disregarded in emerging programs in the schools? This is not a simple question to answer. The United States Congress, through the Smith-Hughes Act, the George-Barden Act, the George-Dean Act, the Vocational Education Acts of 1963 and 1968, attempted to broaden the concept of what schooling was all about, but to little avail. The fundamental problem was that the academicians had a strangle hold on the curriculum, and relating education to life needs was anathema to them. They refused to permit a concept of education separated from its knowledge dissemination functions to prevail. The Bestors, the Adlers, the Rickovers, and the Hutchins were the true villains for the millions of youth who were disenfranchised by an educational system which, as Bruner now sees, was developed to screen them out and freeze them into lowly social stations and economic impotence. The curriculum was conceived in a narrow sense related only to the academic disciplines. I.B. Berkson's great conception of a triune concern for education as a

275

linkage between the individual, the community, and the values which give meaning to life and continuity to civilization was never implemented.

Career education is an endeavor to correct this deficiency. The concept of the curriculum in career education embraces the totality of human life, as well as intellectual and ethical concerns. It attempts to narrow the gap between schooling and total education, and in this view the school would not be a sheltered ivory tower divorced from the community. It should be a part of and related to all of the affairs of the community in which the child lives and through which he must find his fulfillment as a participating, contributing, and hopefully self-fulfilled citizen. The concept of career education includes a social concern for a continuous program of meeting human needs. It establishes a permanent entitlement of the human being at any or all stages of his life to recycle into more meaningful, challenging, and fulfilling activities through his having available educational opportunities which help him acquire the knowledge, skill and competence he needs to achieve his objectives.

Dimensions of Career Education

Career education is not just another addition to the present curriculum. When fully developed, career education will constitute a new paradigm governing the practice of education at all levels and may result in the restructuring of the total educational program. The change does not have to be revolutionary. Career education can be achieved through evolutionary stages as it is integrated within the current curriculum. Cumulative change can take place, resulting eventually in the restructuring of the educational program, based upon experience and the validation of its various elements and processes.

Although there are different patterns through which this restructuring may emerge, experience in formulating approaches to career development and research on career decision-making suggest that there are some general principles or dimensions which will foster the fullest realization of career education. The dimensions which appear to be most significant at the present time are not discrete, but suggest the interlocking and interacting nature of all the elements of career education.

(1) Career education incorporates a view of the curriculum as an integrated and cumulative series of experiences designed to help the student achieve increasing power to make relevant decisions about all his life activities and increasing skill in the performance of his life roles. An integrated curriculum suggests that instead of experiences being presented in indepen-

dent, separate, subject-matter modules, there is an attempt to relate all experience to some central objectives. Each area of study or experience should contribute to the improvement of the student's capabilities. The total curriculum can thus be viewed as having a cumulative impact on the learner. Each successive learning activity can be built upon the previous experiences, the level of accomplishment of the student and his revealed need. The sequencing of educational experiences should be on the basis of each learner's needs, not a pre-established curriculum, and the student's timing as he moves through the sequences of experiences should be individually paced, not rigidly adherent to grade-level norms. Each new experience should be a step toward the learner's next stage of development, particularly with respect to his achieving increased capability to make relevant decisions about his life career and his acquiring increased skill in all the areas related to his life roles. Particular emphasis should be placed upon his skill development and his use of the tools and techniques of learning as well as those related to occupational competence.

(2) Career education in the elementary schools should attempt to achieve pupil *awareness* of himself and of the opportunities available in the universe of productive human affairs. A primary conception of career education is that when an individual is able to synthesize a realistic awareness of himself, his potentialities, his aspirations, and his limitations, along with a realistic perception of the career opportunities available to him, he will then, with proper guidance and through relevant learning experiences, be able to make appropriate decisions about his own life career. An essential aspect of his awareness is his recognition of the social contributions made by all occupations and professions. The first stage in his developing decisional capability is awareness of these two basic ingredients: himself and the world of career opportunities.

(3) In the middle grades career education should emphasize pupil exploration of clusters of occupations as a foundation for each student's eventual selection of a particular career within a general field or cluster. Particular emphasis should be placed upon his *exploration* of various clusters and the preparation requirements and educational opportunities available for his obtaining the necessary training for those of particular interest to him. Inherent in his explorations of various career clusters is an opportunity for him to acquire "hands-on experience" as he experiments with the actual activities, tools, processes, and materials related to the occupations which are involved. The purpose of this exploration and experimentation is to help an individual determine the most desirable fit between himself, his potentialities and aspirations, and the requirements of the careers which he considers within the realm of his possibilities. During this exploratory process, it is essential that students investigate not only their

potentialities in relation to the requirements of each occupation by itself, but also the sequence or levels of other opportunities to which the gaining of skill at an entry level may lead. Each occupation may be conceived as existing upon a particular rung of a career ladder, and each child should become aware of the opportunities for advancing up the career ladder as well as his own potentialities for maximizing the contribution which he can make to his fellow men. In exploring each occupation and the career ladder opportunities available within the cluster of occupations, the learner should also explore the whole range of associated implications of each occupation for his total life style and for his other life roles.

(4) In the upper senior high school the student should begin to narrow his choice within a particular cluster of occupations or to a specific occupation and engage in initial vocational preparation for entry level employment. Some students will complete occupational entry preparation in the high school and will engage in full time employment upon leaving school. For other students the high school will provide an opportunity for the further refinement of career choices and the foundational learning experiences needed for entrance into occupational or professional preparatory programs on the post-high school level.

(5) In a democratic, humanistic society each individual is entitled to receive the education and preparation he needs to fulfil his realistic aspirations and expectations throughout the entire span of his life. From this perspective, post-high school educational programs are necessary to provide for two specific career education functions. First, extensive opportunities must be provided to enable students to obtain the preparation they need for entering into the vocations of their choice beyond the entry rung of the career ladder. Second, post-high school opportunities must be available for helping individuals obtain the preparation they need for continuous advancement upon the career ladder or for recycling into another occupation after some initial on-the-job experiences. The emphasis of post-high school institutions upon career training in no way lessens their obligations for the provision of programs which help an individual gain greater insight into and competence in other life roles.

(6) The emphasis upon career education should not detract from the general education needs of students, specifically as related to life roles other than the occupational. Career education should provide a *focus* for the education of each child, centering concern upon an orientation toward careers. The child's general education should be directed toward building competence in his role as a citizen, a member of a family group, and a participant in avocational, aesthetic, and religious activities. It would be hazardous to conceive of career education as narrowly related exclusively to obtaining occupational competence. A whole range of additional studies

are essential as a foundation for and in support of the individual's acquiring competence in the range of life careers in which he will engage. The advocates of career education do not deny the necessity for a general education. Their criticism is directed toward a conception of general education which is neither focused nor applicative to the problems and needs of society and human beings. By emphasizing applicative rather than descriptive general studies, the advocates of career education hope to provide a more meaningful educational program which leads to the cumulative power of the individual to deal effectively with his environment.

(7) In career education the distinction between the academic and the vocational curricula gives way to the fusion of the two as emphasis for all students is placed upon their career development. No tracks need to be maintained. The program for each student may be developed in accordance with his career development needs. Students will be encouraged to explore among a variety of potentialities, not only to enhance their power to make viable decisions about their own careers, but also to develop avocational interests and competencies to supplement their remunerative careers. The current provisions of different levels of curriculum—the college preparatory, the general, the vocational, the remedial—will give way to a single curriculum within which differentiation may be provided for each student according to his own basic interests, aspirations, and requirements.

(8) Career education necessitates a new definition of the scope and the criteria for the selection of the content of the curriculum. At present, the content of the curriculum consists of a body of knowledge to be acquired by students. As indicated in some of the preceding papers, the existing curriculum is built primarily around discrete subjects, and requirements are determined eclectically in terms of "how much" of each subject the student needs. In career education there need be no courses required as such. The elements of the curriculum are selected to help each student develop the capabilities he needs to become a fully capacitated member of society. The content elements of the career curriculum will include (a) the experiences, skills, and knowledges needed by students to develop understanding of themselves as members of society and to build competence in the performance of the variety of roles which they play as participating members of society; (b) information and experiences that lead to an awareness of the world of productive endeavors and human affairs; (c) skills in making decisions about future careers and choices related to life roles and styles; and (d) skills needed in performing basic occupational processes and the use of relevant tools.

(9) A successful career education program involves the adaptation of all instructional content, material, and processes for the individual needs of each child. Educational philosophy has long held that the child and his

needs should be the central focus of the curriculum, and all instructional elements should be related. However, in practice the curriculum, instructional materials, and instructional strategies have too often been developed without reference to the child and his unique needs. The concept of career education requires the development of instructional strategies to individualize all processes and programs within the school. The central function of instruction is to help the child become capacitated to fulfil his life, achieve his aspirations, and derive satisfactions from his competent performance of his life roles.

(10) Although chronological age may continue to be the basis for administrative grouping of children, grading as such should be of only minor importance. The main criterion for structure of the pupil's time should be the provision of experiences through which he grows in ability to determine his future career goals. A pupil's program at any grade or age level should be determined by his revealed needs. Obviously, there are some natural groupings into which pupils with similar needs will fall. Based upon careful clinical observation of the child and the diagnosis of his needs, a thorough review of his life experiences, interviews and sharing of data with parents, the use of a variety of well-established tests, and the observation of his behaviors both in and out of school, the pupil should be encouraged to select particular individualized or group experiences which seem best to serve his needs. Multi-purpose groupings should be established to serve both the basic learning and the career development needs of the students. Flexibility in scheduling and programming is essential to fulfil this requirement.

(11) As previously indicated, emphasis should be placed upon *applicative* rather than *descriptive* knowledge. No subject matter should be taught as an end in itself. Content should be centered around basic social and personal problems, and students should be helped to find the knowledge and tools they can use to achieve social and personal competence. Subject areas should be fused so that for any problem students can use a variety of data derived from various fields.

(12) Career education requires the development of a clinical mode for the structuring of the schools. The major characteristic of this mode is the emphasis upon the diagnosis of the needs of each child, both for his self-fulfillment and for his capacitation as a contributing member of society. A clinical mode implies that professional resources within the school will be used both to diagnose individual needs and to make individual prescriptions to help the student progress toward his career development objectives.

(13) The clinical mode for the structuring of instructional personnel within the school necessitates the viewing of the teacher, not as a purveyor of knowledge, a disciplinarian, and the evaluator who determines how much

knowledge the students have acquired, but rather as a diagnostician, a prescriber of instructional strategies and interventions, a preparer of materials, a reinforcer of the student's purposes, and an assessor of child growth and development. Teachers, counselors, resource persons, aides, special education specialists, career advisors, and relevant community personnel who can be of assistance in the instructional program should form teams to establish the basis for the proper diagnosis of student needs and the formulation of prescriptions for instructional interventions to improve the student's power to cope with his needs. Career education provides the possibility for developing a true differentiation of instructional roles based upon a set of educational imperatives within the school, rather than a differentiation related primarily to training and salary levels. This differentiation includes the use of professional personnel in specialized roles within the school and requires both a new paradigm for all personnel development programs as well as for the multi-roles within the school which professional personnel are to fill.

(14) As previously intimated, requirements within the school should be stated in terms of performance capabilities of students and the decisions which they are expected to make. Performance capabilities cannot be measured in terms of standardized subject matter, achievement tests. Performance capabilities must be in terms of what the student is capacitated *to do* as a result of the career development and personal life decisions which he has been helped to make. Performance objectives must be stated in applicative rather than descriptive terms. The measurement of achievement or performance capability, then, must be in terms of how the individual applies his knowledge and skill in real life situations.

(15) In career education the *success* of the school should be measured in terms of performance capability of its students, particularly with respect to the manner in which they conduct themselves in roles outside the school and the way in which they are capacitated to perform their several future roles. The criteria used to assess the success of the school now are fictitious. The scores of students on standardized achievement tests, the number of students attending post-high school educational institutions, the honors which athletic or other teams bring back from contests, and the positions to which students are elected in college are not true measures of the school's success. Many students could accomplish the things for which schools receive approbation irrespective of the influence the school may have had upon them. In fact, some of the factors considered measures of the school's success may be an indication of its failure. This is particularly evident in the number of students who are pressured to go to college irrespective of their interests or the relevancy of college for their aspirations. The fact that they go to college is a measure of the school's failure to provide viable

alternatives. The truest measure of the school's success is what it has done for the most disadvantaged child, or the child with the greatest barriers to learning. Emphasis upon performance capability of all students in real life situations requires that the school take into consideration the total range of students needs, rather than catering primarily and giving highest honors to the most elite group.

(16) Each student's program should be developed to help him obtain, among other things, salable skills before leaving school. The most tragic aspect of the present practice in education is that students now either drop out or graduate having had little emphasis placed upon their employability. No matter at what level of competence a student may eventually be able to find his career fulfillment, as several papers indicate, a mark of his career development is his ability to provide for his sustenance first at an entry level of employment. Whether or not the student uses his job skills is not as essential a consideration as the fact that he has them, that he can secure at least avocational satisfactions from them, that he can use them to secure economic independence, and that he has them available in the event he or members of his family face emergencies which require their use. These skills may be the basis upon which the student is able to pay for his continuing education and make a social contribution at the same time that he is increasing his own earning power.

(17) In career education all school personnel have responsibility for the placement, continuing guidance, and advisement of each student throughout as much of his career as he wishes to receive such assistance. The school can no longer consider its job done when the individual "exits" either before or after graduation. To determine the effectiveness of the school program, adequate feedback must be provided for and continuing follow-up must be maintained. Career education places emphasis upon the adaptability of the school program. Such adaptability is based upon a continuous assessment of the validity of its program and how the students use the instruction which the school provided. The modern educational system must provide the mechanisms through which any individual at any stage of his life can obtain the placement, the guidance, and the corrective instructional assistance which he needs to relieve his problems or improve his ability to derive satisfactions.

(18) The school should be "of the community." It should use the resources of the community and the instructional program to extend its instructional capabilities. It should help students plan in conjunction with their parents. It should coordinate the use of other agencies in the community which are also concerned with the proper development of children and youth. In collaboration with other agencies and groups, it should develop programs through which the educational needs of all people, irrespective of

age, can be met. It should use community channels both to assess the reality and appraise the effectiveness of its programs in furthering public purposes in support of education. Schools with adequate career education both use their communities and provide opportunities for all citizens.

(19) Career education necessitates that the entire school program be "people-oriented." Essential to the concept of career education is the principle that the school exists to serve the needs of people and that all of its programs must be adapted accordingly. Within the career education philosophy is a concept that there is a life-long entitlement for every individual in our society to receive, both through his own resources and the resources of the state, the educational programs necessary or desired to increase his satisfactions and enhance his fulfillment. No standards, requirements, or prerequisites are self justified. All can be justified only in terms of the degree in which they help to capacitate human potentialities. To reiterate what has been said before, the present emphasis on the "screening out" functions of education must be replaced with an emphasis which helps an individual maximize his contribution through his identification as a contributing member of society.

(20) The school system which is based upon the career education model is flexible, adaptable, open and pragmatic. By flexible we mean that the school adjusts its use of resources and programs to the individual rather than expecting him to comply with its rules, regulations, prerequisites and requirements. By adaptable we mean that the school program is constantly adjusted to meet the requirements for human resource development imposed by an ever changing society. By open we mean that the school has a program for all individuals, irrespective of their age, irrespective of their academic potential, irrespective of their needs; an open school is one that meets educational needs of all human beings within the community. By pragmatic we mean that the attention of educators is constantly directed toward the consequences which programs have upon individuals through their participation in real life situations. The school is neither a haven from the community nor separated from the problems and needs of society. Career education implies that the school as an agency of society must contribute directly to its human wants and needs.

Basic Issues
in Career Education

When fully implemented, career education will constitute a new paradigm under which educational practice will be developed. There are obviously a number of very critical factors which have to be taken into consideration, and these produce issues to which advocates of career education must respond. Some of these issues are fundamental and can not easily be laid to rest. Some strike at the fundamental values of our society and the legitimated aspirations of individuals within our society. Career education cannot be conceived as a panacea, ready-made to solve all of these problems. However, to the extent that career education enables us to develop a flexible and adaptable educational program, we should be able to have increasing power to control the impact of our problems.

First, career education assumes the centrality of vocation for the determination of all life styles. Common experience indicates the importance of work to an individual's life. To the frequently asked question, "Who are you?" it is presumed that an individual will respond by citing his occupation, "I am a teacher."Evidence from sociology and anthropology indicates that an individual's sense of being and of fulfillment is derived from his vocational status. Occupational competence gives status and prestige to the individual regardless of the artificial social status to which his level in the occupational hierarchy assigns him. The work in which one is engaged governs the income available to his family and to a considerable extent where he might live within the community. It is on the basis of his income and place of residence that an individual is able to develop his total life style and provide the means for the regulation of his life activities.

An individual's identification as a person and an occupant of a particular set of socially approved roles is determined primarily by his occupational orientation. Associations with other people as well as groups are predominantly determined by the work in which one is engaged. What may be an avocational pursuit for some individuals and a subsidiary role may become a primary orientation for other individuals and the consuming factor in their orientation to life. A businessman may try to find release from his tensions by playing golf once or twice a week. No matter how proficient he may become, he is still known primarily as a businessman, while the professional golfer whose business it is to engage in competition for money and provide professional services to others is known as "golfer" by vocation.

No individual can assume a stable position in society except in relationship to the work roles which he performs. His role not only becomes the basis for his establishing meaning in his life experiences, but also conditions his social purposes. His values, political interests, attitudes toward other people and groups, styles for rearing his children and participation in a variety of both social and avocational activities are determined in largest measure by the nature of his vocation. The evidence suggests that even if the number of hours in which he will be engaged in his vocation decreases in the future, this orientation will still be the determiner of most of the activities within his life. Recent futuristic studies tend to conclude that if there is not real work in the future for individuals to perform, some substitute, as yet unidentified, will have to be found to replace it. This does not mean that the work orientation is the sole determiner of one's life style, but it does indicate that it is a primary factor. The only possible alternative which has yet been conceived is the identification with a significant avocational role in which one establishes his career orientations.

As Jerome Bruner has recently observed, a curriculum which does not give centrality to concerns about career or vocation is not likely to provide the relevance necessary both to motivate and fully to capacitate the youngster who is seeking to find his identity in contemporary society.

A second issue arises from the question whether or not career education is anti-intellectual or, at least, non-academic in its perspective. Some critics have suggested that it proposes an end to the study of the academic disciplines. Although career education challenges the concept that the basic function of the school is the sterile transmission of knowledge, it does not alter the concern for using knowledge as the basis upon which rational decisions are made. The average citizen in the post-technological society of the future needs more knowledge to become a fully capacitated and effective participant than does the individual in a simple rural or agrarian society. Although many jobs require complex knowledge of various academic fields, some jobs do not. Although some individuals are engaged in occupations in which the knowledge requirements are relatively simple, other pursuits in which he engages, such as performing his role as a participant in the political life of the community, require more complex and technical knowledge. The avocation in which an individual wishes to engage and from which he derives his feelings of self-fulfillment may or may not require a great deal of scientific information.

Systematic methods for organizing some data on the basis of certain disciplinary boundaries are probably essential for determining the validity and reliability of knowledge. At least for the present, career education will be dependent upon disciplined or subject area specialists to provide the *applicative* knowledge which is required of students to become fully prepared to meet the requirements of their careers. However, the knowledge delivery system in career education will be different than that of the traditional academic, subject-centered curriculum.

For most students applicative knowledge, as previously discussed, requires cutting across disciplinary lines. Most real problems require an interdisciplinary attack drawing from a variety of disciplinary fields rather than self-contained within a single discipline. If the real life problems of society become the central focus of the curriculum, a delivery system which enables an individual to *apply* knowledge from a variety of disciplines which have relevant concepts or research will have to be used. In career education, much lesser emphasis will be placed upon the maintenance of discrete, disciplinary subject-matter areas, and more emphasis will be placed upon problem areas and foundational studies needed to support an individual's preparation for his careers and to enable him to deal effectively with the problems which affect him.

A third concern has arisen with respect to the continuation of vocational education as it is known today. Will the specific job training program, as is generally developed in high schools and community colleges today, give way to a general approach to career development so that specific aspects of job training are delayed until the student leaves school or gets on-the-job training? Career education actually will demand a higher degree of emphasis upon occupational training than now exists, but some modification will be required. The sequence of instructional strategies will be based upon a career development model which provides an individual maximum opportunities for exploring his interests and potentialities in the field before he makes a heavy investment in meeting the more complex, technical knowledge and skill requirements. The emphasis throughout the middle grades will be upon the exploration of clusters or families of jobs with the student obtaining skill in the use of fundamental tools and processes required of most jobs within the family of occupations. In addition to specific vocational skills, the student will have an opportunity to learn some of the more general employability skills related to employment in that particular cluster area. Emphasis within the senior high school will be placed upon the preparation of students for entry level jobs, but instruction will also be designed to help students set goals for securing further preparation for more complex jobs within the occupational ladder for which they have high potentialities for success. The most fundamental change of all will result from the fact that the vocational education teacher will be responsible not only for helping students acquire certain job entry knowledges and skills, but also for providing them opportunities to place these learnings into the perspective of their total career development.

A fourth question is whether or not career education places too much emphasis upon economic man and gives insufficient concern to the total development of the human being, including his social, aesthetic, recreational, and moral interests, needs and obligations. It would be an extremely narrow educational program which did not take into consideration the multiplicity of human needs for capacitation in the performance of all life roles. Career education is founded upon the principle of the school's obligation to facilitate all human endeavors and has a potentiality for being far more humanistic than the traditional academic curriculum, which emphasized the cultivation of mind almost to the exclusion of all other human faculties. The primary deficiency of the general education curriculum today is that it emphasizes man's intellectual development but does not give adequate attention to his vocational, avocational, or ethical development. The emphasis of career education upon an individual's economic career arises from recognition that work is the central focus of an individual's life, but it is essential that he develop interests, skills, understandings which are related to other factors associated with his life, destiny, and his ability to sustain himself through the vicissitudes which he will encounter. There is certainly a greater potentiality for this broader emphasis in career education developed in accordance with the dimensions presented above than is currently true of the typical educational program in the United States.

A fifth problem relates to the relationship of guidance services to instructional functions within the school. Although a considerable emphasis was placed upon vocational guidance (or career development) in the early days of the guidance movement, major emphasis was soon diverted to both educational planning and crisis counseling. Although there was some early emphasis upon the development of a curriculum-based-guidance-model, the field was diverted away from concern for the individual's educational and career development and toward the solution of his more immediate ephemeral and personal adjustment problems. In addition, school officials have been extremely parsimonious in the allocation of resources for the development of adequate guidance programs. Even the most far-reaching recommendations for the employment of guidance personnel have been modest in comparison with the needs for well-trained guidance personnel in the career education program.

Specialized services for educational and crisis counseling will undoubtedly have to be continued either within the school district or through some referral service. But in career education this is not the central function of the guidance program. Career education presupposes that guidance specialists will be specialists in career development and will work closely as members of the instructional team with the teachers and other instructional resource personnel. They will advise teachers on the diagnosis of needs and the prescription of instructional experiences to meet them and assist students and their parents in career decision-making. In career education, guidance is a part of the total curriculum plan.

A sixth problem relates to the effect of career education upon current requirements for graduation and college entrance. No one has been happy with the stultifying requirements for a long time. Numerous studies have shown their inadequacy and particularly the inability to predict success upon the basis of the standards imposed. Yet, the persistence of tradition has maintained these requirements in spite of their inadequacy. A flexible and open career education program will necessitate changes, although it is extremely difficult at this time to predict exactly what these changes will entail. It is apparent that there will be a great deal more flexibility and much greater concern for the demonstration of performance expectations rather than the accumulation of Carnegie units. Career education will undoubtedly facilitate the development of an open system of entrance to educational institutions. As career education emerges, it is entirely likely that the attention of college admissions officers will be upon what the college can do to facilitate human purposes rather than whether or not individuals fit into the traditional, preestablished college mold.

A seventh issue arises from the proposal that every student in high school should be engaged in learning certain job entry skills. Those who object to this requirement hold that many students already have their career plans outlined by the time they enter high school and are destined for college and professional careers. Under those circumstances, they feel that the acquisition of entry level skills is an imposition upon their time and not directly related to their total career development. These students could better spend their time in academic studies or in furthering their general education. Even some who strongly support career education hold that this requirement is not realistic for college-bound students.

Obviously, there are various value perspectives undergirding this proposal. Not the least of them is a concern for the provision of the sense of identity and independence which comes from an individual's earning his own money. There are two other significant responses to the criticism. The first is that the student who is bound for college needs to have a broader perspective of the career ladder and the variety of occupational requirements which are related to his area of professional concern than that which he will have obtained merely by pursuing his narrower professional studies. The development of some entry level skills in a field closely related to his professional choices or involving employment upon a lower rung of the career ladder will help him secure understandings which he might otherwise lack. A future lawyer may well be employed as a clerk in a law office and a future physician employed as a laboratory assistant. There appear to be many advantages for individuals to learn about the services of his professional area from the "ground up" in order to obtain a complete perspective from the client's or patient's point of view.

A second argument is that many students will find the entry level skills advantageous if not essential for securing the funds they need for the completion of their professional degrees. The acquisition of salable skills for many college-bound students may mean the difference between their ability to complete their programs within a reasonable time or the interruption of their college experience prior to completion.

Other subsidiary arguments may be made. Having job entry skills may be the most important insurance policy for a young married woman with children to support, or for a semi-professional or technician who suddenly finds himself out of work as a result of changes in the job market. Many a professional career today has been paid for through the entry level jobs held by the professional's spouse. The knowledges and skills required for job entry into a specific field may never be used on a remunerative basis but may provide the foundation for a very satisfying avocational experience. When one places all the economic as well as the personal development aspects of the acquisition of entry level skills by every individual into proper perspective, the viability of the objective appears to be greatly enhanced.

An eighth issue is the extent to which career choice is "forced" upon a child at a fairly early age. Career education actually does not force a career choice upon the student before he is mature enough to make a responsible decision. The research is not conclusive with respect to when career choices can be most realistically made. Career education does not mean that career choices must be made much earlier than is now the case. The basic rationale undergirding career education is that there will be a period of planning for and developing skill in career decision-making before an individual makes his final choice. Since there will be an emphasis in the instructional program upon becoming aware of one's own potentialities in relationship to the world of human affairs, and since an individual will become increasingly aware of the options open to him as he engages in exploratory studies about vocational opportunities, it seems realistic that a career choice might be made earlier than is now the case. The emphasis in career education is upon providing as realistic and rational a basis as possible for career decision-making. The whole educational system will be based upon the assumption that all of an individual's instruction helps him to determine his career choices. If the program becomes rigid, the emphasis upon career decision-making could constitute a serious impediment. However, to the extent that the program can maintain a desirable flexibility and opportunities for systematic recycling in the event that individuals discover that they have made inappropriate decisions, the decisional structure should remain viable.

A ninth problem area arises out of the feeling of some minority groups that career education is another "put-on" to attempt to force them to remain in lower level occupations and to screen them out of the more prestigious careers. Negative educational counseling has long been one of the serious problems confronting the minority students, and the question which some of these students raise is whether or not career education is a new instrumentality of discrimination against them. No one can guarantee that the purposes of any educational program will not be subverted by individuals with prejudicial attitudes. The best assurance minority groups will have that career education will constitute a barrier to rather than a facilitator of discrimination is in its emphasis upon career education for all students and its elimination of a dual track system in which the prestigious track is reserved for those who have the legitimated personal characteristics. The very idea of career education should be the most forceful factor in minority groups' acceptance because it leaves the career choice open-ended and involves the total breadth and range of vocations open for every child's explorations. In its emphasis upon individualized decision-making about each child, the development of instructional teams, and the flexibility of the instructional program, career education offers far more hope for an open educational system for all groups than does the present educational program.

A tenth issue related to career education is in the charge that career education is too massive an undertaking for a single public agency, and it will, in effect, cause the school to replace the home. This charge has long been made against all developmental programs in education, while in reality the increase in functions by the schools has been rather tardy in response to the abrogation of responsibilities or the accumulation of disabilities in the home and other social agencies for dealing with children's developmental needs. The agrarian model of the functions of the home as distinct from the responsibilities of the school is no longer viable in a complex, pluralistic society. The home is not equipped to deal with all of the child's career development problems, and those individuals who have the most severe deprivation in establishing aspirations which challenge their full potential are the ones most likely to come from homes which can assist them the least. The emerging models of career education put considerable emphasis upon the development of cooperative relationships between the home, the school, and other relevant social agencies. To the extent that the cooperation of the home and other social agencies can be secured, it is possible for the child to be confronted with coordinated rather than disparate or conflicting influences on his career development. Career education undoubtedly is too vast an enterprise for the school to undertake by itself. The home and other agencies within the community must also be involved. Agricultural enterprises, business, industry, government and the professions must also be involved. Emerging exemplary programs in career education tend to emphasize greater coordination with and involvement of broad community resources than is true of the traditional school. Career education may well accelerate the trend toward expansion of the community school concept.

A further issue arises from the criticism that career education will become a major factor for maintaining the present economic system and the *social status quo.* It is argued that students will be locked into the system at a very early age without the provision for them to select viable alternatives. Student self-fulfillment in career education, they argue, is defined in terms of how the individual is "conditioned" to fit into the system. Some of the critics look upon career education as a major move for the indoctrination of students to accept their stations in life, secure their satisfactions exclusively in terms of what the system has to offer them, and to remain the uncritical supporters of a system which uses them to further its own ends by providing them "bread and circuses" to keep them preoccupied. These critics maintain that career education runs against the grain of the counter-culture of youth today who will not *buy* into the system on its present terms.

The advocates of career education accept the responsibility for devising an educational program that will help the present system become viable for all children and youth. This does not mean that they fail to recognize some of the dysfunctionalities and injustices which must be rectified; in fact, they view career education as a major effort to remove those inequities which are produced by educational programs which do not provide the opportunities for youth to benefit fully from the advantages which this system has to offer. Career education is definitely at odds with a counter-culture which advocates a "copping out" from one's obligations and a self-indulgent denial of social responsibility. But there is another aspect of the counter-culture which arises from youth's alienation from the means through which they can benefit from the good things the economic system has to offer. Career education is a response, at least in part, to the counter-culture's demand that youth's interest in being legitimated for their levels of aspiration, and their desire for a relevant concern for solutions to pressing problems of existence, be recognized in the school system.

None of these factors need imply that youth are uncritically locked into this system or are indoctrinated to accept a station in life irrespective of their aspirations. Career education should place a considerable emphasis upon students' explorations of the values and life styles inherent in this and other systems, so that each individual has a basis for making comparisons and determining his own posture with respect to the alternatives available to him. In effect, the student will have a greater opportunity to exercise a meaningful choice because he will have an opportunity to explore the available options.

This is not to say that career education presents a ready solution for all of the human problems of our society. One can anticipate that there will still be some severe problems of achieving identity, of coming to grips with the demands of the external world, or rebelling against the legitimated values and objectives of the adult society. Career education will not provide an aseptic environment in which youth grow to maturity. There will be the normal range of conflicts and frustrations, but, unlike the present system, which has a standardized educational program based upon the structure of knowledge, career education should be designed to organize the school as an exploratory laboratory through which a youth can investigate the problems of his existence and use knowledge in an applicative mode in order to find acceptable solutions. To a large degree, the counter-culture emerges as a result of the closed nature of the school and the irrelevant requirements imposed by the school. Those youngsters who have found a root to their career fulfillment in the present system are not necessarily the subscribers to a nihilistic counter-culture. Because they have learned how to achieve their ends within the system does not mean that they are slavishly uncritical of it. Hopefully, the openness and the flexibility of the career curriculum will give youth the exploratory outlets they need to investigate their life styles in relationships to the pressing problems of existence, so that they find the means not only to establish their own identities, but also to establish the basis upon which they can make the most satisfying and constructive uses of their own lives and energies.

The charge that career education will lock students into their "station" in life is entirely erroneous. Quite the contrary should be the case. The great strength of career education lies in the degree to which the future is open-ended for each student. Every effort should be made to help each student realistically determine how he can maximize his potentialities to achieve the highest career level consistent with his aspirations. Career education has the objective of helping him make his own decisions of how he fits in. Hopefully, through this new educational plan, the past rhetoric of democratic educational opportunities can be made into the realities of the educational system.

Obviously, career education cannot immediately solve all of these issues. It is not a patent response to all of the inadequacies inherent in today's society and educational system. It was not developed to be a fully controlled utopian educational plan. Its virtue lies in the fact that it is less encumbered with traditional approaches than other educational concepts proposed as solutions to the present dilemmas. It has the advantage of advocating an open educational system which is responsive to the needs of all children, youth, and adults who need the services of the educational system. It proposes a *systemic* change in the educational system, a change which diverts emphasis from traditional, fictitious standards and requirements, and places society's obligation to help every individual to become an effective and contributing citizen in the forefront. It suggests that the function of an educational system is that of adapting its resources and programs to the human needs of individuals and society rather than indicting both for its own failures. It is a promise to attempt to find the solutions which are needed in today's world rather than a totally given doctrine and program to which everyone is asked to subscribe. In its simplest form, career education is a plan of action for American education.

Patterns of Installation

As of this writing, there are no known completely installed or fully developed career education programs in the United States. Many school districts, both through their own efforts and with assistance of federal funds, are experimenting with phases of installed career education programs. The United States Office of Education is embarking upon a program for the development of models of career education, and the school-based model is to be installed in six local school districts in September, 1972. Although there are several factors which imply a systemic change in school programs, particularly with reference to the complete installation of the career education concept, there is no reason why school districts cannot make at least partial installations based upon the readiness of the staff and the community to accept phases of the concept under trial conditions. Four patterns of installation can presently be identified. Each of these patterns should be considered a stage working toward the total development of career education in a school system.

The first stage or pattern is the provision of career exploration experiences for students outside of but coordinated with the curricular offerings. Many school districts today have such programs. These involve such things as field trips to businesses and industries, career days, guest speakers on career topics, student interviews with individuals engaged in particular occupations of their choice, career guidance activities associated with other educational and private facilities in the area, and so forth. These types of activities have been provided by many schools for a long time. Although clearly a step toward the incorporation of more emphasis upon careers in the curriculum, these extra-curricular offerings do not generally provide the systematic approach to career development which is essential for helping the student bring together all of the knowledge about himself and the world of work desirable for making a mature decision. The total experience with these modest attempts has been most disappointing. It is too little and too antiseptic an approach to enable educators to deal effectively with the career needs of students.

A second pattern or stage of development is that of integrating certain materials on career education within the existing courses. In some schools students spend a part of their day in a homeroom, a phase of which is the exploration of careers. Some schools make a special effort to incorporate studies about vocations and specific career patterns in areas of the curriculum such as science and the social studies. This can be done from the earliest grades through high school. Some schools make an effort to provide some information about careers related to specific fields of study, resulting in units of work such as employment opportunities in the sciences, in government, in the health fields, and so forth. Vocational courses, particularly, may emphasize the employment opportunities which result from an individual's following through systematically in the acquisition of skills in the particular areas indicated.

Although this pattern has some aspects of a systematic approach, it tends to rely heavily upon the presentation of information in discrete academic modules rather than focused primarily upon the career development needs of students. Career education is subordinated to the academic objectives. It does not provide the breadth of exploration and basic career development elements which are inherent in a total, systemic approach.

A third pattern is that of providing a separate career education sequence or courses from the elementary through the senior high school which tend to emphasize the three basic elements of the career education approach, namely, awareness of self, knowledge of the world of work, and decision-making skills. This approach calls for the incorporation of information from the fields of career or vocational guidance, the vocational knowledge relative to the world of work, and the psychological studies of personal growth and individual assessment.

This pattern can be developed without significantly affecting the established course pattern. Its strength lies in the fact that it offers a systematic approach to career development and provides an area within the curriculum in which the research on career development and the knowledge related to self-awareness and vocational selection can be incorporated into a total program. The weakness of this approach lies in the fact that it may not affect the manner in which the balance of the program is structured or presented; hence, it has the possibility of bifurcating the educational program, of not attacking the basic issues that are related to the development of relevant educational programs, or the use of the basic knowledge fields in an applicative mode related to an individual's finding career relevancy throughout his entire educational program.

The fourth pattern is that of the total restructuring of the curriculum around the career development needs of all students. In this pattern, concern about career development permeates the entire curriculum, and all of the dimensions for career education indicated above can be incorporated. It has the advantage of mobilizing the total instructional resources of the school toward the applicative aspects of career development and constitutes a total systematic program of career education. The weaknesses of this approach may emerge out of the inability of a professional staff to develop fully the new paradigm consistent with the implications inherent within it. The strength of this approach lies in the fact that herein is constituted the fundamental reform of the American school system which is so much needed. It is in this total reform that the school system can become relevant and meaningful in response both to individual needs and to pervasive social issues.

Future and Promise

Career education will not be accepted blindly and without some conflict either by all American educators or the American public-at-large. The reasons are apparent. Many educators will fear the basic changes which will have to take place, at least ultimately, in the schools. Many, if not most, educators will have to adopt new modes of professional performance. The task of re-education and renewal of professional resources will be a massive undertaking. A vast commitment to professional and public renewal in education will have to be made on the federal, state, and local levels, involving numerous public and private agencies as well as the public schools, research and development agencies, and the colleges and universities. A massive new social commitment to education and a recognition of its importance for the maintenance of a democratic society is essential. Teacher education as well as research and development programs in colleges and universities will need revision, and cooperation of public schools, parents, the agencies of the private economy and government will be required to accomplish the desired ends. Professional associations of educators will have to play a responsible role and lend their support, for unless career education is accepted by teachers and other educators, local negotiations and bargaining are likely to constitute severe obstacles.

Some long accepted educational values must be examined. American education has long been dominated by the academic tradition in which schooling below the college level is conceived as primarily preparatory for college admission. Educators and the public-at-large must examine this traditional concept. Career education cannot achieve its total promise if the central function of the schools is to transmit academic subject-matter regardless of its relevance both for the needs of children and the human requirements of society. Since the existing power structure in education has controlled the sanctions which the public has come to value, it will be a very difficult transition both in values and aspirations not only for the educational establishment but for the public as well.

More than government support and publicity campaigns will be necessary. Efforts must be made to obtain broad involvement in decision-making affecting both total systems and individual attendance centers. Programs which characteristically have had very low support and prestige in schools will need much higher support levels and much greater legitimation.

Can it be done? An affirmative answer depends upon an assessment of how effective both governmental and educational leadership will be. The intensity of current educational and social problems calls for a similar intensity of leadership on all levels of affairs. Only with the emergence of the rudimentary concepts of career education have the American public and the educational profession been confronted with what appears to be a new and viable educational paradigm. Career education is not just more of the same! Not more variations upon the same irrelevant theme! If career education as presently conceived cannot deliver what it promises, then our society faces two alternatives—either adapt career education so it can *or* invent new institutions to replace the entire range of agencies which now constitute the American educational system. The challenge calls for the concerted effort of all those interested in the perpetuation of an educational system which can build a stronger democratic society. It cannot be evaded.